216 W. 42d
King's
Oxygen

218 W. 42d
Stancourt
Laundry

220-222-224 W. 42d
Central Baptist
Church

226 W. 42d
N. Y. Free Circulating
Library

THE STORY OF

42ND

STREET

THE STORY OF 42ND STREET

STREET

THE THEATRES, SHOWS, CHARACTERS, AND SCANDALS OF THE WORLD'S MOST NOTORIOUS STREET

MARY C. HENDERSON and ALEXIS GREENE

BACK STAGE BOOKS

AN IMPRINT OF WATSON-GUPTILL PUBLICATIONS / NEW YORK

Editor: John A. Foster
Designer: 3&Co.
Production Director: Alyn Evans

First published in 2008 by Back Stage Books,
An imprint of Watson-Guptill Publications,
Nielsen Business Media, a division of The Nielsen Company
770 Broadway, New York, NY 10003
www.watsonguptill.com

Library of Congress Cataloging-in-Publication Data

Greene, Alexis, 1950-
 Henderson, Mary C., 1928-
 The story of 42nd Street : the theatres, shows, characters, and scandals of the world's most notorious street / Mary C.
Henderson and Alexis Greene.
    p. cm.
 Includes index.
 ISBN-13: 978-0-8230-3072-9
 ISBN-10: 0-8230-3072-5
 1. Theater—New York (State)—New York—History—20th century. 2. Theaters—New York (State)—New York—History—20th
century. 3. Forty-second Street (New York, N.Y.)—History—20th century. I. Greene, Alexis. II. Title.
 PN2277.N5H43 2008
 792.09747'1—dc22

                            2008001594

Watson-Guptill Publications books are available at special discounts when purchased in bulk for premiums and sales promotions,
as well as for fund-raising or educational use. Special editions or book excerpts can be created to specification. For details,
please contact the Special Sales Director at the address above.

Printed in Singapore

First printing, 2008
1 2 3 4 5 6 7 / 14 13 12 11 10 09 08

Mary C. Henderson and Alexis Greene extend their thanks to Furthermore, a program of the J. M. Kaplan Fund for its support.

TO MY SISTER, CHRISTINE M. WILSON.

—MARY C. HENDERSON

TO MY FATHER, WIL GREENE.

—ALEXIS GREENE

CONTENTS

PREFACE ·········· 8

ACKNOWLEDGMENTS ·········· 9

THE HISTORY OF THE STREET OF DREAMS ·········· 11

THE AMERICAN, **1893** ·········· 35

HAMMERSTEIN'S VICTORIA, **1899** ·········· 49

THE THEATRE REPUBLIC, **1900** ·········· 61

THE LYRIC, **1903** ·········· 77

THE NEW AMSTERDAM, **1903** ·········· 95

THE LIBERTY, **1904** ·········· 109

THE LEW FIELDS, **1904** ·········· 125

THE ELTINGE, **1912** ·········· 141

THE CANDLER, **1914** ·········· 157

THE SELWYN, **1918** ·········· 173

THE TIMES SQUARE, **1920** ·········· 193

THE APOLLO, **1920** ·········· 209

THE NEW FORTY-SECOND STREET ·········· 221

WORKS CITED ·········· 230

PHOTOGRAPHY CREDITS ·········· 234

INDEX ·········· 236

PREFACE

Theatre, it has frequently been noted, is one of the most ephemeral of the arts. No camera can capture the unique sensation of a stage performance, which lives more vibrantly in one's memory than in an image preserved on videotape or film.

By the start of the twenty-first century, few people knew that, once upon a time, from 1893 to around 1930, Forty-second Street between Seventh and Eighth avenues had been the center of the country's theatrical universe, with twelve theatres, each more lush than the next, hosting a wealth of musicals and plays.

So the authors wrote this book to tell the story of these Forty-second Street theatres, and of the men who built and managed them, the dramatists and composers who created for them, and the actors who brightened their stages. Truly, it was a street of dreams.

We wanted to convey, through words and photographs, the astounding variety that these theatres presented, from Shakespearean tragedy to heart-tugging melodrama, from George M. Cohan's patriotic musical extravaganzas to the roughhouse comedy of immigrant vaudevillians Weber and Fields. We wanted to describe the personalities that created Forty-second Street, both behind the scenes and onstage: the singularly imaginative and obsessive producer Oscar Hammerstein I; feisty comedic playwright Anita Loos; the charismatic dancer Bill "Bojangles" Robinson; and genuine American luminaries such as handsome but self-destructive John Barrymore and the enticing female impersonator Julian Eltinge. Long before television soap operas there was Anne Nichols's *Abie's Irish Rose.* Long before Paris Hilton there was the notorious Evelyn Nesbit.

As fast as the flicker of a celluloid image, the Forty-second Street theatres flourished and waned, victims of a revolution in popular entertainment and an economic collapse called the Great Depression. As Americans flocked to talking pictures and then, after the Second World War, strayed from movies to huddle around television's electronic fire, Forty-second Street entered its period of greatest decline.

But this dynamic block has come back, thanks to public money and private initiative. And theatre was the spark that ignited the reclamation. Once again, long-running commercial shows play the street of dreams, as do nonprofit revivals of gems of the American theatre. Courtesy of the New 42nd Street Inc., the Walt Disney Company, the Roundabout Theatre Company, and the Hilton Theatre, Forty-second Street has rejoined New York City's world-famous theatre district. What is more, the revival has spurred the renovation and upgrading of other historic theatres that decorate the Times Square area.

So this is the story of Forty-second Street, its good times and bad, its wild successes and downright failures, and its comeback. In its glory, Forty-second Street was a cradle for the talented women and men that brought American theatre into the modern era. Now, replenished, the street lives as a vibrant entertainment center for audiences of all ages, from all over the world. It is a story like no other.

Mary C. Henderson and Alexis Greene

ACKNOWLEDGMENTS

Several years ago, while in the process of researching and writing this book, I was diagnosed with Parkinson's disease. For the first few years following the diagnosis, I functioned somewhat normally, but more recently, I have felt the true impact of the disease, which has turned my life upside down. I was seriously considering abandoning this project when by some sort of divine intervention the name "Alexis Greene" was whispered into my ear. With the blessings of my editor, Mark Glubke, I sought her out, gave her a portion of the book to read, and presto! I had a coauthor. Alexis, an excellent, established author in her own right, has been a joy to work with, and this book represents the fruit of our collaboration. I thank her from the bottom of my heart.

With the care and concern of my wonderful doctors, David Hodes, Marianna Golden, and Lois Kroplick, I have managed to keep body and soul together since the diagnosis. With the help and support of my devoted friend and housemate, Jean Porter, I have been able to live a comfortable life, which has allowed me to carry on with my writing. My gratitude to her is boundless.

For making this book possible, we are indebted to the Furthermore Foundation and its inspired founder, Joan Kaplan Davidson. Her staff, Mike Gladstone and Ann Birckmayer, has been extremely helpful, and we thank them both. Cora Cahan, president of The New 42nd Street Inc., graciously consented to administer the fund, making the whole experience pleasant and painless. I welcomed a small grant from the Carnegie Fund for Authors.

I cannot forget my agent, Carolyn French of the Fifi Oscard Agency. Fifi is gone now, but Carolyn keeps her spirit alive with her encouragement and dedication to her authors. Carolyn is truly the epitome of a great agent.

This book benefits from the vast resources of the New York Public Library for the Performing Arts and from the help and cooperation of its staff: the curator, Bob Taylor; staff members Karen Nickeson, Barbara Knowles, Amy Schwegel, Rod Bladel, Dan Patri, Christine Karatnytsky, Annette Marotta, Jeremy Megraw, Susan Chute, Elizabeth Elkind, Louis Paul, Christopher Frith, Louise Martzinek, Olive Wong; and staff volunteers Rosalie Spar and Donald Fowle.

At the New York Public Library we would like to thank Wilson Project Director Mary Ellen Rogan. At the Tamiment Library and Robert F. Wagner Archives of New York University, our gratitude goes to K. Kevyne Baar for trawling through the early files of the Actors' Equity Association and uncovering information that no one else could find. The book also benefits enormously from the knowledge and meticulous skills of theatre architect and historian Craig Morrison, who generously and painstakingly read our manuscript.

Jennifer Bright, intrepid picture researcher, who has worked tirelessly on several of my books, has—as usual—enriched this volume with her unerring eye for just the right picture to enhance the text. What would this book be without the images culled from her treasure trove of resources? The help from curator Marty Jacobs of the Theatre Collection of the Museum of the City of New York in ferreting out many wonderful pictures from that extraordinary resource is deeply appreciated.

My final gratitude must be tendered to two people who have become fast friends, advisers, and indispensable aides: Camille and Norman Dee. When I am missing an important nugget of information, I can always depend on Camille to find it in her uncanny way. When my computer misbehaves, which is often, Norman diagnoses its neurotic quirks (and mine, too) and fixes them. They are treasures, and I will never undertake another project unless I know they are available.

Finally, but very importantly, we thank our families, particularly Alexis Greene's husband, Gordon R. Hough, for his unstinting support.

DENTAL INFIRMARY
INFIRMARY.
DENTAL INFIRMARY.
STANCOURT & STANCOURT
LAUNDRY. LAUNDRY.

The History of the

Street of Dreams

The forty-second street on Jonathan Randel, Jr.'s map began as a thin line on his grid, which in 1811 extended to 155th Street. At that time, residents of New York City had started the move north from the southern tip of Manhattan, but had gotten only as far as City Hall Park—which occupied less than a mile of the 13.4-mile–long island. Appointed by a special New York State commission to study the island and devise a plan to hasten its development, Randel and his associates spent four long years tramping through forests and underbrush, scrabbling over rock encrustations and hills. After Randel completed his study, the commissioners took his drawings and laid out a grid of avenues and streets that eschewed "circles, ovals, and stars." What they created was a future city that was entirely utilitarian, politically correct, and uniform. A generation later, Henry James decried it as "the city's primal topographic curse, her old inconceivably bourgeois scheme of composition and distribution, the uncorrected labor of minds with no imagination."

Unimaginative it might have been, but the grid lent itself to uniform blocks that could be cut into rectangular lots, which would be easy to sell and build upon—and developing the island was the uppermost consideration of the commission.

Like a giant branding iron, a grid pattern was stamped upon the topographical map of Manhattan drawn by the surveyor Jonathan Randel, Jr. in 1811.

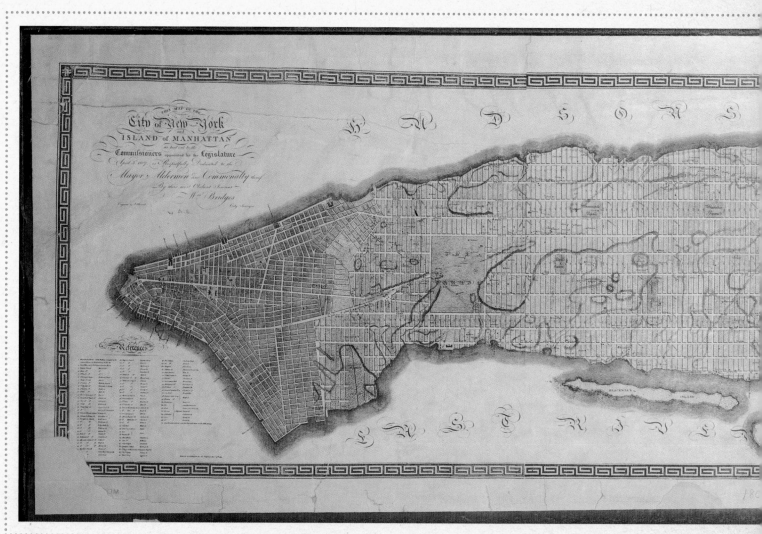

According to the earliest city records, the western side of Forty-second Street was part of a huge tract of land awarded to a group of patentees in 1667 by New York's British colonial governor, Sir Richard Nicolls. Much of the tract, including the "Street of Dreams," became the property of Johannes Van Brugh, one of those patentees. That piece of land would soon change hands in a dizzying succession of sales and legacies.

To begin the tale, Van Brugh left the land to his daughter Maria, who willed it to her son, who then sold it to one Joseph Murray in 1748. By 1792, it was owned by John Leake. Childless, Leake left the tract to his niece Martha Norton. Martha had two sons, between whom she divided the property in her will. The elder, John Leake Norton, received the parcel that attached to what is now Thirty-ninth Street and extended north in a diagonal to what is now Forty-eighth

Street, ending at the Hudson River. John kept his inheritance in the family for a while; he created a farm, which he named Hermitage, and built a house somewhere in the middle of present-day Times Square. His brother Robert's tract bordered John's farm on the south. John kept reducing the size of his property as the economic winds changed course, cutting it up into parcels and leasing them to farmers.

By 1807 John Jacob Astor, the richest man in the country, owned the piece of land slightly north of Hermitage farm, which he had acquired for $25,000 from the heirs of Medcef Eden. Astor's farm extended northwest from Forty-second to Forty-sixth Streets and all the way to the Hudson River. Part of Nicolls' original 1667 tract embraced the rest of what we now consider New York's theatre district. Astor, the most acquisitive landlord in the city, exhorted his heirs not to sell

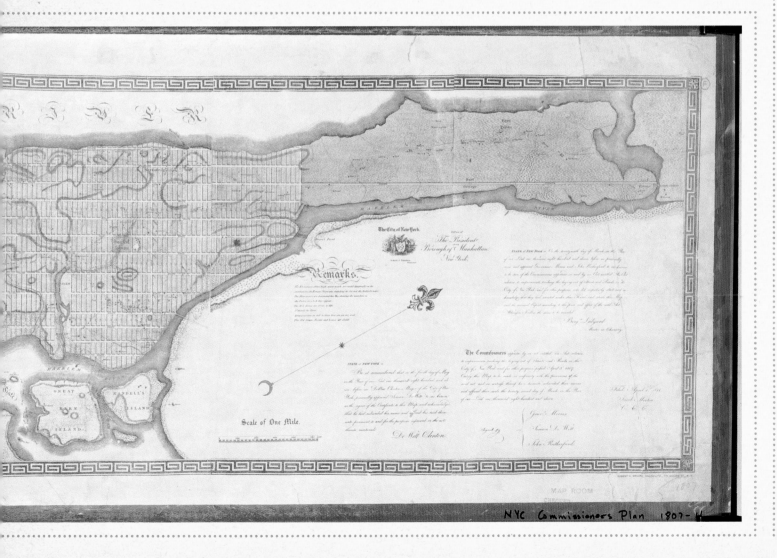

NYC Commissioners Plan 1807-4

the land he had accumulated but instead to lease it and sell only when its value had increased significantly. The Astor heirs would heed this advice and wax even richer in subsequent generations.

A cabbage farmer named Wolfert Webber, whose family had occupied a large tract from the original patentees, lived somewhere near today's Times Square and Forty-second Street (the boundaries of the colonial farms are no longer clear). Blending fact and fiction, Washington Irving, the nineteenth-century writer and chronicler of old New York, concocted the following story about Wolfert. Some say he wrote it to tease his close friend Astor. Wolfert had heard tales of treasure buried in various spots on Manhattan Island both by the crotchety Dutch governor Peter Stuyvesant and

by pirates who had roamed the Hudson River in earlier days. After dreaming three nights in a row that there was treasure under the cabbages in his garden, Wolfert began digging up his garden and farm, only to come up empty-handed. So consumed was he with the idea of buried treasure that he began digging farther and farther afield until, with his spirit broken and his farm in ruins, he became deathly ill. The lawyer summoned to draw up Wolfert's will told him that his daughter would probably be a rich woman after his death, since the Corporation of the City of New York was buying up land to lay streets. Making a miraculous recovery, Wolfert left his bed and began planning the disposition of his farm. We'll let Irving finish the story:

The first millionaire in America, John Jacob Astor, made his money by buying as much real estate as he could, then leasing it lot by lot and pocketing the rent money dollar by dollar.

John Jacob Astor found his treasure above the land, not in it, as he collected the rents from his tenants.

"Before many months had elapsed, a great bustling street passed through the very centre of the Webber garden, just where Wolfert had dreamed of finding a treasure. His golden dream was accomplished; he did indeed find an unlooked-for source of wealth; for, when his paternal lands were distributed into building lots, and rented out to safe tenants, instead of producing a paltry crop of cabbages, they returned him an abundant crop of rent; insomuch that on quarter day it was a goodly sight to see his tenants knocking at the door from morning till night, each with a round-bellied bag of money, a golden produce of the soil."

—from the short story
    "Wolfert Webber, or Golden Dreams"

Although this drawing of the Medcef Eden Farmhouse is conjectural, the artist wanted to convey the essentials of early Dutch architecture: hipped roof, porch, dormer, and other typical features. Eden sold the farm to John Jacob Astor.

A century later, another notable event occurred within the vicinity of what would one day be Forty-second Street and Times Square. It happened in the early years of the Revolutionary War, and it is not a tale of triumph. Fully cognizant of the value of New York as the most strategic port of entry into the colonies, the British sent troops to take over the island in 1776. Since the American forces were greatly outnumbered and outgunned, the wisest action that General George Washington could respond with was to retreat with his ragtag troops to what was then called Harlem Heights. General Israel Putnam, commanding his small army in the southern part of New York, was alerted to move out quickly before being surrounded. Guided by Aaron Burr's scouting, Putnam moved his troops rapidly north on crude, barely passable roads, narrowly escaping the advancing British.

The present-day theatre district stands on land where Israel Putnam, a veteran of the French and Indian War, parleyed with General George Washington.

While Washington was trying to keep his men together, General Sir William Howe landed at Kips Bay on the East River to squeeze Washington from the east. Sensing a complete rout, Washington nearly surrendered to the British. Legend says that he was saved by one of his own men, who grabbed the bridle of his leader's horse and urged him to flee. Later, Putnam and Washington met to parley among the cornfields of the future Times Square to prepare their orderly retreat

to what is now Washington Heights so that they could live to fight another day. More than a century later, the Sons of the Revolution erected a plaque just above Forty-second Street in Times Square to mark the occasion.

These two events, one real and one legendary, marked the most benign, if not quiescent, periods in the history of the area. During the next two centuries it was transformed many times, metamorphosing from farmland to a city center bustling with human activity, complete with all the improvements the modern age has thrust upon it. The transformations of just one block of Forty-second Street—that between Seventh and Eighth avenues—has created a history notable for its diversity and urban dynamism.

The building boom, which made the fictional Wolfert Webber's fortune, gathered speed after the Revolutionary War. New York rebuilt itself from its ashes. One-fourth of the city had burned as a result of two disastrous fires during the war, and it was looking to expand. By 1800 the city had reached the area known today as City Hall Park, and was rapidly moving north. In a few more years, the planning commission began putting its proposition in motion. It devised a street grid that called for longitudinal avenues one hundred feet wide and latitudinal streets sixty feet wide, except for fifteen that were to be as wide as avenues: 14th, 23rd, 34th, 42nd, 57th, 72nd, 79th, 86th, 96th, 106th, 116th, 125th, 135th, 145th, and 155th. In 1811 they were only lines on paper—it would take more than forty years for civilization to reach Forty-second Street.

Broadway, the pre-Revolutionary city's rambling "Main Street," survived the plan's stern discipline, becoming a major artery along which people, businesses, and culture moved out of the old haunts to create a vast new city. Jonathan Randel, Jr., had intended Broadway to be a dead end at Fourteenth Street and to merge with Bowery Road (the old Boston Post Road, which later became Fourth Avenue). Instead, Broadway was allowed to turn westward at this point, forming a parallelogram, or "bow-tie," at Fourteenth Street before heading west again up the island. The place where the two wide avenues met was originally called Union Place, but later named "Union Square." During the subsequent decades, each time Broadway crossed one of the wide thoroughfares, the space created was always called a square, with one exception: at Fifty-ninth Street it was called a circle.

From 1800 to 1850, the city marched relentlessly up

Manhattan Island, filling Randel's numbered streets and avenues with houses, offices, and shops, which would be replaced by larger structures in the decades that followed. Impermanence became part of the city's psychology: tear down the old or not-so-old, put up the new, and wait for the next round. For a time, the rural, more northern parts of the city were used as retreats from the dirt, dust, and bustle of everyday life, and were fair game for squatters' shacks. Much as they disliked it, the good and respectable burghers had to share the sun and fresh air with the transient folk. When the builders moved in, however, civilization evicted the squatters from their shanties.

During the second half of the nineteenth century, public transportation improved throughout Manhattan. Lumbering horse-drawn omnibuses plied the avenues and wide cross streets on routes that extended ever farther as the population shifted and accommodated itself, bringing lifeblood to the city plan. In 1836 double tracks for streetcars were installed along Broadway up to Fifty-seventh Street. In 1871 the Harlem Railroad Company opened Grand Central Depot on East Forty-second Street, the precursor of Grand Central Terminal. For a while, New York became the country's leading manufacturer of horse-drawn vehicles, and the area around Forty-second Street and Broadway (dubbed Long Acre Square after London's livery and carriage-making district) was dominated by the industry. Unfortunately, this also meant that the square's side streets were frequently used as dumping grounds for manure and garbage.

In 1825 John Leake Norton received permission to divide his farm into 310 parcels, each large enough for a building. For a small consideration he also agreed to have the city increase the width of Forty-second Street to one hundred feet in accordance with the commissioners' plan. By the middle of the nineteenth century, Forty-second Street between Seventh and Eighth avenues began filling up with brownstone and brick residences. Two churches appeared on the block: the Bloomingdale Baptist Church in 1841 (renamed the Central Baptist Church in 1868) and, in 1854, the Forty-second Street Presbyterian Church (rededicated as St. Luke's Lutheran Church in 1875). At mid-century, a retirement home, the Methodist-Episcopal Asylum, opened on the street and was later converted into the Clinton Apartments—a portent of what was to become the dominant mode of living for New Yorkers.

LADIES UNION AID SOCIETY, WEST 42 ST EAST OF 8TH AVENUE.

The Ladies' Union Aid Society gave Forty-second Street respectability.

The brownstones of the West 200 block of Forty-second Street were originally intended to serve single families, and for many years they did. *The Elite Private Address and Carriage Directory and Ladies' Visiting and Shopping Guide for New York City Containing the Names of the Upper Classes of Society Arranged in Street Form (1874 – 5)* listed residents of the street by name, usually with only one surname appearing at each address. Whether or not they were the upper class of the time cannot be ascertained. One thing was certain: many of the names were followed by MD, and for reasons unknown, for many years the street continued to attract doctors and dentists. In 1883 additional respectability arrived with the appearance of a circulating library.

The history of one building encapsulates the rise and fall of the brownstone and brick era on Forty-second Street as well as in other areas of the theatre district. In 1872 a school for boys from respectable Roman Catholic families was erected at 230 West Forty-second Street. Twenty years later it was sold to a banker named Percival Wood Clement. He hired the prestigious architectural firm of McKim, Mead and White to convert the six-story building into a bachelor apartment house—the Percival—with an apartment for himself, which he kept until 1918, when he became governor of Vermont. Meanwhile, a gentleman named John L. Murray took over the Percival in 1907, and asked the architect Henry Erkins to convert the lower stories into a lavish facsimile of a Roman garden and the several floors above into private—equally elaborate—dining rooms. Murray's Roman Gardens, a restaurant for theatre folk and aficionados, became a theatre district landmark and lasted almost until the death of its proprietor in 1927.

By 1900 the single families departed from West Forty-second Street, and the *Elite Private Address and Carriage Directory* was listing sometimes two or more names to a building. At the Clinton Apartments at 253 West Forty-second Street, more than two-dozen tenants were calling the place home. Now shorn of their stoops, the lower stories of the brownstones in the area were occupied by businesses, while residents lived in the upper stories. Some buildings were converted into rooming houses that offered bed and board to aspiring thespians on the lookout for acting jobs. Soon the area was bustling with carpenters, sign painters, restaurants, laundries, clothing stores, and even a manufactory of mantels. The churches moved out, and a Franklin Bank moved in. The real change, however, arrived when theatrical entrepreneurs began to eye the street as an anchor for a new theatre district.

In 1883 the Metropolitan Opera House, made famous in Edith Wharton's novels, opened its doors on Broadway between Thirty-ninth and Fortieth streets, replacing the Academy of Music. Disenchanted with the area around Fourteenth Street and Union Square, which was becoming increasingly déclassé, opera lovers and patrons decided to underwrite a new building uptown. Although most of the city's theatres remained clustered around Union Square, the entertainment district's tentacles were extending farther and farther up Broadway, to Madison Square at Twenty-third Street and to Herald Square at Thirty-fourth Street.

When plans were announced to build a new theatre one block north of the new opera house, most New Yorkers doubted that it would draw audiences. James Bailey, a partner of circus impresario P. T. Barnum, may have had second thoughts, too, because he pulled out of the project, leaving it in the hands of three experienced Broadway veterans—Frank Sanger, T. Henry French, and Elliott Zborowski—who brought the Broadway Theatre to completion in 1888.

As if to validate the movement uptown, Charles Frohman, arguably the most respected producer on Broadway, decided to build *his* new theatre, the Empire, at Fortieth and Broadway. Opening in January 1893 with David Belasco's hit *The Girl I Left Behind Me,* the Empire would become one of the era's most influential playhouses. Later that year, T. Henry French, whose father, Samuel French, had founded a play-publishing company, gambled on a site even farther away from the hub of activity. His huge theatre, the American, on Forty-first Street and Eighth Avenue, was designed expressly for melodrama, which was the most popular type of theatrical entertainment throughout the nineteenth century. The theatre contained seats for more than two thousand customers, and had three entrances: one on Forty-first Street, another on Eighth Avenue, and a third through a door in the narrow façade on Forty-second Street. It also had a roof-garden theatre that catered to those whose appetite for entertainment was insatiable late into the night. Electric lights shone throughout the building, and elevators—the first to be installed in a New York City theatre—carried ticket-holders to the balcony and the roof.

Frohman and French led the march uptown, but it was Oscar Hammerstein I (grandfather of the renowned lyricist)—the grand opera impresario, inventor, real estate speculator, publisher, and theatre builder—who staked out the area above Forty-second Street that soon would be known as Times Square. Even if he did not actually invent the latter (as some chroniclers have alleged), he received most of the credit for laying the foundation of the new theatre district.

OSCAR HAMMERSTEIN I

A sixteen-year-old runaway with little more than the clothes on his back and a few pennies in his pocket, Oscar Hammerstein I had left Germany and arrived in the United States in the momentous year of 1863. Although he did not speak English, he found work immediately with a German-speaking cigar manufacturer in lower Manhattan. He then devised methods that improved the performance of the machines that rolled tobacco into cigars while inventing new means to refine the process. Unsophisticated when it came to business dealings, Hammerstein at first practically gave away his early inventions, though he acquired more business sense in regard to leasing his patents. He would, even later, return to the cigar-making industry and develop moneymaking ideas whenever he needed cash for his theatrical ventures.

No one could possibly miss the robust figure of Oscar Hammerstein I, clad in his "uniform": Prince Albert coat, silk top hat, and gold-tipped cane. His office was the sidewalk, in front of his theatre.

Hammerstein explored several careers before he began to build theatres, such as publishing a tobacco journal, developing real estate, and writing music, but presenting opera to the public in English was to become his lifelong passion. Finally, in 1889, he built the Harlem Opera House on West 125th Street, which at that time was amid a white, middle-class neighborhood. Soon he added a second auditorium to the opera house and opened yet another theatre, the Columbus, to offer lighter fare—for he had discovered that grand opera did not pay in that milieu.

In 1892, having found property on Thirty-fourth Street near Herald Square, Hammerstein built the Manhattan Opera House, hoping this time to lure the public with low prices. When the venture also failed, Hammerstein struck a deal with the producers John Koster and Rudolf Bial, who were running a restaurant/theatre on Twenty-third Street, to turn the Thirty-fourth Street building into Koster and Bial's New Music Hall. For a while, the hall was successful, but a falling-out with his partners terminated Hammerstein's interest in the enterprise.

Never one to run out of options, Hammerstein was clearly ahead of his time when he decided to build an entertainment mall on the east side of the square stretching out along the entire block between Forty-fourth and Forty-fifth streets. The space had previously been occupied by the 71st Regiment Armory, which had burned to the ground.

Hammerstein's second theatre on Forty-second Street was the Theatre Republic, shown here in a later incarnation as the first legitimate theatre on the street to run pornographic movies. Had Hammerstein seen his theatre in this state, he would have been horrified.

The huge building he proposed would encompass two theatres, an enclosed roof, and embellishments such as an Oriental café, lounges, a billiard parlor, and a Turkish bath. All of these attractions, he decided, would be available to the public for the price of one ticket.

Investing $2 million into the enterprise—every cent he could muster— Hammerstein named his entertainment hall-of-plenty the Olympia, unconcerned that the neighborhood still had no street lamps and was considered disreputable at best. More important, it was also a daunting distance from the established theatre district at Fourteenth Street. For a while, Hammerstein confounded the naysayers. At the time the Olympia opened on November 25, 1895, the paint was not quite dry on the walls when eager patrons started pouring through the doors. There was room for six thousand, but true to his fashion, Hammerstein had sold ten thousand tickets— and chaos reigned. Unfortunately, the fervor of interest soon began to wane; month after month, customers stopped coming to the Olympia. Finally, in 1898, the mortgage company foreclosed on the property, which quietly slipped into other hands.

Unfazed, Hammerstein secured a lease on the northwest corner of Forty-second Street at Seventh Avenue and somehow raised the money to build another theatre, which he called Hammerstein's Victoria, perhaps as a thumb-to-the-nose directed at his doubting colleagues. There, with the assistance of his son Willie, Hammerstein at last discovered success and poured the money he was making into a spate of theatre building. In 1900 he secured the foundation of the new district by building the Theatre Republic, which abutted the Victoria on the north side of Forty-second Street. Four years later, he would slip the Lew Fields Theatre into place on the south side of the street.

Hammerstein married twice and had six children, but his obsession with theatre kept him from being much of a family man. He kept an apartment in the Victoria and conducted most of his business on the sidewalk that fronted it. He became a familiar figure in the neighborhood with his signature goatee, Prince Albert coat, silk top hat, and gold-tipped cane. When he died in New York in 1919, a career of failure and success, fame and excess, fortunes lost and gained, died with him.

In August 1903, *The Theatre*, a magazine that had been launched in 1900 for the delectation of an increasingly avid theatregoing public, announced that six playhouses were either planned or already going up in the new district forming around Long Acre Square. One by one, the brownstones lining the square disappeared, and theatres rose in their places. That fall, the Lyric Theatre and the New Amsterdam opened on Forty-second Street within days of each other.

Broadway cognoscenti recognized that more than a theatrical building boom was occurring on Forty-second Street. A war was brewing behind the two new theatres' imposing façades. Forty-second Street was about to become the battleground of two rival camps for the American theatre: the Shubert brothers, and the Theatrical Syndicate. The Lyric, built with money that composer Reginald De Koven had made from his operetta *Robin Hood,* had been leased by Sam S. Shubert and his brothers Lee and Jacob J., or "Jake," who were on their way to accumulating a vast theatrical empire. Across the street, the New Amsterdam, a splendid art nouveau palace, was the flagship of the Theatrical Syndicate, a show-business monopoly that had been established in 1896.

KLAW, ERLANGER, AND THE THEATRICAL SYNDICATE

The story of the Theatrical Syndicate, containing a mixture of legend and fact, began on August 31, 1894, at a luncheon in New York City's famous Holland House. In attendance were six men: Charles Frohman, the astute and charismatic Broadway producer; Samuel Nixon, a former notions salesman; J. Frederick Zimmerman, a baker turned theatre owner; Al Hayman, who would remain in the shadows but probably supplied the Syndicate with money, either his own or the bank's; a lawyer named Marc Alonzo Klaw; and his partner, Abraham Lincoln Erlanger, best described as a theatrical opportunist extraordinaire.

For years, the American theatre had been structured along the lines of the "stock" system inherited from England. There was an acting company, a repertory of plays to which each actor was assigned roles according to her or his type (leading lady, villain, ingénue, juvenile), a manager, and a

223 W. 42d
George W. Thedford
Coal

7th Ave. & 42 l	204 W. 42d	208 W. 42d	210 W. 42d	212 W. 42d	214 W. 42d
MacDermot's	The Garrick	William D. Grant	The Royal		
Cafè	Chop House	Tiles			

A panoramic view, circa 1900, of both sides of Forty-second Street shows
Oscar Hammerstein I's Victoria dominating the North side.

SEVENTH AVENUE.

7th Ave. & 42d
Victoria Theatre

216 W. 42d
King's
Oxygen

218 W. 42d
Stancourt
Laundry

220-222-224 W. 42d
Central Baptist
Church

226 W. 42d
N. Y. Free Circulating
Library

theatre that the manager either owned or leased.

The system had begun to break down in the second half of the nineteenth century, when managers discovered that they could send "duplicate companies" of their most successful productions—their hits—to theatres outside their usual territory and reap financial benefits. The managers in different cities frequently joined forces to form an exchange of productions, or "combination system," to ensure their audiences had a supply of new plays and faces. Eventually, the managers created what became known as "the road."

In its early days, that is, in the 1870s, the combination system was wildly haphazard and wasteful. There was no guarantee that managers would get the hits they wanted, and sometimes the distances that a company traveled were enormous. So the system eventually created the "booking agent," whose job involved setting up a schedule for theatres in the towns and cities along railway lines, to make tours reliable and efficient.

Enter Klaw and Erlanger, who had supposedly met during the 1880s while working a dusty Texas town for Effie Ellsler, a popular actress who was touring that part of the country. Whether that tale was true or not, it was certain that the pair officially joined forces in New York in 1888, after purchasing a booking agency called the Taylor Theatrical Exchange.

The partners proceeded to establish a central clearinghouse, which funneled productions to regional theatrical managers. Producers of touring productions were notorious for making double bookings and last-minute cancellations. Klaw and Erlanger replaced handshakes with written, binding contracts; created an in-house promotions staff (the precursors of today's press agents); and guaranteed production dates. Erlanger's special talent was for organization. His command of railroad timetables (committed to memory during his years as an advance man) was legendary; at a moment's notice, he could reroute a production if a theatre became unavailable or the owner changed his mind.

Erlanger had also studied the methods of American industry and believed that they could be adapted to the theatre. As he persuaded his colleagues at the Holland House, by controlling the product (the show), the workers (the actors), and the outlets for the product (the theatres), a syndicate could bring order out of chaos and—so the men told themselves—provide a service to the American theatre.

A syndicate could also make a lot of money. The six men at that August luncheon pooled their resources and eventually created a monopoly. They badgered theatre owners, producers, and actors into signing exclusive contracts with the Syndicate. On paper, this theatrical trust was to receive a commission exclusively from the gross receipts of the theatres. But the partners also extracted under-the-table commissions from the producers of the shows they booked. Although Klaw, Erlanger, and the Syndicate dictated all terms—lowering salaries and increasing their own profit shares—the Syndicate was able to lure independent producers with the promise of increased earnings. By offering continuous employment, the Syndicate also attracted a sizable pool of actors, composers, lyricists, directors, scenery and costume designers, and choreographers.

And woe to anyone who rebelled. Intractable theatre owners would be frozen out of a steady stream of productions, noncompliant producers would not be able to send their shows out on the road, and defiant actors—stars included—would be unable to work. A few producers were courageous enough to launch legal battles to break the Syndicate's hold. But even the independent producer-managers who owned theatres had to compromise in order to get the right play or star for their audiences—and the public had developed a taste for stars.

Klaw and Erlanger's tactics were reviled by the theatre community, and a scathing press corps directed particular venom at the tyrannical Erlanger. His derogatory nicknames included "Dishonest Abe" and "Little Napoleon." The partnership was also visited with undisguised anti-semitism.

Still, by today's accounting, at its height the Syndicate controlled a theatrical empire worth more than several billion dollars.

The Syndicate finally dissolved in 1916. Charles Frohman died in the sinking of the SS *Lusitania*, in 1915. The Klaw-Erlanger partnership was breaking up, and competition was fierce from the increasingly powerful Shubert brothers—Sam S., Lee, and Jacob J. or "Jake." Looked upon at first, in 1900, as saviors of the American theatre, the Shuberts would prove to be even more rapacious than the corporate rulers they dethroned.

But in 1903, when the Lyric and the New Amsterdam went up on Forty-second Street, both the Syndicate and the rivalry with the Shuberts were at their height. Looking out from their office windows on opposite sides of the street, Klaw, Erlanger, and the Shuberts could survey each other and plot their next moves. A third but lesser rival, David Belasco, could observe both of the warlords from his perch at the Republic/Belasco, next to the Lyric, and from time to time he leaped into the fray to protect his flanks. It was Belasco who led the march to the courts, armed with a long list of Syndicate abuses. The response of the State of New York was to institute a suit against the Syndicate "for criminal conspiracy in restraint of trade." But to the surprise and dismay of practically everyone in the theatre, Judge Otto Rosalsky dismissed the case, deciding that "plays and entertainments of the stage are not articles or useful commodities of common use" and that owning theatres and producing plays does not constitute *trade* and therefore is not subject to the restraint of trade under the laws of the State of New York. The men of the Syndicate fairly danced in the street.

THE RISE OF THE THEATRE DISTRICT

That very street was rapidly becoming the prime locale for playhouses. Just as importantly, the bow tie formed by the streets flowing north from Forty-second became home to a New York institution. In 1904, the fifty-year-old *New York Times* pulled its headquarters out of lower Manhattan to take over a site at the base of Long Acre Square. Honoring this move, and at the same time expressing their faith in New York's progress, both culturally and geographically, the City Fathers christened the area "Times Square," a name that has become synonymous with the central locus of New York entertainment.

The year that the *New York Times* relocated, Klaw and Erlanger opened the Liberty Theatre a couple of doors from the New Amsterdam, to install the Rogers Brothers, a comedy team, as the principal attraction. A year later, Oscar Hammerstein I erected the Lew Fields Theatre on the same side of the street, and in 1912, producer A. H. Woods established the Eltinge Theatre, named for his star Julian Eltinge, whose extraordinary popularity as a female impersonator had made Woods a rich man. Two years after

that, the southern businessman Asa Candler, who had amassed a fortune manufacturing a drink called Coca-Cola, erected the Candler Theatre in the lower part of a five-story office building, next to the twenty-three-story Candler Building—the only skyscraper on the block—that he had built in 1912. The theatre opened with a movie but, under the leadership of entertainer George M. Cohan and his partner Sam H. Harris, soon turned to presenting musicals and plays.

With the block now rich in theatres, the brothers Edgar and Archibald "Arch" Selwyn amassed the few possible sites left, on the north side of Forty-second Street. The first of these producers' three playhouses, the Selwyn, opened in 1918, followed two years later by the Times Square and the Apollo.

With the building of the Apollo in 1920, theatre construction on Forty-second Street's theatrical Rialto came to a halt. For a number of years, Oscar Hammerstein, Klaw and Erlanger, the Shuberts, Al Woods, George M. Cohan and Sam H. Harris, Florenz Ziegfeld, and many other prominent producers—all had offices in or near Forty-second Street theatres. (Was this "the gang" that George M. Cohan referred to in his song "Give My Regards to Broadway"?) Play brokers, agents, publicists, photographers—anyone connected with show business—maintained an address on Forty-second Street. There would never again be a patch of city pavement quite like it.

As the theatres went up, the area in and around Forty-second Street and Times Square blossomed. Hotels, restaurants, souvenir shops, and other businesses that would attract crowds by day and night replaced the brownstones and other low buildings. On the Broadway side of Times Square, the Knickerbocker Hotel joined the Hotel Cadillac, which, when known as the Barrett House, had been the birthplace of Eugene O'Neill in 1888. Nearby, two prominent restaurants, Shanley's and Rector's, drew in stars and their followers. On the Seventh Avenue side of the square, the Astor Hotel went up between Forty-fifth and Forty-sixth streets and, like the Knickerbocker, flourished as a haven for producers and celebrities.

On Forty-second Street, Murray's Roman Gardens, near the New Amsterdam, was the smart watering hole. Atop the American, Victoria, and New Amsterdam theatres, rooftop stages—the prototypes for nightclubs—provided places for post-midnight revelry in the never-sleeping city. During this period, it became easy to reach Forty-second Street to savor its delights. By 1904, a long-awaited subway had arrived at Forty-second Street from its starting point downtown at City Hall (elevated trains along Sixth and Ninth avenues had been carrying passengers to Forty-second Street since 1881). With Grand Central to the east and Pennsylvania Station eight blocks to the south, commuters and out-of-towners found the new theatre district easily accessible. Forty-second Street, by 1920, had become the hub of mass transit in the city.

BETWEEN THE WARS

New York City's theatre district entered its fabled era after World War I. Between 1920 and 1930, a total of 2,174 productions found their way into the playhouses on Forty-second Street, Broadway, and Broadway's tributaries, from West Thirty-eighth to West Fifty-eighth streets. The dynamism of the Broadway theatre in the Roaring Twenties has never been matched. The American theatre, like the country, had come of age.

In those days, everyone went to the theatre for entertainment and escape. The top ticket price for a play was $4, and usually $5 for a musical. At that rate, a family with an annual income of $5,000 could easily afford $1 balcony tickets and go to shows on a regular basis. And for really cheap seats, young people, students, and true aficionados could try the downstairs booth at Gray's Drug Store on Times Square at Forty-third Street. There, Joe Leblang, an entrepreneur who obtained last-minute, unsold tickets from producers anxious to fill their houses, offered steep discounts. Today's half-price ticket booths are a direct descendant of Leblang's well-patronized business.

Successful shows in New York's theatre district were sent on tour through a network of playhouses across the nation, and the proceeds from the road swelled the coffers of the producers. Theatre in the United States had always been a commercial enterprise more than a high art, but during the 1920s it was the fourth largest industry in America. And producers came in all varieties. There was the proper Boston Brahman in the person of the eminent Winthrop Ames, and then there was the flamboyant, newsworthy Florenz Ziegfeld. Each producer specialized in a certain type of stage show.

Ames preferred polite, preferably English, drawing-room comedies and Gilbert and Sullivan revivals; Charles Dillingham presented lavish musicals at the gigantic Hippodrome on Sixth Avenue between Forty-third and Forty-fourth Streets; Arthur Hopkins assisted young, untried playwrights and failed as often as he succeeded at his Plymouth Theatre on West Forty-fifth Street, which he managed for the Shuberts; Al Woods produced lurid melodramas and bedroom farces; and each season, Ziegfeld and his imitators produced new editions of musical revues, the most popular kind of entertainment.

The 1920s ushered in the careers of playwrights Eugene O'Neill, Maxwell Anderson, and George S. Kaufman, and of composers and lyricists George and Ira Gershwin, along with Richard Rodgers and Lorenz Hart. The decade cemented the careers of Irving Berlin, Jerome Kern, and Victor Herbert. But these were only a few of the many who plied their trade on the city's stages.

Through it all, Forty-second Street remained the anchor of the theatre district and the true Rialto of show business. There were ominous signs on the horizon, but no one seemed to be paying much attention. D. W. Griffith's *The Birth of a Nation*, a silent movie that was three hours long, premiered at the Liberty Theatre in 1915, launching an era of serious filmmaking. Griffith presented a massive, coherent drama of the Civil War in striking scenes that could never be duplicated on the stage. Above all, *Nation* told a complex story, unlike earlier films that were often no more than episodes strung together. In 1927, Warner Bros., a motion picture company, produced *The Jazz Singer*, a movie about a cantor's son caught between the traditions of his Jewish roots and the lure of show business. Starring Al Jolson, the film contained snippets of synchronized song and dialogue, heralding the emergence of talking pictures and posing a serious threat to theatre. But Broadway seemed untroubled.

A few producers actually entered the new field, and many theatre owners booked silent films into their playhouses, to fill slack periods when stage shows suddenly failed or were unavailable. At the two largest theatres on Forty-second Street, the American at one end and Hammerstein's Victoria at the other, movies became a permanent fixture. When Marcus Loew took over the American from William Morris in 1911, he brought movies to both the main stage and the rooftop playhouse. Oscar Hammerstein ceded control of the Victoria to S. L. "Roxy" Rothafel, who rebuilt it as the Rialto and replaced vaudeville with movies in continuous showings.

Despite these cracks in the solid wall of live entertainment on Forty-second Street, in 1925 the Forty-second Street Property Owners and Merchants Association marked the street's centennial with a celebration that honored the thoroughfare from the East River to the Hudson. Events included a historical pageant and programs featuring performers from the Metropolitan Opera and Broadway. The importance of show business on the street was obvious from the programming, some of which was broadcast over the radio: there was a New York Hippodrome Night, a Charles Dillingham Night, a Grand Opera Night, a Shubert Night, and a David Belasco Night. A Motion Picture Night rounded out the events.

Four years later, in 1929, the stock market crashed, and the changing world of entertainment could no longer be ignored. Producers found themselves in bankruptcy court, banks took over theatres, and stars decamped for Hollywood, along with writers, composers, designers, and the people who worked backstage. They deserted Broadway for the movies and for radio, some never to return.

After the Crash, it became apparent that the theatre district contained more playhouses than could be filled, either by productions or patrons. Broadway on both sides of Times Square became the domain of the new motion-picture palaces: huge, ornate edifices that contained thousands of seats priced within everybody's reach. They offered audience amenities that the aging Broadway houses could never provide. In this new entertainment culture, the small, antiquated playhouses—many of which were located on Forty-second Street—had become an endangered species.

Forty-second Street's transformation was amazingly swift. Because some theatre owners had already presented movies or vaudeville as a substitute for legitimate theatre during slow times, the buildings were ripe for conversion. In many cases, when owners or lessees lost their theatres, the buildings passed into the control of banks and holding companies, which divested these properties without much concern for who was buying them. That is how burlesque came to Forty-second Street.

In February 1931, the most colorful burlesque producer of all, Billy Minsky, invaded the New York theatre district. He leased the Republic on Forty-second Street, presenting two shows a day and charging only $1 for matinees and $1.50 for evening performances. His burlesque, which included striptease and comedians providing risqué patter, played to packed houses, and police raids served only to pull in more customers.

One month after Minsky opened at the Republic, the motion-picture operator Max Rudnick secured a lease on the Eltinge and presented a combination of movies and burlesque. Observing this success, another movie-house owner, Max Wilner, took over the Apollo Theatre and presented "glorified" burlesque. Although only three of the Forty-second Street playhouses were actually offering burlesque, few were producing "legitimate" theatre anymore. The public received the impression of a street totally given over to an unpalatable form of show business. Forty-second Street was branded the "cesspool of filth and obscenity." Somehow, it had to be stopped.

Attacks on burlesque began to appear frequently in the press. The Forty-second Street Property Owners and Merchants Association, the same group that had celebrated the street's centennial in 1925, launched a fierce attack on the burlesque houses, which, they said, were hurting conventional businesses. It became routine for the police to raid the Theatre Republic, the Eltinge, and the Apollo, and it became just as routine for the charges to be dropped after defense teams cited First Amendment rights and were supported by civil libertarians. A group of civic-minded citizens and clergy—the Society for the Suppression of Vice—appealed to the City government, which promptly stopped issuing licenses to operate the burlesque theatres, and for a while the producers cleaned up their shows. But their regular customers stayed home, and so when no one was looking, Minsky and his colleagues reverted to offering their customary fare. Like mushrooms appearing overnight on a wet stump, burlesque quietly reemerged on the street when the public hue and cry had abated.

In 1934, Fiorello H. La Guardia became mayor of New York City and the self-described guardian of public morals. One of his first acts was to appoint a license commissioner named Paul Moss, who shared the mayor's stance on burlesque. The men decided that, if they could not take the legal high road and win their case in court, they could certainly harass burlesque to death—and almost succeeded in doing just that. Still, not until La Guardia was elected for the third time, in 1942, did burlesque operators surrender to the inevitable and close shop in New York City, taking what was left of their shows to locales across the Hudson, in New Jersey and beyond.

THE DECLINE OF A GREAT THOROUGHFARE

Burlesque had exited Forty-second Street, but legitimate theatre did not rush to fill the void. Where once there had been stages alive with actors, dancers, and singers, movie screens now flickered in darkened auditoriums. The Lyric, the Liberty, the Times Square, the Selwyn, the Candler (now known as the Harris), and the Lew Fields (renamed Wallack's)—all hosted first- and second-run movies from morn until past midnight. The glorious New Amsterdam, home of the *Ziegfeld Follies*, had withstood the pressure of conversion until 1937, when it was taken over by Max Cohen, who announced that he would make the house available for live presentations whenever the right show came along. It never did. Cohen also controlled Wallack's, which he dubbed the Anco and substantially rebuilt in 1940 just for movies.

With movies now the primary entertainment, Forty-second Street once again changed. During and after World War II, new audiences invaded the neighborhood. There were servicemen briefly in town for a good time, and families visiting the city on the weekends. The street remained respectable but was perceived as honky-tonk. At Hubert's Museum, on the site of what had been Murray's Roman Gardens near the New Amsterdam, ten cents bought the casual visitor a show with trained fleas, or sideshows featuring assorted freaks, pitchmen, belly dancers, and sword swallowers. The streetscape comprised a welter of penny arcades, hot dog stands, candy shops, souvenir and novelty stores, and other enterprises geared to crowds of passersby.

Ironically, the entrepreneurs who had brought movies to the block's theatres were soon suffering from the impact of another revolution in popular American entertainment: television. In a desperate attempt to lure people away from their living rooms, and with television sets proliferating throughout the nation, the Hollywood studios, led by 20th

Century Fox, secured the option on a wide-screen system called CinemaScope. In the 1950s, the owners of most of the movie houses on Forty-second Street—Max Cohen and his partner Mark Finkelstein, and the Brandt family—brought CinemaScope to their theatres. To accommodate the wide screens, they tore out the theatres' remaining boxes and made other alterations. These alterations, in the long run, did little to wean the public from television but would certainly make it difficult to reclaim Forty-second Street's legitimate theatres, if and when tastes in entertainment changed again.

Movies were not the only attractions on the block during the 1960s. Pornography vendors took over empty storefronts; shops that used to sell miniature replicas of the Statue of Liberty and the Empire State Building began to stock drug paraphernalia and sex-oriented merchandise. By the end of the decade, the lowbrow but harmless Hubert's Museum had disappeared, replaced by Peepland, which catered to more prurient tastes. (It was later razed to make way for the New York edition of Madame Tussaud's wax museum.) Prostitutes and drug pushers worked the street, and the Rialto movie house, on the site of Hammerstein's flagship theatre, the Victoria, at the corner of Forty-second Street and Seventh Avenue, screened pornographic films under the guise of "art" (the first Rialto movie house had been demolished in 1935). Emulating the Rialto's success, other theatre owners on Forty-second Street were emboldened to change their booking policies. Garish billboards and marquees advertised sex, gore, and violence.

THE NEW FORTY-SECOND STREET

In March 1960, an article in the *New York Times* declared that Forty-second Street was "unsightly, raucous, offensive and, at times, dangerous." It was an urgent call to New Yorkers to pay attention, and indeed everyone agreed that something had to be done about Forty-second Street. But no one had the solution. During the next thirty years, private and public groups would propose an array of plans. Then, for one reason or another, the schemes would be shelved. A veritable alphabet soup of agencies sprang up to tackle the problem.

One plan called for the demolition of all the theatres on the block. Office buildings, each required to include a legitimate playhouse within its structure, would supposedly replace them. But the vagaries of the economy and New York's real estate market squelched that proposal.

Project followed upon project. In 1978, a strategy dubbed the "Times Square Action Plan" was launched. One year later, the Ford Foundation granted $150,000 for "The City at 42nd Street," a plan to revive the block between Times Square and Eighth Avenue and create a kind of urban theme park of theatres, multimedia displays, exhibitions, and studios that would reconfigure the street as a gateway to city life. Not forgetting that the business of New York is business, the planners made room for three office towers and a fashion mart—and, of course, a new tower for the *New York Times*. The suggestions drew the contempt of many, but it was Mayor Edward I. Koch who administered the coup de grâce when he rejected the idea outright.

The Ford Foundation proposal, like all the others, achieved no tangible results. But at least it spurred the City and State to become seriously involved. Reluctantly, successive mayors realized that the only way to rescue Forty-second Street from the mire was to pledge taxpayer money.

Prompted perhaps by public interest in the Ford Foundation's rehabilitation project, the Brandts announced their intention to renovate two of their Forty-second Street theatres: the Apollo, and the Lyric. Beginning with the Apollo, the Brandt organization gave it a $350,000 face-lift, switched the main entrance to Forty-third Street, and announced that the house had been booked for a new play for general audiences: Edward Thompson's *On Golden Pond*, which opened in February 1979. The production's success led to several more bookings. The owners of the Rialto at Forty-second Street and Seventh Avenue decided to follow suit, renovating the smaller of two movie theatres to house a legitimate production—a revival of the musical *Canterbury Tales*. Despite the overall popularity of the legitimate presentations, within a few years both houses had reverted to showing movies.

These setbacks aside, public and private awareness of New York's "sore thumb" pushed the reclamation along. In 1980, the City and State jointly launched the 42nd Street Development Project as a special agency of the New York State Urban Development Corporation (UDC), charging the agency to come up not only with a plan but with estimates about costs and funding. The resulting scheme called for four office towers on the Forty-second Street corners of Seventh Avenue and Broadway; the renovation of the historic theatres; and the construction of a trade mart and hotel at Forty-second Street and Eighth Avenue. Financial estimates exceeded the billion-dollar mark.

By 1984, the renewal of Forty-second Street had been approved by the Municipal Board of Estimate, and for the next few years it looked as if the street's problems would be solved. On the wings of a real-estate boom in the early 1980s, the Times Square Center Associates, an amalgam of Park Tower Realty (the developer) and the Prudential Insurance Company (the financer), struck a deal with the 42nd Street Development Project to build the four office towers, and the world-renowned architects Philip Johnson and John Burgee were commissioned to design them. The 42nd Street Development Project was also charged with finding tenants or other uses for the midblock theatres.

During the next few years, the public and the press subjected the redevelopment project to intense scrutiny, with mixed results. Civil libertarians decided that cleaning up Times Square and Forty-second Street was nothing short of a violation of First Amendment rights. If citizens wanted smut, they had a right to it, and the redevelopment plan to rid the area of the pornography purveyors was simply a ploy to trample constitutional guarantees of freedom of expression. For their part, the owners of the businesses affected by the condemnation went to court to protect their very lucrative livelihoods (porn tenants, it seems, paid exceedingly well). Still another vocal group, architecture critics (who number in the millions in New York), attacked the towers as sterile monoliths. Johnson and Burgee eventually agreed to modify their designs.

The battle between the "no-gooders" and the do-good-ers seemed to be at a stalemate, until fate intervened. The economic recession of the mid-1980s brought about a re-trenchment in building, as in other types of city improvement. The New Amsterdam Theatre, a designated landmark that was now controlled by the Nederlander Organization, a company that owned and operated theatres around the country, had been closed for a renovation that was never completed. When construction of the new office towers at Times Square was postponed, the entire area's cachet sank even lower.

An impressionistic proposal for the new Forty-second Street, as envisioned by Robert A. M. Stern, Architects, showing the northwest corner of Forty-second Street and Seventh Avenue.

The planners returned to their drawing boards. The State acquired condemnations of Forty-second Street properties site-by-site and inch-by-inch. Then, as the economy began rebounding, the redevelopment plans were dusted off and again put into play. By 1990, however, tenants for the proposed office towers had melted away. So the focus turned to the block's antiquated theatres: at this point, the key to revitalizing Forty-second Street lay in *their* future.

In 1990, the UDC and the 42nd Street Development Project created an independent nonprofit organization called The New 42nd Street Inc. in order to oversee the disposition of six theatres so that the two agencies could focus on the bigger redevelopment picture. Under the terms of a master lease, the State now held control of the block's nine surviving theatres, and the appointed board of directors of The New 42nd Street Inc. was charged with deciding the fates of six of them. After much discussion and negotiation, the board and president of the new agency, Cora Cahan, announced that they had received serious proposals for revitalizing the block's theatres as well as other property along the famous street.

In 1993, the Walt Disney Company indicated its interest in acquiring the New Amsterdam Theatre, which Disney intended to restore as a playhouse for large musicals. Shortly after receiving *that* firm commitment, The New 42nd Street announced that Forest City Ratner, a Cleveland-based company specializing in entertainment malls, would be building a huge center on the south side of the street, to be anchored by a New York outpost of London's famous wax museum, Madame Tussaud's, along with a multiplex movie emporium. True to its word, the Walt Disney Company proceeded with the painstaking renovation of the New Amsterdam, which opened to the public in May 1997. Forest City Ratner's project would end up destroying all of the Candler except the façade, while incorporating the historic Eltinge Theatre and parts of the Liberty.

In 1995, Livent Inc., a Canadian firm that produced live entertainment and created its own venues, signed an agreement to build a large musical house on the north side of Forty-second Street. Two years later, the brand-new Ford Center for the Performing Arts—built by Livent on the sites of the Lyric and Apollo, and incorporating some of their architecture—was ready to accept audiences for Livent's new musical, *Ragtime*.

As part of its mandate from the City and State, The New 42nd Street promised to dedicate two of the theatres under its aegis to nonprofit use. To establish a paradigm for the redevelopment, Cahan and her board decided to renovate the Victory movie theatre, which had been built by Oscar Hammerstein I as the Theatre Republic in 1900 and was the oldest extant house on the block. Restored at a cost of $9.2 million by the architectural firm of Hardy Holzman Pfeiffer, the playhouse reopened in December 1995 as the New Victory, a theatre dedicated to entertainment for children and families.

During a fierce storm in the winter of 1997, a building on the street's north side that used to contain the offices of Selwyn and Company, collapsed. It was replaced by a new structure that houses offices and rehearsal studios for

Cora Cahan, president of The New 42nd Street Inc. had the unenviable job of lifting the street out of its squalor by rehabilitating as many theatres as she could.

nonprofit organizations, and a 199-seat black-box theatre called The Duke on 42nd Street (named for a substantial grant from the Doris Duke Foundation), built and operated by The New 42nd Street.

The Selwyn Theatre was leased to New York City's well-established Roundabout Theatre Company, which raised $17 million for its restoration from a variety of sources. One contributor, American Airlines, donated a hefty sum and was duly rewarded by having the theatre's name changed to the American Airlines Theatre, which opened in June 2000.

Early in 1998, construction began on "E Walk," which is today a series of retail establishments surrounding a multiscreen movie complex on the north side of Forty-second Street. Among the last of these stores to open was Ecko Ltd., on the site of the Times Square Theatre. At the northeast corner of Forty-second Street and Eighth Avenue stands a new hotel, which extends to Forty-third Street and finishes off the redevelopment of the north side of the block.

As for Forty-second Street's pornography venues, they departed. Although the First Amendment challenges persisted and made their way up to the appellate courts, Forty-second Street's properties, now among the most expensive in the world, had already been priced beyond the reach of the porn purveyors by the time the matter was finally resolved. Most of these businesses had already packed up their wares and moved to other parts of the city or gone online. As of the new millennium's first decade, traces of the old "naughty, bawdy, gaudy, sporty Forty-second Street" of song and legend had all but disappeared.

What had begun as a thin line on an engineer's drawing became, in successive eras, a middle-class enclave, a world-famous Rialto, and an infamous hub for pornography and crime. Today, as a corridor for family entertainment, Forty-second Street has actually returned to its historical role as anchor of New York City's Theatre District—which was born in the late nineteenth century, when adventurers turned shovelfuls of earth to build twelve theatres on one Manhattan block, creating the world's most famous theatrical boulevard.

AMERICAN THEATRE

42ᵈ STREET BET 7ᵗʰ and 8ᵗʰ AVES.

THE AMERICAN

1893

A view of the entrance added to the American Theatre (in center of photograph), the bulk of which was actually on Eighth Avenue and extended to Forty-first Street.

The American Theatre possessed two dubious distinctions: it was the first theatre to reach Forty-second Street, which in 1893 might as well have been the antipodes; and it would be the first Forty-second Street theatre to be torn down. Several other distinctions also bear noting: the American was equipped with the most efficient ventilating equipment then in existence, the house was entirely wired for electricity, and elevators whisked patrons from ground level to the balcony and the roof. The huge auditorium contained 2,064 seats and room for two hundred standees.

T. HENRY FRENCH

The American was built by T. Henry French, the son of Samuel French, the publisher of inexpensive play script editions, and Count Elliott Zborowski, a millionaire. The men had been partners before in the building of the Broadway Theatre at Forty-first Street in 1888. In the case of the American, Zborowski appeared content to be a silent partner until circumstances forced him to play a more active role; French was a notable theatrical producer with an established reputation. Still, many thought his move to Eighth Avenue and Forty-second Street to erect a theatre was a foolhardy one. French reasoned, however, that the Metropolitan Opera House had already been located "uptown," and that Charles Frohman was planning for his Empire Theatre to be placed in the upper reaches of Broadway. Also, only a few desirable lots were left in the old theatre district, which stretched from Union Square on Fourteenth Street to Herald Square at Thirty-fourth. French envisioned the American as a house of melodramas, which he rightly perceived were the most popular theatrical fare at the time. By mounting these productions with lavish scenery and stunning stage effects, and by dressing actors in beautiful costumes, he hoped to lure audiences uptown. He also planned to offer his productions at prices that everyone could afford.

French's architect, Charles Coolidge Haight, was a respected designer who had college buildings, churches, and other institutional edifices to his credit. Because of the lot's three-pronged shape, Haight put the main façade (and bulk)

of the theatre on Forty-first Street and provided corridors to entrances on Eighth Avenue and at 260–62 West Forty-second Street. The façades were covered with a light-colored brick ornamented with terra-cotta decorations. Like many buildings of the period, the style was eclectic, incorporating both Italian Renaissance and Gothic touches. French had had success with roof garden theatres, and so he built a terrace atop the American. Patrons were to sit at tables scattered around the garden and enjoy light refreshments along with the light entertainment.

The interior of the main theatre pleased the *New York Times* reporter who covered the opening. He was impressed by there not being a bad seat in the house despite the slim columns supporting the balcony. (The age of the cantilever had not yet arrived.) He noted that the theatre was large but projected a feeling of intimacy because it was more broad than deep, and because the balconies had been brought close to the stage. He described the color scheme as pleasant to the eye: a palette of red tones with plenty of gilding, but not enough to be overwhelming.

The *Times* man commented on the giant mural painting over the proscenium "representing the daughters of Eve employed in some sort of function." (It apparently was not important to specify which one.) The only jarring note in this journalist's estimation was the painted drop curtain which, he strongly felt, did not belong in such elegant surroundings. The vast stage, on the other hand, was conducive to permitting "stirring pictorial representations"—exactly what French had in mind.

The opening-night production on May 22, 1893, was *The Prodigal Daughter*, an English melodrama about a girl named Rose who is disowned by her father for eloping with the wrong man. The play's climax is a steeplechase that calls for real horses, riders, and hurdles over which the horses are supposed to jump. The race has been fixed, but Rose's husband saves the day by riding his own horse and winning the race, turning out to be the very man Rose's father had wanted for her all along.

Audiences were thrilled when the racehorses (set on treadmills) seemed to be heading right into the orchestra. Although the critics did not entirely approve, the melodrama was a tremendous popular success and ran for more than seven months. French charged $1.50 for orchestra seats, $1 for the balcony, and 25 to 50 cents for seats in the gallery, all

Atop the American, owner and manager T. Henry French built a roof garden theatre, which he promptly leased to another manager, who chose to present vaudeville-type fare.

below the usual cost of Broadway tickets, which mostly had an upper limit of $2 and a low of 50 cents.

The roof garden—an open terrace rather than a conventional theatre—was launched that June, and eventually attracted a different audience than did the American's main hall. French leased the roof to another manager while he ran the main theatre downstairs and, catering to the area's local inhabitants, the manager presented variety acts that ranged

from a fake bullfight, to performing dogs, to the boisterous Irish singer Maggie Cline singing the crowd's favorite, "Throw 'Em Down, McCloskey." For anyone holding a ticket to the main theatre, admission to the roof was free—everybody else paid fifty cents.

French had difficulty finding another melodrama to equal the success of *The Prodigal Daughter*. *The Voyage of Suzette* involved a circus and allowed French to include a couple of spectacles. There was a parade of real animals, including an elephant and a marching band. But alas, *Suzette* failed within two weeks. *Poor Girls*, a drama about two sisters, one of whom is seduced by the other's fiancé, followed. Another

The American Theatre opened with the melodrama *The Prodigal Daughter*, but the play was not the success that owner-manager T. Henry French had hoped for, despite a climactic scene featuring a real steeplechase with real horses.

Maggie Cline, an Irish ballad singer, never failed to thrill the roof garden crowd with her rendition of "Throw' Em Down, McCloskey," about a savage prize fight between a white man and a black man that lasted forty-seven rounds.

suitor comes forth, threatening to shoot the seducer, but as the final curtain falls, all is forgiven, and the sisters pair off with the right men. One of the play's highlights was a meal cooked onstage (a touch worthy of that master of surface realism, David Belasco). The meal consisted of fried eggs and ham, perhaps an inadvertent comment on certain participants in the play. *Poor Girls* shuttered after two weeks.

French was running out of money to launch any more spectacular melodramas. To keep his theatre afloat, he began booking other producers' shows into the house. Most either began their tours at the American or were booked

there when they returned to New York City from the road, and the shows tended to change weekly. (Joseph Jefferson's production of *The Rivals* stopped by for only one night in 1896.) Occasionally, French booked a production that roused uncommon interest: the young Florenz Ziegfeld, Jr., presented the Sandow Trocadero Company, a kind of variety show that presaged things to come from this budding theatrical entrepreneur. But most of the entries did not draw audiences.

The American's roof garden, despite a succession of managers, was not profitable either, and what is more, the perfor-

After declaring bankruptcy, T. Henry French sold his half-interest in the theatre to his partner, Elliott Zborowski, who began negotiations to bring Henry Savage's Boston-based Castle Square Opera Company to the American Theatre.

"THE MERCHANT OF VENICE"

When opera disappeared from the American's stage, the theatre passed
into the hands of several managers. One of them produced *The Merchant
of Venice* with Jacob Adler, star of the Yiddish stage, seen here brilliantly
performing Shylock in Yiddish.

mances occasionally got French into trouble. To bring in audiences, one manager presented a sketch called "Ten Minutes in the Latin Quarter; or a Study in the Nude," which brought in the local police inspector. The inspector decided that the show violated public decency laws and closed it down, arresting both the promoter and the performer.

By 1897, it had become clear to T. Henry French that his magnificent theatre was, unfortunately, also a white elephant. The newspapers reported his financial difficulties in great detail, and the *Times* critic went so far as to offer suggestions, advising French to make the American a house for all sorts of dramas: melodramas, comedies, classics, new plays, well — but not lavishly produced. It was too late for French: he declared bankruptcy and saw his theatre put up for auction.

T. Henry French went into his father's business, attempting to protect, to little avail, the publishing company's licenses to American, British, and European plays. Pirating plays was an established practice among producers, flouting the copyright laws already on the books. It would take many years to effect change and to draft laws that were actually enforceable. French, who died in 1902 at the age of fifty-four, would not see it happen.

ELLIOTT ZBOROWSKI AND HENRY SAVAGE

French's erstwhile partner, Elliott Zborowski, bought the American and immediately began negotiations with Henry Savage to bring his Boston-based Castle Square Opera Company to the theatre. Savage had been enjoying great success presenting operas in English, and Zborowski nourished hopes that Savage would also attract audiences to the American, especially at ticket prices that ranged from 75 cents for the orchestra to 25 cents for the gallery.

Savage and Zborowski were off to a good start in January 1899 with a revival of Johann Strauss's *The Queen's Lace Handkerchief,* an operetta involving a compromising royal message written on a stolen handkerchief. When introduced in Vienna, the operetta had provided its composer with his biggest success in years, and when produced in 1882 at the

Casino Theatre, at Thirty-ninth and Broadway, it had proven popular with American audiences as well. The new partners reasoned correctly that it would make a good beginning to their stewardship of the American.

The repertory of the Castle Square Opera Company was impressive. Bills ranged from Gilbert and Sullivan to grand opera, and for three seasons at the American, both the theatre and the company fared well, drawing favorable comparisons with the Metropolitan Opera. The company's greatest contribution was to make opera fans out of audiences who would not have ventured into the more exclusive Metropolitan. Whether the American showed a profit—a dubious possibility considering the price of the tickets— seemed unimportant and was not reported in the press. Presumably, Zborowski was content simply to see his playhouse lighted and active.

After the Castle Square Opera Company departed in the spring of 1900, Zborowski leased the American to Henry Greenwall, a theatre manager who had begun his career in Galveston, Texas. Greenwall and his stock company returned the house to melodramas and kept admission prices low. Ticket prices ranged from 50 cents for the orchestra to 25 cents for the gallery; the result was that, for the three seasons of Greenwall's tenure, performances tended to attract rowdy patrons. Still, the American's main stage fared better than its roof garden, which was plagued by bad weather, bad management, and a dwindling audience. Zborowski closed the roof garden in 1902; it would not reopen until 1909.

During the 1901–02 season, Greenwall presented a revival of *Carmen* by Henry Hamilton and interjected a short film of a bullfight in Cordova, Spain. Whether this was done to introduce a note of authenticity or to entertain Greenwall's typical audience, the event presaged the future of the American. Then, in the spring of 1903, the manager actually won positive critical attention for a production of *The Merchant of Venice*, with Jacob P. Adler, a star of New York's Yiddish theatre, acting the part of Shylock. Adler spoke his lines in Yiddish while the rest of the cast played in English(!), but the critics hailed Adler's portrayal nonetheless.

In 1903, Count Elliott Zborowski was killed in an automobile race in France, and his son inherited the theatre. The American would remain part of the Zborowski estate until the theatre was torn down in 1932, but the estate seemed to provide little leadership. Greenwall gave up his lease, and

Hoping to duplicate the success of *The Merchant of Venice* in Yiddish, another manager brought Yiddish theatre star Bertha Kalich into a production of *Fedora*, which Sarah Bernhardt had made famous. Kalich played the role creditably, in perfect English.

in the fall of 1903, the American began its journey through a succession of managers and producers, each striving to find audiences that would keep their productions afloat. George Fawcett's stock company, which had originated in Baltimore, briefly took over the theatre in 1905. That May he presented Bertha Kalich in *Fedora*, a melodrama written by Victorien Sardou for Sarah Bernhardt and acted in this country by the American star Fanny Davenport (*Fedora* contained a death scene that few actresses could resist). The critics, charmed by Kalich's accented but perfectly understandable English, applauded her performance.

A. H. Woods, who would later become a formidable Forty-second Street theatre owner and producer, discovered a formula that seemed to appeal to the American's audiences. Beginning with Theodore Kremer's *Bertha, the Sewing Machine Girl*, he presented melodramas that revolved around young, innocent women exposed to the perils of the Big City and its less-than-reputable citizens. Caught in the toils of intrigue, which invariably led to life-threatening sequences, the heroines were portrayed as indomitable and indestructible, and invariably ended up in the arms of their male saviors, to the cheers of the American's spectators. After *Bertha* came *Edna, the Pretty Typewriter*.

WILLIAM MORRIS

Finally, in 1908, William Morris, who was known in the theatre world as a booking agent without peer, took over the American and brought about an inventive change of policy. Morris invested $50,000 on renovations. An ivory and green color scheme gave the house a new look; seats were reupholstered, and 160 were added; carpeting was replaced, and a new heating and ventilating system was installed. Morris changed the theatre's name to the American Music Hall and began booking vaudeville acts. The Scottish performer Harry Lauder played the theatre, singing, dancing, joking, and telling stories with his Scottish burr. Audiences were delighted. Morris booked Sophie Tucker, who entertained the crowd with ragtime melodies and suggestive lyrics. Billed as the "Last of the Red Hot Mamas," Tucker would see her career endure for more than fifty years, from the vaudeville stage on through the television age.

When William Morris took over the American in 1908, he spent thousands to renovate the theatre and installed vaudeville acts. One act starred the multitalented Scottish comedian Harry Lauder, who charmed audiences with his Scottish burr.

Always on the hunt for new acts and performers, Morris brought in Fred Karno's English Comedy Troupe and gave the American's audience its first taste of Charlie Chaplin. At the American, Mack Sennett saw Chaplin for the first time, and after the director co-founded the Keystone motion picture company, he remembered Chaplin and gave him the starring roles that made the great comedian famous.

Tackling the roof garden, which had been closed for seven years, Morris hired the rising young theatre architect Thomas Lamb to enclose the space and turn it into a second playhouse, which sat 1,147 patrons in the orchestra and single balcony. When the rooftop theatre reopened on July 19, 1909, patrons walked into a rustic environment. The décor called to mind an Adirondacks lodge, foliage twined around supporting columns, and lights suspended from the ceiling twinkled like stars.

Despite intense competition from the vaudeville presentations down the block at Hammerstein's Victoria, William Morris did moderately well at both the Music Hall and the new rooftop theatre. But he received an offer that apparently he could not refuse. Marcus Loewe, who had begun his rise in the movie world as the owner of a string of nickelodeons (usually storefront theatres that presented movie "shorts" for a five-cent admission charge), bought out Morris's interest in the American. Loewe and Morris established offices at the theatre, and in 1911, converted both houses to movies and small-time vaudeville. William Morris died in 1932, and his son, William, Jr., inherited the father's talent agency, still one of the foremost in the business.

MARCUS LOEWE

Loewe eventually would control some four-hundred movie theatres in the United States. To ensure a steady flow of films into his venues, he bought out several movie studios and

Morris also booked an English comedy troupe, thus introducing a very young Charles Chaplin to U.S. audiences. Chaplin caught the eye of filmmaker Mack Sennett, and the rest, as they say, is history.

consolidated them as the film production company Metro-Goldwyn-Mayer, or MGM for short. Dropping the "e" from his surname, Loew created an entertainment empire that endured until 1952, when the federal government forced Loew's, Inc., to divest itself of MGM.

Renamed Loew's American Theatre, the old American stayed in the movie fold until 1929, when burlesque began a premature move over to Forty-second Street. For a year, the main stage was taken over by a stock burlesque company, until one night a fire began in the gallery after a performance and spread throughout the empty theatre, utterly destroying it. Still owned by the Zborowski estate, the building's charred hulk was torn down in 1932. The land on which the American had stood became a parking lot, and so it remained for decades.

In 1983, the Milstein family, which owned real estate throughout New York City, bought the parking lot for $5 million after the State, on account of a cash shortage, demurred. Development languished while the Milsteins sorted out family disputes and waited on plans for the Times Square area to materialize. When that lot became the only parcel in the thirteen-acre redevelopment zone for which there were still no firm intentions, the Milsteins settled their family differences and announced in 2002 that they would break ground on a thirty-five-story building that would "combine office space, street-level stores, and possibly apartments on the site of the former parking lot"—previously the site of the American Theatre. (One of the Milsteins' proposed designs included a giant aquarium).

However, as the New York Times reported in August 2006, the Milsteins "never got beyond erecting a blue construction fence." In July 2006, Howard and Edward Milstein sold the property for $305 million to SJP Properties, named after its chair and CEO, Steven J. Pozycki, and primarily known for developing suburban office parks in New Jersey and Pennsylvania.

When SJP Properties builds its planned $1 billion office tower, that will complete the reclamation of Forty-second Street.

Marcus Loewe, at his desk in the American. He left theatre and moved to
the nascent motion picture industry, eventually building a chain of four-
hundred movie theatres, some of which still bear his name—minus
the final "e."

HAMMERSTEIN'S

VICTORIA

1899

The Victoria, at the corner of Forty-second Street and
Seventh Avenue, was the gateway to the new theatre district.
Hammerstein built it with used construction materials,
salvaged seats, and appointments from demolished theatres.
Even so, everyone agreed it was a handsome house.

Like the mythic phoenix, Oscar Hammerstein I seemed to rise from the ashes of his failed enterprises and move on with renewed vigor and endless faith in theatre and in himself. And so it was with the building of the theatre he called Hammerstein's Victoria, at 201-205 West Forty-second Street. He named it the Victoria because he wanted to proclaim his triumph over the moneylenders who had foreclosed on the Olympia, his grandiose complex on Broadway.

When Hammerstein became aware that the lots on the northwest corner of Forty-second Street and Seventh Avenue were available, he knew that he had found the site for his next theatre. A stable and a few dilapidated buildings occupied the land when Hammerstein secured a lease on the property, which, he discovered, was owned by heirs who squabbled among themselves and paid little attention to it. Making a trip to Albany to meet with the administrator of the owners' estate, Hammerstein, whose powers of persuasion were legendary, wangled a twenty-year lease with an option for another twenty years, all at very favorable terms.

Hammerstein quickly formed a company with his sons Willie and Arthur so that he would not personally be liable if things did not work out, using them to forestall creditors. He raised $25,000 by selling his patent for a machine that utilized all of the tobacco leaf in the manufacture of a cigar. That was not enough to build a theatre, but somehow he raised an additional $50,000. The funds were only a fraction of what a theatre in that era cost to build, but they were enough to launch his venture.

The architectural firm of J. B. McElfatrick and Son ostensibly designed the Victoria, but Hammerstein insisted on being listed as the de facto designer and architect, and involved himself in all phases of the construction. By not designating the building a theatre, he could erect it under the less stringent building code for concert halls. So he declared the project to be a concert hall, a typical Hammerstein ruse that enabled him to do things his way and save money as well.

Working on a shoestring budget, Hammerstein salvaged anything that was usable from the buildings that had been torn down on the property—including the hay from the stable, which he used for insulating the walls. He found carpeting from a transatlantic ocean liner, a secondhand heating system,

secondhand fixtures, used seats, and bought whatever else he could acquire cheaply. Believing that his sons should have trades to fall back on in case of hard times in the theatre, he had seen to it that Arthur was trained as a plasterer. As a result, it was Arthur who designed the molds used for the theatre's decorations. It was Arthur who suggested that the color scheme be white with gold accents. (The walls were already white, so why paint them?) It was Arthur who found a way to avoid buying expensive light fixtures, by leaving holes in the ornamental plaster into which ordinary light bulbs could be placed. The scheme turned out to be unexpectedly effective.

Whether it was McElfatrick's design or Hammerstein's, the interior did not follow a conventional pattern. To reach the orchestra seats, ticket-holders passed through a vestibule, a lobby, and then a promenade that surrounded the orchestra on three sides. Separated from the orchestra only by a heavy marble balustrade, the promenade accommodated tables and chairs at which patrons could eat and drink and still watch the show. From the promenade, two marble staircases rose to the mezzanine and the gallery. The mezzanine was formed by a horseshoe-shaped ring of boxes and backed by its own promenade; the gallery was also horseshoe-shaped, but was outfitted with regular seats. The nearly square proscenium was surrounded by an ornate plaster frame—perhaps more of Arthur's work.

The theatre's façades were intended to be colonial in design, but what with fire escapes crisscrossing them, and big signs covering large portions of them, the architectural style was indistinguishable. Hammerstein didn't mind. The style of the building was eclectic, practical, and served his purpose.

Despite the secondhand, improvised décor, opening night audiences were impressed by the beauty of the 950-seat theatre. Some even paid $100 per ticket to be present at Hammerstein's new creation and to revel in the glow emanating from the hundreds of lights embedded in the walls.

Hammerstein opened the doors of the Victoria on March 2, 1899, with a three-act vaudeville show called *A Reign of Error*, featuring the Rogers Brothers, a comedy duo whose specialty was a "Dutch" act performed in a heavy German accent, with much mauling of the English language. But the highlight of the evening occurred when Hammerstein appeared before the curtain during an entr'acte and brought down the house by expressing his gratitude for the audience's faith in him. New Yorkers love a success story.

Hammerstein next turned his attention to the roof, atop which he had also built a venue. Called the Venetian Terrace, despite a design that was supposed to represent "the grand promenade at Monte Carlo," the roof opened on June 26, 1899, after Hammerstein had shuttered the main theatre for the summer. (In those pre–air-conditioned days, the theatre season ran from September to June, or until warm weather made auditoriums unbearable.)

Elevators whisked patrons to a covered enclosure at the west side of the terrace. A raised platform that served as the stage was located in the center of the roof and was ringed by a gravel walkway and a series of rising terraces, all equipped with tables and chairs so that spectators could eat and drink while enjoying the show. (A second stage apparently was built to one side, but seems to have been rarely used.) The entire roof was decorated with plants and beautifully, if simply, lighted. The only drawback: the acoustics of the open-air stage were poor. To compensate, Hammerstein booked highly physical vaudeville acts (animals, acrobats, jugglers, and the like), which the public adored. The roof theatre was such a success, in fact, that it led to an abbreviated season for its main competition, the roof garden atop the American Theatre, at the west end of Forty-second Street.

By 1901, Hammerstein had joined the Victoria's open-air venue to that of his Theatre Republic, moving the stage to the east end and erecting a shed roof that provided shelter for six hundred fixed seats. Known now as the Paradise Garden, it offered both sideshow acts and large-scale burlesques of Broadway productions. For a time it was the most popular rooftop theatre in New York City.

The roof theatre's drawing power was not equaled downstairs in the main hall, where Hammerstein could not find entertainment to fill the seats. To make good on earlier obligations, he moved several of Theodore A. Liebler's productions into the Victoria during the 1901–1902 season. But whatever personal satisfaction Hammerstein derived from Liebler and Company's high-quality productions, they did not add much to his coffers. He presented Liebler's well-cast, splendidly mounted, serious dramas, *Pelléas and Mélisande* and *Francesca da Rimini*, and Eleonora Duse's company performing *La Gioconda*—with little financial success.

To Hammerstein's amazement, the trend almost reversed

As if to confirm his sophistication and dispel the notion that he catered only to vulgar tastes, Hammerstein continued his season of tragedies by presenting a dramatization of Leo Tolstoy's *Resurrection* with Blanche Walsh.

when an adaptation of Tolstoy's portentous novel *Resurrection* proved so popular early in 1903 that it ran for eighty-eight performances.(This was an era when one-hundred performances was the measure for a hit.) *Resurrection* played New York at the same time that the great actor-manager Sir Herbert Beerbohm Tree was mounting the London production. Tree played the leading part, a master of the house who seduces a serving girl, causing her descent into prostitution and incarceration in Siberia, and then repents. At the Victoria,

With a cast headed by the extraordinary Italian actress Eleonora Duse, George Henry Boker's *Francesca da Rimini* was revived at the Victoria shortly after the theatre opened.

Joseph Haworth and Blanche Walsh played the main roles; both were fine actors, but neither was a bankable Broadway star.

Hammerstein concluded that, since vaudeville seemed to work well on the roof, perhaps he should also try it in the main venue. He was not alone in thinking this. Hammerstein and his shows were drawing the attention of the Theatrical Syndicate, which was poised to add vaudeville to its empire. Marc Klaw and Abraham Erlanger had already lured the Rogers Brothers from Hammerstein, who now pondered whether he would benefit from allying himself with the Syndicate.

Ultimately, Hammerstein decided to remain in the ranks of the independent producers, or "indies." But in February 1904, he rechristened his building the Victoria Theatre of Varieties, dedicated to featuring the best in vaudeville acts.

His first show after the renaming was a resounding success, and Hammerstein knew that he had finally hit upon the right formula for his theatre. A succession of stars from both the vaudeville and legitimate stages appeared at the Victoria, and all contributed to Hammerstein's enrichment. The canny Hammerstein had also cut his admission prices in half, to his great advantage. He made deals that allowed him to present Marie Dressler, the young Charlie Chaplin, Harry Houdini, Will Rogers, Buster Keaton, Bert Williams, Mae West, Fanny Brice, Irving Berlin, and a seemingly endless list of rising stars and established celebrities. Willie Hammerstein hired a European scout to find the finest acts abroad. Learning of the bountiful salaries paid to these variety artists, many Broadway stage stars joined their ranks, eager to appear at the Victoria in a one-act play, a sketch, or a famous scene from the classics. Frequently, however, the Victoria simply featured record-breakers—prize fighters, channel swimmers, Olympians, stunt airplane pilots, and bridge jumpers—who, it would appear, evidently did nothing except stand on the stage.

Miss Prinnt, a musical comedy by George Hobart, offered a change of pace. It featured talented Marie Dressler, a whiskey-voiced comedienne whose career in theatre, vaudeville, and motion pictures lasted for decades.

Will Rogers, just barely out of his teens, joined a Wild West show. His prowess with a lariat, accompanied by his unique homespun patter, drew the attention of vaudeville producers and of Willie Hammerstein, who signed him and made Rogers a star attraction.

Always on the hunt for the unusual performer, Willie Hammerstein hired voluptuous Mae West for her nuanced, suggestive renditions of songs.

Harry Houdini, who frequently appeared at Hammerstein's theatres, was the greatest escape artist of his time. Facing the audience, he would wrap chains around his body, submerge himself in a tank of water, and resurface without the chains.

WILLIE HAMMERSTEIN

Despite his father's disapproval, Willie began to book people who had made headlines for less glorified reasons. He hired them to tell their (usually lurid) stories firsthand, onstage. These "real acts" pulled in the audiences, whose prurient interest seemed unquenchable. Acquitted murderers and assorted criminals were highlighted along with the freaks that Willie found in circuses, museums, and carnival sideshows. Willie also ran film shorts in the Victoria, never anticipating that one day they would become the main attraction, ousting the vaudeville acts.

Piling up a fortune, which Oscar Hammerstein I quickly spent on opera projects, his son Willie ran the Victoria from 1904 until he died in 1914 of a kidney ailment. The elder Hammerstein was heartbroken.

Willie Hammerstein

From 1904 to 1914, the Victoria, under Willie's management, became Oscar's private money tree. Recognizing his son's genius (and because the theatre was making so much money), Oscar tried not to interfere. Some of Willie's practices may have been questionable, but apparently they were not illegal. For instance, the admission price was never printed on the face of a ticket, thus allowing Willie to adjust the price up or down depending on a bill's popularity. Willie dealt similarly with performers' salaries: if an act proved to be a real draw, he would tear up the contract and raise salaries during intermission, to prevent other producers from poaching on his acts.

Serendipity played a major part in the popularity of one of Willie's reality acts. He happened to book Evelyn Nesbit and her dancing partner Jack Clifford into the Victoria at the same time that Nesbit's erstwhile husband, Harry K. Thaw, escaped from an asylum for the criminally insane. (Newspapers accused Willie of having engineered the whole event, but he interpreted it as merely a lucky break.)

Lovely Evelyn Nesbit, an artists' model and chorus girl, had been at the center of a sensational murder trial. At the age of sixteen, she had been either seduced or raped (her version) by the architect and socialite Stanford White, who, having despoiled her, made her his mistress. The tabloid press described White's dinner parties as alcohol-laced sex orgies, during which young, pretty women sailed above the dinner table in a red velvet swing attached to the room's balcony. Thus did Evelyn acquire the sobriquet "The Girl in the Red Velvet Swing." Predictably, White, losing interest in her, found another young woman, and in 1905 Evelyn managed to find a husband: Harry Kendall Thaw of Pittsburgh, heir to an industrial fortune.

But Thaw was mentally unbalanced. After hearing his wife's tale of seduction and debauchery, Thaw stalked White. On the evening of June 25, 1906, Thaw found the architect at the roof theatre atop Madison Square Garden, watching a performance of *Mamzelle Champagne*, and shot White three times during the song "I Could Love a Million Girls." White fell over, dead.

The subsequent trial revived interest in the dark details

Willie Hammerstein lured potential headliners with the promise of hefty paychecks. He added comedienne Fanny Brice to his shows long before Florenz Ziegfeld "discovered" her.

Fanny Brice—Now One of the Boys

Vaudeville Has at Last Captured One of the Best Comedians and Truest Artists on Our Stage

With two hit musicals to his credit, up-and-coming composer Irving Berlin
was in great demand. But Willie managed to get a few songs from him
before Berlin departed for the Ziegfeld Follies.

of Stanford White's life and his affair with Nesbit. Although Thaw was indisputably guilty, mental instability was cited as the cause of his violence, and he was sent to a state hospital for the criminally insane in Beacon, New York, where he apparently enjoyed all sorts of privileges because of his wealth and social standing. In 1913, he escaped from the hospital at the very moment when his former wife was performing at the Victoria for Willie Hammerstein. Willie had hired Nesbit and Clifford for two weeks, but when Thaw reentered the picture and brought more press attention (he had always threatened to kill Nesbit if he ever got out), Willie capitalized on the coincidence, extended the performers' contracts, and reportedly took in $175,000 at the box office. After that, Hammerstein raised Nesbit's salary and, paying her $3,500 per week, sent the notorious chorine on tour.

It was well known in the theatrical community that Oscar was systematically raiding the Victoria's till to build an opera house on Thirty-fourth Street and Eighth Avenue, near the magnificent Pennsylvania Railroad Station. Oscar knew that Arthur and Willie were unalterably opposed to his desire to produce opera, but the sons knew that they were fighting a losing battle. Dutiful children that they were, they helped their father when he needed them. When the Manhattan Opera House opened in December 1906, Arthur was installed in the box office, and Willie was called upon to produce greater and greater profits at the Victoria and funnel them into his father's new venture.

Willie Hammerstein was an ingenious producer, and under his direction the Victoria evolved into one of the finest, and most profitable, vaudeville houses in the country. But in 1913 it suddenly became harder for Willie to turn the profits that his father required of him. That year B. F. Keith and Edward F. Albee, proprietors of the most extensive vaudeville circuit in the United States, began to operate the Palace at Broadway and Forty-seventh Street. The Victoria could not compete with the Palace's stars and stupendous settings. And in any case, during the spring of 1914, Willie became seriously ill. He died on June 10, 1914, at the age of forty-two.

Arthur took over the roof theatre in that summer of 1914, but it did not prosper, and in August, Oscar closed it for renovations. The 1914–15 season was a poor one for both the Victoria and Oscar Hammerstein personally, for he became entangled in legal and financial problems. Regaining control of the Victoria from Arthur, he announced alterations

that would include erecting an office building on part of the Victoria's site. But before he could bring any of that to pass, he fell ill, and his businesses went into receivership. He died in 1919.

The season of 1914–15 was the Victoria's last. A group of Wall Street businessmen leased the Victoria for movies, and eventually S. F. "Roxy" Rothafel was charged essentially with tearing down the Victoria and building the Rialto movie palace on the site in its stead. When the Rialto opened on April 21, 1916, this "Temple of the Motion Picture," as Rothafel called it, sat two thousand people and had no stage, although there was space for a full orchestra to provide musical accompaniment for silent films.

The Rialto lasted until 1935, when Forty-second Street was at a low point. In its place rose a building that contained offices and a seven hundred-seat movie theatre, also called the Rialto, which changed hands until, in the 1950s, the Brandt Organization bought the property. The Brandts built a second, smaller movie theatre on the site of the building's Forty-second Street side, and both movie houses showed "art films," as sex films were called at the time. In 1980 the Rialto's owners briefly turned the larger house into an Off-Broadway theatre, but then it reverted to movies. The building on the site of what had once been Hammerstein's Victoria came down in 2002, as part of the reclamation of Forty-second Street and Times Square.

ARCHITECT AND MISTRESS had met when White was 47, Evelyn 16. He was immensely successful designer of Pennsylvania Station, Washington Square Arch. She was in chorus of musical which featured Florodora Sextet.

In one attempt to fill seats, Willie Hammerstein sought vaudeville acts based on lurid stories lifted from the tabloids. His most famous coup was luring to the stage Evelyn Nesbitt, whose husband, Harry K. Thaw, had been imprisoned for murdering Evelyn's lover, Stanford White.

REPUBLIC
Theatre

OLIVER D. BAILEY
SOLE LESSEE

42nd STREET
West of Broadway

THE THEATRE

REPUBLIC

1900

Oscar Hammerstein I's new playhouse was known almost from its beginning as the Theatre Republic. Its façade was probably the handsomest on Forty-second Street.

Whatever Oscar Hammerstein I's reasons for building the Theatre Republic adjacent to his Victoria Theatre, the result was providential. He expanded the Victoria's roof garden onto the roof of the new building, enlarging his profits as well as the space.

As was usual for those times, the plot of land had dictated the size and shape of the new theatre. The frontage on Forty-second Street was approximately seventy feet wide; the rest of the theatre extended back one-hundred feet. Hammerstein and his architect, Albert E. Westover, put together a design that combined the façade of the new theatre, at 207–211 West Forty-second Street, with the Forty-second Street façade of the Victoria.

The new theatre was to be a small venue suitable for dramas and comedies—not exactly in keeping with Hammerstein's usual taste, which ran to grand opera and spectacle—and Hammerstein crammed as many seats as possible into the house. People sitting in the back rows of the orchestra were so close to the street that outside noise often drowned out the voices of the actors onstage. Out on the sidewalk, two staircases led to the balconies inside, freeing up even more space for seats, and in another space-saving bit of design, Hammerstein tucked the box office underneath the staircases.

The façade was largely unadorned, except for an elaborate, sculpted doorway and a series of round-headed windows separated by the pilasters that supported the main cornice. At the center of this row of windows, a medallion bore the name "Theatre Republic" and the year: 1900. (No adequate explanation has been found for Hammerstein's unconventional transposition of the theatre's name.) Almost halfway up the façade, four small, round windows continued a line of windows on the neighboring Victoria. Five stories above the street, archways topped by large urns surrounded the roof garden.

The interior, which sat 1,050, looked very much like the inside of the Victoria, without the promenade surrounding the orchestra floor. The Republic contained two curved balconies, and six boxes flanked each side of the proscenium. A large central dome was divided by decorative ribs that culminated in a lyre embraced by a pair of cherubs. The interior's dominant colors were green, ivory, and old gold.

Solid rock lay beneath the site of the proposed theatre, but Oscar Hammerstein's budget precluded blasting it away to give the theatre an orchestra pit beneath the stage, nor did he want to give the musicians valuable space in front of the stage. Instead, Hammerstein installed a gallery for the musicians just above the proscenium. Audiences and critics accustomed to the traditional placement of the orchestra were not quite enthusiastic about this new arrangement; one can only imagine how the musicians and conductor felt.

Hammerstein opened the playhouse on September 27, 1900, with *Sag Harbor* by James A. Herne, who, at the time, was one of the few American dramatists giving playwrights some stature in this country. This was Herne's last play and his last appearance in New York as an actor. He himself admitted that his plot about two brothers in love with the same woman was not very original, but he had imbued the story with an honesty that the critics appreciated, even if they did not appreciate the performance of a young character actor named Lionel Barrymore. *Sag Harbor* ran through seventy-six performances before going on tour.

For the rest of the 1900–01 season, the Republic presented plays mounted by independent producers. Among the most interesting offerings were *In the Palace of the King* (produced by Liebler and Company); *Under Southern Skies* (produced by William A. Brady and starring his wife, Grace George); and Mrs. Patrick Campbell in a repertoire that included Arthur Wing Pinero's *The Second Mrs. Tanqueray* and *The Notorious Mrs. Ebbsmith*, Hermann Sudermann's *Magda*, and Björnstjerne Bjornson's *Beyond Human Power*. The spirited Henrietta Crosman appeared in three plays, including Shakespeare's *As You Like It*, in which she played Rosalind. The productions failed to make her a star, but they did boost her career.

For Hammerstein, the most important part of the new theatre was the roof that adjoined the Victoria next door. Now called the Paradise Roof Garden, this was the field in which Hammerstein let his imagination run wild. With its multiple attractions—the vaudeville theatre presenting every type of variety act, a restaurant with singing waiters, and a working Swiss farm on the Republic roof (!)—the Paradise Roof Garden became a magnet for tourists. Even blasé New Yorkers apparently could not resist taking a look at the "farm" in the middle of the city. Where else on Forty-second Street could

a visitor find a real cow, a milkmaid, and vegetables growing in neat rows? In 1904, Hammerstein spirited the Swiss farm to Holland and made it a "Dutch farm," complete with windmill and water wheel. More farm animals were added, and crops were harvested in full view of a curious public. With the addition of other novelties that Hammerstein thought up from time to time, the Paradise Roof proved a gold mine.

DAVID BELASCO

Only two years after building the Theatre Republic, Hammerstein relinquished control of the main stage to the charismatic producer David Belasco—and probably breathed a sigh of relief. The terms could not have been better: Hammerstein received $30,000 annually plus ten percent of the gross receipts from each performance; Belasco received a playhouse from which he could battle the Theatrical Syndicate. Belasco's lease extended for five years, with an option to renew for another five.

Belasco planned extensive renovations for the theatre and, not surprisingly, the cost outran his original estimates. When he discovered that he would not be able to present his scenic magic within the confines of the existing structure, he had the area under the stage excavated so that he could install elevators to handle scene changes more efficiently. But when digging below the stage, Belasco's workmen hit a spring of water that had to be closed off before the elevators could be installed. Above the stage, Belasco built a new, higher gridiron; a counterweight system; and a catwalk, along which stagehands could move to control special effects such as a setting sun or a rising moon. He improved the stage lighting by using resistance dimmers capable of lowering or raising the intensity of the illumination—a new development in theatre technology.

Thanks to the newly excavated area under the stage, musicians could return to their usual place. On the building's top floor, Belasco carved out special quarters for himself and for his star, Mrs. Leslie Carter.

Hammerstein fulfilled his dream of an expanded roof garden by taking over the roof of the Theatre Republic.

David Belasco in his usual, affected attire: turned-around collar and black suit.

The domed ceiling decorated with plaster cherubs was a notable feature of the Theatre Republic.

David Belasco made alterations, including the addition of an elevator beneath the stage. For eight years, the Republic was called the Belasco.

The interior of the Republic, now called the Belasco.

Legend has it that Mrs. Leslie Carter threw herself at Belasco's feet and begged him to make her an actress.

The final Belasco touches were reserved for the décor of the auditorium, for which the producer and his architects, Bigelow, Wallis and Cotten, chose autumnal shades of red, gold, brown, and green, with splashes of rose du Barry, Mrs. Carter's favorite color. Green French tapestries covered the walls of the orchestra level; a rose-colored faux tapestry was painted onto the walls of the second balcony. And nothing was spared for the comfort of the audience: there were a gentlemen's smoking room, a beautifully appointed ladies' room, a telephone for the use of patrons (highly unusual at the time), an electric carriage call, and other amenities

For Belasco's *The Darling of the Gods*, the playwright-producer cast Blanche Bates, another of his retinue of leading ladies, as a kind of Japanese Tosca. The drama's ending surpassed even Puccini's tragedy.

designed to create a welcoming atmosphere.

After a year of planning and construction, the theatre now known as the Belasco opened on September 29, 1902, with Mrs. Carter starring in *Du Barry*, which ran for sixty-three performances. It was followed by a spectacular production of *The Darling of the Gods*, starring another of Belasco's favorites, Blanche Bates, that lasted 182 performances, largely because of the lavish scenery and costumes. In September 1903, Belasco, who was also a dramatist, turned playwright again with *Sweet Kitty Bellairs,* starring Henrietta Crosman, which held the stage for more than three-hundred performances. In the cast was a newcomer named Jane Cowl,

who was destined for stardom in later years on Forty-second Street.

Before his lease with Hammerstein ran out, Belasco forged several other successes at the Belasco. His melodramas *The Girl of the Golden West* and *Rose of the Rancho* each ran for almost an entire season. William C. De Mille's *The Warrens of Virginia* went through almost two-hundred performances, adding to Belasco's record of successful seasons at the theatre.

Doubts linger about David Belasco's place in the history of American theatre, but these derive in large part from the uneven quality of the plays he produced. All were written, coauthored, or liberally doctored by Belasco to fit his formula: a large portion of sensationalism combined with a double-serving of melodrama. Even so, two of Belasco's own scripts achieved immortality as the bases of operas by

Giacomo Puccini: *Madame Butterfly* and *The Girl of the Golden West*. Belasco also produced Eugene Walter's *The Easiest Way*, often cited as among the earliest experiments in realism in American dramatic literature. Its naturalistic dialogue, a surprise (unhappy) ending, and a plot that hung on the redemption (that never occurred) of a beautiful demimondaine made the play unique for its time.

But Belasco really made his mark in the realm of stage technology. Upon his death in 1931, the young turks of the New Stagecraft—a group of American stage designers led by the visionary Robert Edmond Jones—paid tribute to Belasco's genius, even if it had been lavished on hokum. Belasco had been aided by inspired, loyal assistants who translated his ideas into tangible results. His principal scene painter, Ernest Gros, and his lighting expert, Louis Hartmann, had had long careers with Belasco and always attested that they were only doing the Master's bidding. Hartmann later revealed in a book on stage lighting that he had induced Belasco to install a shop in the Republic/Belasco dome, to test the latest technical advances in lighting apparatus before using them onstage. Following Belasco's orders, Gros got rid of painted wings and drops—tired holdovers from previous eras—and instead provided box sets equipped with movable windows, working stoves, real flowers in window boxes, faucets that actually spouted water, and other realistic touches to titillate audiences. Indeed, it was at this theatre that the producer famously replicated Child's Restaurant, one of his favorite Manhattan eateries.

Belasco transformed the Theatre Republic into a laboratory, and when he built the Stuyvesant Theatre on West Forty-fourth Street to his own specifications, he brought along the ideas in stagecraft that had matured at the Forty-second Street house.

The Stuyvesant opened in 1907, and in 1910 Belasco's new theatre acquired the producer's name, while the Belasco on Forty-second Street reverted to Theatre Republic. David Belasco still held the lease on the Republic, however, and in January 1914, he subleased it to the Universal Film Manufacturing Company for the presentation of movies—over the objections of Oscar Hammerstein I, who still owned the theatre. Hammerstein took Belasco to court, but the matter was ultimately settled when Belasco surrendered his lease in March 1914, ending his producing days at the Republic after twelve years of extraordinary success.

A.H. WOODS

The producer A. H. Woods leased the theatre, presumably to present legitimate attractions but, like Belasco, promptly surrendered it to a film company. This time there were no objections from Hammerstein, and anyway Woods soon reclaimed the venue for legitimate theatre with the beginning of the 1914–15 season. One of his productions, Willard Mack's *Kick In*, is notable only because John Barrymore appeared in the cast—the second Barrymore to appear on the Republic's stage.

Woods enjoyed greater success the following season with a production of *Common Clay*, written by a student in George Pierce Baker's prestigious Workshop 47 at Harvard. The play was a mushy melodrama made palatable by the appearance of Jane Cowl, who helped the show run for more than three hundred performances. In October 1916, Arthur Hopkins booked the Republic for Clare Kummer's light comedy *Good Gracious Annabelle*, launching Kummer's career as a popular dramatist.

Unable to produce all the entries at the Republic, Woods continued to lease the house to keep its stage busy, ending the 1916–17 season with *Peter Ibbetson*, produced by the brothers Shubert and starring both Barrymore brothers, John and Lionel. Woods had not gained his reputation as a smart producer for nothing, and for the next several years, whether booking the house or producing the shows himself, he continued to feed the Republic's audiences a diet of bedroom farces and melodramas.

ANNE NICHOLS'S *ABIE'S IRISH ROSE*

In 1922, Woods leased the theatre to author-producer Anne Nichols for *Abie's Irish Rose*, her mindless but warming comedy about the difficulties that ensue when an Irish Catholic girl marries a Jewish boy. The play, which had opened at the Fulton Theatre on Forty-sixth Street in May, moved into the Republic that July and remained there for five years, toting up 2,327 performances and making Nichols a millionaire. This sentimental drama held the record for the longest-running play on Broadway, until *Tobacco Road* opened in 1933 and surpassed it.

The success of *Abie's Irish Rose* was attributed at the time to Nichols's relentless publicity campaign. But as months

After Belasco had moved on, the theatre's name reverted to the Republic.
Arthur Hopkins booked it for Clare Kummer's *Good Gracious Annabelle*, a
light comedy about friends who hire themselves out as servants.

passed, the production gathered its own momentum and
became self-sustaining. During the mid-1920s, immigrants
and their children were settling into patterns that were
distinctly American. Not only were Old World traditions being
cast aside by first-generation Americans, but the émigrés
were also accepting the new order. This is reflected by the
end of Nichols's play, when the bride's Irish father and the
groom's Jewish father forget their differences. The men are
reconciled over the cribs of their grandchildren, whom the
young parents have named Patrick and Rebecca, representing
the two families' cultures and religions. The American melting
pot had succeeded in absorbing them all.

Abie's Irish Rose did not exit the Republic's stage until
September 1927, but by then the theatre's lease had been
passed to the producer Oliver D. Bailey. Under his tenure,
the Republic hosted the Theatre Guild's production of *Porgy*,
the Dorothy and DuBose Heyward drama that had opened
at the Guild Theatre on October 10, 1927. *Porgy*, the play
that George and Ira Gershwin would transform in 1935 into
the rich, lyrical opera *Porgy and Bess*, completed its 367-
performance run at the Republic. That was the lone hit at that
venue until *My Girl Friday*, a drama with a titillating plot that
kept customers coming back for 253 performances, more than
William A. Grew's script was worth. Subsequent bookings
were mostly short-lived, and in December 1930, Depression
economics forced Bailey to surrender his lease to Arthur
Hammerstein.

Oscar Hammerstein I had died in 1919, and Arthur had become custodian of his father's estate. In late December 1930, with the theatre world struggling amid the fierce onset of the Depression, Arthur announced that he intended to wire the Republic to accommodate motion pictures. Then, to everyone's surprise, he granted a twenty-year lease to Billy

Minsky and Joseph Weinstock. The Minsky brothers—Billy, Abe, Herbert, and Morton—were the entrepreneurs who had made "burlesque" a household word; Weinstock was a financial backer. At the Republic, Billy Minsky built two well-lit runways from the stage into the orchestra, to bring the girls closer to their cheering male public.

The profitability of a hit show would often be prolonged by moving it to Forty-second Street. Anne Nichols's *Abie's Irish Rose*, a comedy about an Irish lass and a Jewish lad who marry despite their parents' objections, completed its record 2,327-performance run at the Republic.

Rose McClendon played Serena, Frank Wilson acted Porgy, and Evelyn Ellis was Bess in the Theatre Guild's 1927 production of *Porgy*. George and Ira Gershwin would later turn the love story into the ground-breaking opera *Porgy and Bess*.

THE MINSKY BROTHERS AND AMERICAN BURLESQUE

American burlesque undoubtedly had its good points. Ann Corio, one of the great stars of burlesque in its heyday, and someone who appeared frequently at the Republic, once stated what has since become a historical verity: "Burlesque was the breeding ground . . . for the great comics." Among the comedians who performed off-color routines in burlesque were W. C. Fields, Bert Lahr, Ed Wynn, Bobby Clark, Eddie Cantor, Phil Silvers, Jimmy Durante, and Abbott and Costello.

Porgy, a drama of black American life by Dorothy and DuBose Heyward, adapted from their novel, also finished its run at the Republic.

But by the time Billy Minsky leased the Theatre Republic and instituted a two-shows-a-day policy, charging $1 and $1.50 for tickets, the entertainment value of the form had begun to decline. During a performance in April 1931, the police raided the house, charged the manager and a number of the girls with public indecency, and hauled them off to jail. Of course, in that line of work, a raid was the best publicity, ensuring full houses for the next performances. Bad notices also served as magnets.

Billy Minsky died in 1932, but his brothers kept the business going. Their success at the Republic only brought more burlesque to Forty-second Street. Managers and owners of the Eltinge and, later, the Apollo, noting the Minskys' overflowing box office, surrendered their stages to striptease.

After burlesque entrepreneur Billy Minsky took over the Republic, Ann Corio was a frequent performer.

THE REPUBLIC'S REINCARNATION

Even a whirlwind force named Mayor Fiorello H. La Guardia, who crusaded to rid New York City of immorality, had difficulty ousting burlesque. The Minskys finally capitulated when La Guardia was reelected for a third term, in 1942. Still, the Republic was one of the last burlesque theatres in the city to surrender its license and close.

By the spring of 1944, the Brandt Organization had acquired the Republic and turned it into a "grind" house presenting movies from morn to midnight, and with the country deeply engaged in World War II, the Brandts renamed the theatre the Victory. The Brandts were perhaps under the impression that the block would recover some of its respectability. But instead, Forty-second Street continued to deteriorate, and by the end of the 1960s, the Victory's owners had surrendered it to pornographic films.

In the 1990s, after The New 42nd Street Inc. acquired the lease to the Victory as part of its commitment to reclaim the block's legitimate theatres, the organization selected the Victory for renewal as a nonprofit theatre designated for the city's youth. The internationally known architectural firm of Hardy Holzman Pfeiffer was engaged to bring the Victory back to life without sacrificing what remained of its historic details, and Hugh Hardy, a former scene designer and one of the principals of the firm, was charged with designing the restoration.

Hardy's plan reduced the number of seats to 499, freeing up space for a small lobby at the rear of the auditorium. Excavation beneath the auditorium provided room for amenities such as a concession and a lounge, and an elevator tower constructed in an alley adjacent to the building made the whole venue accessible to the handicapped. What was left of the antiquated backstage equipment was replaced by state-of-the-art technology.

The décor of the restored theatre preserves the central dome embellished with cherubs while retaining much of the elegance of the Belasco era: the wrought-iron stanchions decorated with bees; and the two balconies, but only one tier of elaborate, domed boxes on each side of the proscenium. Hardy and his interior designer chose a color scheme of deep reds and gold, with subtle touches of purple and green. Stripping the exterior of all its accretions from movie theatre days, Hardy returned the façade to a reasonable facsimile of Hammerstein's original, outside staircases and all. Paul Goldberger, architectural critic of the *New York Times*, summed up Hardy's improvements: "It is a restoration that uses the architecture of the past to create a viable 42nd Street for today, and that is a different enterprise altogether from the architecture of make-believe."

On December 11, 1995, the reincarnation of Hammerstein's Theatre Republic, now hailed as the New Victory—with all that the name implied—opened with *Cirque Éloize,* a dazzling production by a Canadian company that was transforming circus performance into high art. Subsequent presentations continued to draw on international artists who could create dynamic works for young audiences and their families. One of the earliest entries was Julie Taymor's

experimental staging of Carlo Gozzi's eighteenth-century fable *The Green Bird.* Pieces choreographed and performed by New Vaudeville artist Bill Irwin comprised another eye-catching program at the reborn theatre.

In 2005, the New Victory celebrated its tenth anniversary. It has emerged not so much as a children's theatre as a place to provide young audiences with high-quality performances by multitalented artists from many disciplines. Under the aegis of The New 42nd Street, this new theatre has reached out with affordable entertainment to the city's schools, the families of its student population, and the general public.

The New Victory exemplifies how a historic playhouse with a battered past can successfully reemerge, when reinvented by visionary leadership and a sympathetic but hands-off government.

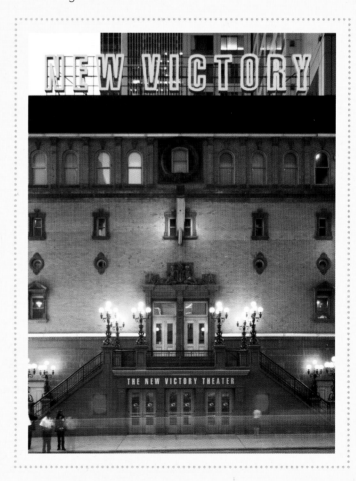

Freed of its tawdry past, the current incarnation of the Republic—the New Victory—has acquired a new purpose as a nonprofit venue dedicated to fare for youngsters and their families.

LYRIC THEATRE

SAM S. AND LEE SHUBERT INC. MANAGERS

REGINALD DE KOVEN
PROPRIETOR

THE LYRIC

1903

The wide, elaborate façade of the Lyric on Forty-third Street still remains, long after Richard Mansfield acted there.

They were a study in contrasts: Reginald De Koven—cultured and poised, an Oxford graduate and music scholar, at home on the highest levels of polite society from birth, impeccably groomed and mannered, reserved and self-assured; and Sam S. Shubert—small and wiry, uneducated and streetwise, born and raised in abject poverty, at home in the rough-and-tumble of show business, dynamic, and charismatic.

These were the partners who built one of the most impressive venues in the theatre district forming around Long Acre Square. De Koven, recently made wealthy from the success of his romantic light operetta *Robin Hood*, supplied the money; Shubert handled the business affairs and apparently supervised the construction. This improbable partnership seemed to work.

The architect they chose was Victor Hugo Koehler. If his extant buildings are representative of his work, he was a captive (as were many of his colleagues) of the Beaux Arts style and may well have made a pilgrimage to Paris's École des Beaux Arts for his training. Having set up practice in 1886, Koehler later established a partnership with another architect, but in 1903 he was working alone when approached about the Lyric. His bread-and-butter practice consisted of churches and synagogues, department stores, and apartment buildings, but he seems also to have gained a reputation for designing theatres.

By 1903, sites in the fast-growing new theatre district were becoming scarce. But Sam Shubert had been able to acquire a T-shaped lot that ran from Forty-second to Forty-third Street between Seventh and Eighth avenues, with the bulk of the land lying along Forty-third. Part of the site was taken up by a one-story brick structure with a tin roof that was listed in the city's records as a "manufactory-workshop," possibly associated with the carriage-building business around Long Acre Square. Koehler was commissioned to design a playhouse that would cover the entire plot of land.

This requirement resulted in an unorthodox plan. Koehler created two façades: one, twenty-feet wide, provided an entryway on Forty-second Street; a larger, more imposing façade provided an entrance on Forty-third Street. A lobby that stretched from Forty-second to Forty-third linked the two entrances and provided ingress into the side of the auditorium. (In more conventional theatre layouts, an audience entered the auditorium at the back of the orchestra.)

The façades were works of art, their style best described as Italian Renaissance approached via the Beaux Arts. On the Forty-third Street façade, an ornate terra-cotta cornice surmounted five arched entryways, and, set in keystones above the three central doors, the ancient deities Apollo, Hermes, and Athena looked down on the street below. The words "Music" and "Drama" were carved in stone above the two side doors.

The building's second story, which was faced in rose-red brick and framed in gray brick, featured a colonnade set with three windows behind a low balustrade. Niches above the windows contained busts of De Koven, William S. Gilbert, and Sir Arthur Sullivan, a tribute to the theatre's owner and two of his idols. Above the niches and below a cornice, carved letters proclaimed "The Lyric Theatre." Three round windows, each wreathed with terra-cotta fruits and capped by a lion's head, rose above the cornice. To the right and left of the colonnade, Koehler placed a rectangular window framed by pilasters and topped by an ornate entablature; above each entablature, he put a circular window, surmounting one with the mask of Comedy and the other with the mask of Tragedy.

A third story contained high windows set between columns and fronted by a wrought-iron railing decorated with the lyre, the Lyric Theatre's symbol. A red-tiled roof with overhanging eaves completed the Forty-third Street façade, although for the protection of patrons alighting from their carriages, Koehler provided a wrought-iron and glass canopy over the arched entryways.

The narrow façade at 213 West Forty-second Street did not allow the architect similar flights of fancy, but a two-story arched window framed by pilasters gave the front of the building a distinctive appearance. The first story featured a stone portico framed by two columns and surmounted by a frieze into which "The Lyric" was inscribed. A riot of terra-cotta decoration completed the façade's ornamentation.

Also, as protection against the elements, a canopy of wrought iron and glass jutted out from the portico to the curb. To light an audience's way, two electrified globes flanked the portico, and a sign framed in electric lights and bearing the image of a lyre towered above the portico.

The interior of the Lyric, by contrast, was conservative,

The handsome Lyric Theatre, built by Reginald De Koven using the profits from his operetta *Robin Hood*, initially opened onto Forty-third Street. The popularity of Forty-second Street led De Koven and his business partners, the Shuberts, to construct a Forty-second Street entrance instead.

although once more, the architect's Beaux Arts predilection influenced the décor. Laurel-leaf molding surrounded the proscenium, which measured forty feet in width by thirty-five feet in height. On each side of the house, nine boxes were set into a vaulted arch that filled the wall between the proscenium and the two balconies, and columns with spiral fluting and ornate capitals framed each of the three tiers of boxes. (The vaulted arch also served as an acoustical sounding board.) The balconies, one atop the other, rounded out the seating in the Lyric, which originally accommodated some 1,349 playgoers. Fully cantilevered balconies had not yet been introduced in New York theatres, and the Lyric's balconies were supported by narrow columns that extended from the orchestra floor up through the first balcony—a less-

than-happy solution in a theatre, where an audience's ability to see the stage is all-important.

Over the auditorium floated a shallow dome set into a flat ceiling. Once again Koehler chose a laurel-leaf motif for the decorative molding, into which he placed tightly spaced incandescent lamps. A stenciled border ringed the dome, and a painted ribbon united the images of lyres and Greek masks. Ornamental moldings and stenciling were also applied to other parts of the auditorium. Over the proscenium, a mural depicted the Greek hero Orpheus playing his lyre, surrounded by maidens cavorting in the clouds.

Koehler's color scheme for the interior was somewhat unusual in that era of red plush and gold. He chose light apple green and rose for the general palette and old ivory tinged with gold for the ornamental plasterwork. Rose-colored satin damask was applied to the walls of the boxes and the first balcony, and the seats were covered in an apple-green fabric. The rose-hued main curtain was embroidered with gold thread. The overall effect was one of restraint and delicacy.

THE SHUBERT BROTHERS

When, on October 12, 1903, the first-night audience passed through the doors of the new theatre to see the popular actor-manager Richard Mansfield in a revival of *Old Heidelberg,* they may have appreciated the splendor of the playhouse as much as they did the production. Certainly the newspaper critics found the theatre attractive and comfortable, and were quick to point out the " absence of extravagance and gaudiness in the decoration." The arch-curmudgeon, Alan Dale of the *New York American,* described the color scheme as "tomatoes and lettuce" but did not begrudge his admiration. The side entrance into the auditorium confused several reviewers, though it did not lessen their enthusiasm for the new theatre. And all the critics approved the production and its star.

The exterior of the Lyric's Forty-second Street entrance.

The interior of the Lyric Theatre, with its three rows of elaborate boxes.

It had been no small triumph for the comparatively un-tested Shubert brothers to lure Mansfield into their theatre, for the British-born actor had been one of the first stars to refuse to submit to the Shuberts' archenemy, the Syndicate. He was saving the day for Sam, Lee, and Jacob. J. "Jake" Shubert by appearing in *Old Heidelberg*. The Shuberts had produced the drama the previous season, and it had been deemed a failure. This time they hoped that Mansfield's skill-ful acting would rescue it. The Shuberts not only gave Mans-field the honor of opening the Lyric, they also promised him yearly bookings for his company at the new house.

Then in his mid-forties, Mansfield was acting the part of a nineteen-year-old prince in *Old Heidelberg*. But he astonished audiences with his youthful makeup, energetic movement, and altogether graceful performance. *Old Heidelberg* would figure again in the Shuberts' saga: in 1924 it was set to music by Sigmund Romberg and, as *The Student Prince*, became one of the Shuberts' enduring successes. Mansfield, ironically, never again appeared at the Lyric (he died in 1907 at the age of fifty-three).

But other repertory companies headed by famous actors did become staples at the new theatre. In January 1904, Ada Rehan and Otis Skinner, two popular actors then in their forties, played Shakespeare in repertory and were followed by the famous Parisian comedienne Gabrielle Réjane, who starred in no less than thirteen French plays. Coasting on their reputation as independent producers, the Shuberts even enticed Sarah Bernhardt back to America for one of her numerous "farewell" tours, booking the French star and her company into the Lyric in 1905.

The brothers enjoyed a double victory in signing up the Divine Sarah. Not only did she agree to appear under their management, but the Shuberts reaped immensely favorable press when the Syndicate refused to allow the celebrated actress to appear in any of its theatres. Unruffled, Lee Shubert announced that he and his brothers would rent circus tents if Bernhardt played a town where a Syndicate theatre shut its doors and a non-Syndicate house was unavailable. The tour proved a public relations triumph, but Sam Shubert did not live to enjoy the victory over the brothers' rivals. Bernhardt took the stage of the Lyric in December 1905, but Sam had died in a train accident the previous May.

It was a time when the idea of "hits" and "flops" did not dominate theatrical production. Plays and musicals could

Bound by family ties and possessed of unbridled ambition, the Shubert brothers descended on Broadway to beat the Theatrical Syndicate at its own game. The organization they founded has outlasted its rivals and spanned several generations.

have short runs without being considered outright failures, and repertory companies alternated plays on a nightly basis, extending audiences' options. Early in 1907, the famous company headed by E. H. Sothern and Julia Marlowe came into the Lyric with Shakespeare and contemporary plays in repertory. When they left, the Italian Ermete Novelli arrived. Renowned on the Continent for his protean talents—Novelli could play Shakespeare, dramatizations of French and Italian novels, and monologues of his own devising—he was performing in America for the first time, courtesy of the Shuberts. Like Réjane, Bernhardt, the Italian actor Tommaso Salvini, and other non–English-speaking stars from abroad, Novelli played in his native language, and American audiences did not seem to mind.

Mrs. Patrick Campbell, considered in her day one of the most brilliant English actresses, led another admired repertory company. Brought to the Lyric in November 1907 by Theodore A. Liebler, Mrs. Campbell played a short engagement of four plays, including Ibsen's *Hedda Gabler* and Hermann Sudermann's *Magda*, both tours de force for the actress. Deeply admired by George Bernard Shaw, Mrs. Campbell kept up a lively correspondence with that great playwright and would become the inspiration for Eliza Doolittle in Shaw's *Pygmalion*.

New York audiences would eventually tire of repertory companies, but while they were in vogue, they brought the Lyric and other Broadway theatres a range of offerings and a display of histrionic talent rarely matched in subsequent decades.

Before he died in the spring of 1905, Sam Shubert brought in a number of major stars who were opposed to the Theatrical Syndicate: Otis Skinner, Arnold Daly, James O'Neill, Laurette Taylor, Minnie Maddern Fiske, and Walter Hampden. One such star, the comedian and singer Jefferson De Angelis, opened in January 1905 in *Fantana*, the most successful of the Lyric's early productions. Billed as a "Japanese-American Musical Comedy," this confection, which Sam produced—and supposedly coauthored with Robert Bache Smith—featured tuneful music and a bevy of pretty girls. It stayed on for nearly three-hundred performances.

Channing Pollock's *The Pit* contained a vivid scene depicting the floor of the stock exchange, when the hero fails to corner the market in wheat. In the end, he loses everything but his wife.

Happyland, a new comic opera by Reginald De Koven, followed *Fantana* but did not fare nearly so well. The composer whose money had largely built the Lyric was, in fact, having a rough time of it. Back in 1903, his light opera *The Red Feather* had moved into the house after *Old Heidelberg* departed, but *Feather*, while glorious visually, was not a success otherwise. What the show did accomplish was to further the reputation of its producer, Florenz Ziegfeld, Jr., as a man of exceptional, if lavish, taste. Audiences and critics kept hoping that De Koven would write another *Robin Hood*, but he never did. In 1907, *The Girls of Holland*, De Koven's final entry at the Lyric, also fizzled.

Producers on the cusps of their careers, producers and stars who were fighting the Syndicate—these were the mainstays of the Lyric during its first decade. After Ziegfeld came another born gambler, William A. Brady, with an adaptation of Frank Norris's novel *The Pit*, which featured mustachioed Wilton Lackaye, a star under Brady's management. The play, a moderate success, told the unhappy tale of a man so driven by ambition and greed that he attempts to corner the wheat market on the stock exchange and ends up losing everything except his loyal wife. In those

Playwright Langdon Mitchell tailored *The New York Idea* for Minnie Maddern Fiske, the first lady of the Broadway stage. In this satire of upper-class New York, various married pairs uncouple and recouple before the final curtain.

Scenes in Mrs. Fiske's New Play "The New York Idea"

Ida Vernon   Emily Stevens   Blanche Weaver   Mrs. Fiske   Charles Harbury

ACT I. The Phillimore family discussing their wedding announcement list, while the Judge reads his evening paper, and Mrs. Karslake, his prospective bride, gets an insight

years of corporate trusts and monopolies, the theme must have resonated among a sizable share of the audience.

In 1906, Syndicate foe Arnold Daly produced and starred in George Bernard Shaw's *Arms and the Man* and *How He Lied to Her Husband*. (From time immemorial, anything British was considered the height of sophistication on Broadway.) Also in 1906, Harrison Grey Fiske, another staunch Syndicate antagonist, brought his wife, the famed Mrs. Fiske, to the Lyric in Langdon Mitchell's *The New York Idea*, a clever satire about marriage and divorce. The following season, Mrs. Fiske demonstrated her versatility and what she called "natural, true acting" by moving from the comedy of manners to serious drama, taking on the role of Rebecca West in Henrik Ibsen's *Rosmersholm*.

But the play that succeeded best during this opening decade of the Lyric's existence was *The Blue Mouse*, a German comedy Americanized by the prolific and popular dramatist Clyde Fitch. Blessed with the skill to create unforgettable characters, excellent dialogue, and well-structured plots, as well as the ability to direct his own plays, Fitch staged *The Blue Mouse* in November 1908. Like all farces, *Mouse* served up an abundance of swinging doors and coincidences, and a plot that defied logic. The production proved so successful that it ran through the season at the Lyric and moved on to another theatre.

A little more than a year later, in December 1909, Fitch's *The City*, probably his strongest play and by far the most interesting production of the Lyric's early years, was introduced with a stellar cast that included Walter Hampden. Fitch's drama showed the effects of city life on a small-town family, with grim results. Lauded by the critics for its honest appraisal of the human condition, *The City*, like *Mouse*, enjoyed such a long run that the Shuberts moved it to another venue to free up the Lyric for other productions.

A woman authored the last of the significant dramas presented at the Lyric during this time. Rachel Crothers, whose work is now being rediscovered by feminist scholars, was an actress, director, and commercially successful play-wright. In Crothers' *Ourselves*, which opened at the Lyric in November 1913, a society matron with a social conscience brings a prostitute into her home in order to reform the lady, but the experiment fails after a tryst with the woman's brother is exposed. A product of America's first wave of feminism, Crothers tackled social problems, and did so with-out sentimentality.

Mixed among the Lyric's comedies and dramas were light operas, operettas, and comic operas. Some, like De Koven's last efforts, have passed into history leaving barely a trace. Others were instant hits. Best remembered (and still revived) is *The Chocolate Soldier*, loosely based on Shaw's *Arms and the Man*, with music by Oscar Strauss. Producers who had rejected it as a risky enterprise, because of its association with a Shaw thesis play, later rued their decision. Fred C. Whitney, an independent producer who gambled on its success, had first taken it to Marc Klaw and Abraham Erlanger, but they could not guarantee him a playhouse in those days of theatre shortages. The Shuberts could and did, producing it at the Lyric in September 1909. Although *Soldier* had to vacate the Lyric to make room for another production, it returned for a second stay before moving on to other theatres (including the Lyric Theatre in London), making money for all concerned.

Three years later, the Lyric hosted another musical success when Arthur Hammerstein, producing his first Broadway show, commissioned Rudolf Friml to compose his first Broadway score. The delightful result was *The Firefly*, with book and lyrics by Otto Hauerbach (later Harbach).

The show's temperamental star, Emma Trentini, played an Italian street singer in love with a social-register yachtsman, in a Cinderella story that few in the audience could believe. But the music and the singing entranced critics and public alike and kept the show running at the Lyric for more than one-hundred performances. In a kind of testimony to these musicals' longevity, in 1937 and 1941, Metro-Goldwyn-Mayer adapted *The Firefly* and *The Chocolate Soldier* into movies, starring, respectively, Jeanette MacDonald and Risë Stevens.

The years spanning 1915 to 1920 saw only two notable successes at the house De Koven built, and neither was a musical. In 1915 came *Abe and Mawruss* (later renamed *Potash and Perlmutter in Society*), a comedy by Roi Cooper Megrue and Montague Glass that depended on the comic bumbling of the two leading characters, partners in a cloak-and-suit company. When Mawruss quits the firm to "go high society" on Wall Street—and goes broke—Abe rides in to the rescue. The other hit, *The Unknown Purple*, starred Richard Bennett in a dark tale of revenge. Playwrights Roland West and Carlyle Moore employed flashbacks and simultaneous action to convey the plot's twists and turns, as the hero is transformed from a decent man into a calculating avenger obsessed with his wife's treachery. Melodramatic but effective, *Unknown Purple* lasted at the Lyric for almost the entire 1918–19 season.

Reginald De Koven died on January 15, 1920, but his estate had already sold the Lyric in the previous year to the sportsman E. E. Smathers. In 1921, Smathers leased the house to the producer Harry H. Frazee, but when it was noted that the Shuberts still had several more years of *their* lease to complete, Frazee withdrew, and the Lyric continued under the Shuberts' management.

Long before the sale of the Lyric, however, the brothers' attention had shifted to their new theatre and offices on West Forty-fourth Street. The fortunes of the Syndicate had ebbed—the last Syndicate agreement expired in 1916—and it was the two remaining Shubert brothers who now held a monopoly on theatres around the country. They were also the major force on Broadway, expanding north of Forty-second Street and gobbling up the leases of many extant playhouses. They used their properties like pieces on a checkerboard, moving productions from one theatre to another as they saw fit. As far as they were concerned, keeping a presence on Forty-second Street was no longer important.

THE LYRIC'S PRODUCTIONS

There were worthy productions at the Lyric during the 1920s, and some actors, singers, and dancers who would later attain fame on Broadway—or in motion pictures—appeared on the Lyric's stage. In 1922, Fred and Adele Astaire arrived in *For Goodness Sake*, a cheerful vehicle for their singing and dancing talents. Performers since childhood, the brother and sister had become the young favorites of Broadway audiences and reviewers. One particularly effusive critic wrote that the Astaires' show was "the kind of musical comedy that makes Broadway the theatrical centre of the world."

In 1925, the four Marx Brothers took over the Lyric's stage with *The Cocoanuts*, which then finished its long run at another theatre. Having cut their teeth on vaudeville, the brothers were bringing their particular brand of antic comedy to Broadway. When they were onstage, nothing else

mattered—neither the music by Irving Berlin nor the book by George S. Kaufman. Indeed, Kaufman professed to be amazed when, sitting in the audience, he occasionally heard his own lines being spoken by these outrageous ad-libbers.

Whether it was the mood of the Roaring Twenties that accounted for it or some other factor, comedy went over well at the Lyric, as witnessed by the reception given the comedy team of Bobby Clark and Paul McCullough in a musical called *The Ramblers*. Graduates of minstrel shows, circuses, and vaudeville, Clark and McCullough had delighted New York audiences in revues before becoming Broadway headliners. Their clowning, described as "amiable tomfoolery," laid waste to the plot, but audiences did not appear to mind that the comedians' hijinks constituted the whole show.

In the spring of 1927, the producers Jacob and Joseph Oppenheimer bought the Lyric and announced their intention to demolish the building and replace it with an office tower that would include a seventeen hundred seat playhouse for musical comedies. Fortunately, their plans fell through, and E. E. Smathers reclaimed the theatre just a year later. Saved from destruction (at least for the time being), in 1928 the Lyric hosted the return of Florenz Ziegfeld, who produced a musical version of *The Three Musketeers*, starring Vivienne Segal, with Dennis King as D'Artagnan. With music by Rudolf Friml, lyrics by P. G. Wodehouse and Clifford Grey, and scenery by Austrian-born Joseph Urban, the show was a solid hit and remained at the theatre for more than three-hundred performances. Gloriously overproduced in the Ziegfeld manner, it ran for almost four hours. The love duet "One Kiss" would have an even longer musical life.

Close on its heels, in 1929 came *Fifty Million Frenchmen*, with music and lyrics by Cole Porter and a book by Herbert Fields. Arriving at the Lyric about a month after Black Friday at the stock market, the musical perhaps provided audiences with a respite from the grim realities of post-Crash life. Although the critics were not unanimous in their praise, they found much to like about the musical and encouraged audiences to attend. At least one song, "You Do Something to Me," was vintage Porter. Set in Paris, which seemed far

Owners and managers came and went at the Lyric, but the theatre survived. In 1922, one highlight occurred when Fred and Adele Astaire danced across the Lyric's stage in *For Goodness Sake*.

from the anxieties of Wall Street, and lavishly produced, the show provided pure escapist theatre.

But the country's economic tailspin had caught up with the Lyric. After *Fifty Million Frenchmen* closed in July 1930, the house went dark for almost a year. When the Lyric reopened, under a lease held by William and Harry Brandt, it seesawed back and forth between vaudeville and movies before switching entirely to films. It reopened as a legitimate house briefly in 1931 and again in 1932, when it was rented to the impresario Sol Hurok for Teatro dei Piccoli, an Italian marionette troupe.

Then in March 1933, *Run, Little Chillun!*—a drama by the famous choirmaster Hall Johnson—arrived on the Lyric's stage. Billed as "A Negro Folk Drama in Four Scenes" and hailed as a worthy successor to *The Green Pastures* (the Pulitzer Prize–winning success of 1930), the show was widely considered an epochal event in the American theatre, bringing, as one critic put it, "reverence to an infidel season on Broadway." *Run, Little Chillun!* filled the house with spirituals magnificently sung by Johnson and his Hall Johnson Choir, and dances choreographed by Doris Humphrey. Many in the audience paid more than one visit to the Lyric to see the show, which was forced to close after only 130 performances because of its overwhelming production costs: counting the choir and the dancers, there were 175 people in the cast.

Run, Little Chillun! was the last event of importance to take place on the Lyric's stage. Vaudeville returned briefly, then an experiment with tabloid or "tab" shows (shortened versions of well-known plays), and finally movies. By July 1934, the Lyric was just another movie house on the street; ten years later, it had become part of the Brandt movie chain, which from time to time made careless physical alterations to the theatre. The boxes were removed when wide-screen projection came into vogue; the original seats and carpeting wore out and were replaced; water damaged V. Hugo Koehler's ornamental plaster; and in the lobbies and the auditorium, any decoration that had not been painted over was covered with plywood.

With the reawakening of interest in Forty-second Street during the late 1970s, the Brandts toyed with the idea of returning the Lyric to legitimate drama, but changed their minds after their anticipated success with the converted Apollo Theatre never materialized. A study of Forty-second Street playhouses in the 1980s brought about another spate of attention, and the Lyric was assessed for a possible return to live productions. The theatre was deemed salvageable, although it would require an immense amount of restoration at high cost. However, no one came forward to rebuild and restore it, and so the antique theatre became a condemned property and was acquired by the State of New York; in 1990, its fate fell into the hands of The New 42nd Street Inc. The Canadian entertainment company Livent leased the property in 1996, and in 1997, a great theatrical heritage was lost when the stage and the auditorium were demolished to erect the Ford Center for the Performing Arts. Parts of the Lyric live on in the venue's subsequent name: the Hilton Theatre.

In 1929, the Lyric's days were numbered, but just before the stock market crashed, Cole Porter's *Fifty Million Frenchmen* opened, and Porter enjoyed his first major success.

An elaborate scene from *Fifty Million Frenchmen*, seemingly with fifty million actors on stage.

One of the last productions at the Lyric was Hall Johnson's *Run, Little Chillun!* Johnson, a composer and the founder of the Hall Johnson Choir, called his play a folk drama. It involved a conflict between Christian and African religious sects.

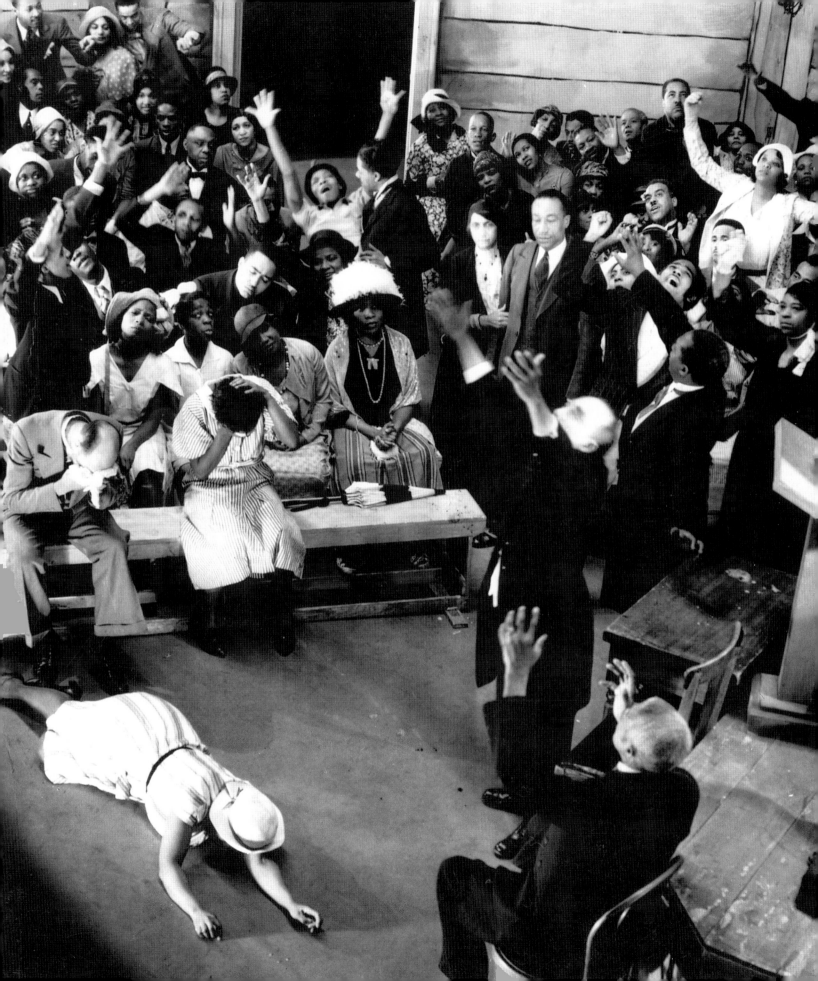

NEW AMSTERDAM THEATRE

42D ST. WEST OF BROADWAY

NEWAM THEATRE CORPORATION

ERLANGER, DILLINGHAM & ZIEGFELD

DIRECTORS

THE NEW

AMSTERDAM

1903

A view of the New Amsterdam Theatre from Seventh Avenue.

A turn into West Forty-second Street from the southwest corner of Seventh Avenue—and a few steps down the street—brings today's theatre patron face to face with a pink-neon art deco sign announcing the New Amsterdam Theatre. But in 1903, when the theatre at 214 West Forty-second Street was new, a grand entrance three stories high greeted the theatregoer. Built of gray limestone and sculpted terra-cotta, it sported an ornate, free-standing sculpture by the noted artist George Gray Barnard, and this elaborate decoration rested atop a curved, bronze window frame. The theatre's name was writ in lights within a diadem above the entrance doors.

The architects had incorporated the theatre within the ten-story office building that served as headquarters for the new theatre's owners, and at night, lights on the ten-story façade illuminated the marquee. All in all, the New Amsterdam's entryway was the most impressive on Forty-second Street.

In the early years of the new century, when Abraham Lincoln Erlanger and Marc Klaw decided to build their flagship theatre, they did not fail to notice that the old theatre district around Union Square was rapidly becoming passé. Two auspicious events had occurred: The Metropolitan Opera House on "upper" Broadway (at Fortieth Street) had supplanted the Academy of Music on Fourteenth Street, and one of their colleagues, the producer Charles Frohman, had built his Empire Theatre almost directly across the street from the Met. The Forty-second Street presence of Oscar Hammerstein I's two stages—the Victoria and the Theatre Republic—and of Henry French's American Theatre, were also good reasons for Klaw and Erlanger to consider locating their new house "uptown." If a new theatre district was to develop along Forty-second Street and Long Acre Square, this opportunistic pair wanted to play a part in it—a large part. As if to establish themselves as men of good taste, the partners hired the architects Henry B. Herts and Hugh Tallant to design their playhouse, after acquiring property that fronted on Forty-second Street and stretched through the block to Forty-first Street.

Ground was broken in the spring of 1902, but the doors did not open until October 26, 1903. And what an opening it was! The first-nighters walked under the brilliantly lighted

A detailed view of the New Amsterdam's façade.

Wagner's great opera cycle *The Ring of the Nibelungs.*

From the lobby, the audience passed into the entrance foyer, which included a refreshment bar. More panels adorned the walls, each featuring allegorical themes and embellished by intricate designs of flowers and entwined leaves. Topping off the foyer, a ceiling dome of stained glass depicted "The Song of the Flowers."

Leaving the foyer, patrons entered a grand promenade on the orchestra floor, where they could savor the full effect of the magnificent domed auditorium. Here, too, art nouveau pervaded the décor: in the murals; interlaced with wrought iron on the balustrades and railings; and in the boxes, each of which was encrusted with flowers. The floral theme was woven into the stage curtain, and allegorical figures dominated the murals over the proscenium and on the sides of the auditorium. Everywhere, it seemed, twisted vines, leaves, and flowers mingled with ethereal figures. (Art nouveau was more a decorative mode than an architectural style, and some critics likened it to a "strange decorative disease" because of its overwhelming reliance on nature.)

No theatre built during the Gilded Age could match the sumptuousness of the New Amsterdam. The carefully wrought murals, friezes, and reliefs; the molded plaster and terra-cotta; and the painted glass and ironwork—all had been fabricated and installed by master craftsmen and women, part of the thousand-person workforce responsible for the splendor of the place. New Yorkers are unyielding architectural critics. For some, the profusion of art nouveau combined to endow a spectacular palace; for others, it was an exercise in monumental bad taste.

For the more than sixteen hundred spectators the theatre accommodated, every section offered unobstructed views of the stage, thanks to the architects' use of cantilevered and suspended balconies. And because of Tallant's special knowledge of acoustics, the audience could hear an actor's every word and the orchestra's every note. Herts and Tallant devised an advanced system of heating and ventilating the building, by locating ducts in the walls and grilles in the floor for the even distribution of filtered fresh air. The comfort of the audience was a high priority for Klaw and Erlanger.

Backstage, the latest technology was employed to manipulate the scenery in such a way that it would delight the spectators. The ample stage, one hundred by fifty-two feet, was equipped with plateaux elevators that raised,

marquee through the open-air vestibule, then entered a long lobby. There, along the left wall, were bronze office doors and three elevator doors decorated with floral motifs characteristic of the art nouveau style. On the right wall, mirrored panels set between terra-cotta pilasters were also ornamented by intricate floral and leaf patterns. Twelve pale-colored panels below the dark coffered ceiling depicted scenes from Greek drama, Shakespearean drama, and Richard

VIEW TOWARD STAGE NEW AMSTERDAM THEATER, NEW YORK

THE INLAND ARCHITECT
AND NEWS RECORD

The owners of the New Amsterdam—the barons of
Broadway—Marc Klaw and Abraham Erlanger spared no
expense on their sumptuous theatre.

The elaborate proscenium of the New Amsterdam offered
audiences murals and art nouveau décor, design that was
replete throughout the ornate theatre.

lowered, and—perhaps unique in the United States—tilted across the entire stage from side to side. These elevators could effect scene changes by lowering the entire stage and scenery by thirty-three feet. No theatre in New York—or in the entire country for that matter—could equal the stage facilities offered at the New Amsterdam. The total cost of this theatrical marvel was reputed to have been more than $1.5 million, in an era when theatres could be erected for less than one quarter of that amount.

An interior view of the New Amsterdam showing the proscenium boxes, each decorated with a floral motif.

KLAW AND ERLANGER'S PRODUCTIONS

For the opening production, Klaw and Erlanger chose Shakespeare's *A Midsummer Night's Dream,* starring the comic actor Nat C. Goodwin as Bottom, the weaver who is temporarily transmogrified into an ass. Victor Herbert was engaged to adapt Mendelssohn's music for full orchestra, and Ned Wayburn, the leading Broadway dance master, staged the chorus of 150 dancers and singers in eye-popping musical numbers. The entire spectacle cost $50,000—about five times the usual outlay for a Broadway production.

A Midsummer Night's Dream, unfortunately, was not as huge a success as the theatre in which it opened. Goodwin's fans found his offstage antics endlessly fascinating (he'd been married five times), but many in the audience and among the critics remembered only his early career as a vaudeville comedian and could not accept his playing Shakespeare. In addition, theatregoers generally felt that the elaborate production overshadowed the play.

Despite their legendary business acumen, Klaw and Erlanger did not fare well as artistic managers, perhaps the result of their divergent tastes. Erlanger favored spectacles and musical extravaganzas, while Klaw preferred Shakespeare and contemporary Continental playwrights. Both, however, ascribed to the power of stars at the box office. *Midsummer Night's Dream* was quickly followed by the English Christmas pantomime *Mother Goose,* and as insurance, the partners engaged Broadway's leading man-about-theatre, George M. Cohan, to give the show the Yankee touch. The nursery rhyme–themed show had a somewhat more respectable run than the Shakespeare play.

During the spring of 1904, Klaw and Erlanger brought the actor-manager Richard Mansfield to the New Amsterdam, perhaps to counter their rivals across the street at the Lyric, where the Shuberts had engaged Mansfield during the previous fall in the Lyric's opening production. (Mansfield had initially opposed Klaw, Erlanger, and the Theatrical Syndicate, but this time around, his principles apparently stopped at the stage door.)

After Mansfield's company had departed, Klaw and Erlanger revived the melodrama *The Two Orphans* with an all-star cast and, to round out their first season, brought in the popular comic duo of Joe Weber and Lew Fields in *Whoop-*

Dee-Doo, in the comedians' last joint appearance before severing their partnership.

Inevitably, Klaw and Erlanger realized that they could not produce every show in their house, not only because of the cost but also because it distracted them from their other theatre activities. To continue offering a steady flow of plays and musicals, the partners opened the New Amsterdam to other producers and managed their theatre as a booking house to ensure that rental fees would always be forthcoming.

Because of its stage facilities and splendor, the New Amsterdam was eagerly sought after by Broadway's leading producers. But Klaw and Erlanger picked and chose among the contenders to be sure that outsiders' productions merited a run at the beautiful theatre. In 1907, Henry W. Savage, one of the producers "anointed" by Klaw and Erlanger, presented the New Amsterdam's first solid hit—Franz Lehar's delightful *The Merry Widow*. Based on a Viennese operetta and receiving a first-rate production from Savage, *Merry Widow* ran for more than four-hundred performances. New Yorkers were humming Lehar's tunes, particularly "The Merry Widow Waltz," for months.

Indeed, musicals adapted from European sources were a popular item on Broadway in those years. In 1910 and 1911, respectively, *Madam Sherry* and *The Pink Lady* also proved hits at the New Amsterdam, and since Klaw and Erlanger were actually the producers of *The Pink Lady*, they finally had achieved the success for which they had yearned. But it was not until the arrival of the whirlwind named Florenz Ziegfeld, Jr., that the pleasure palace created by the partners would become the new theatre district's most celebrated venue.

FLORENZ ZIEGFELD, JR.

Florenz Ziegfeld, Jr., was born in 1867 to a prominent musical family in Chicago. His father was a classical musician who had founded the Chicago Musical Academy, but the younger Ziegfeld's tastes ran to popular music, ballroom dancing, and Wild West shows. During Chicago's 1893 World's Columbian Exposition, Ziegfeld, Sr., briefly ran a nightclub to finance

Nat Goodwin played Bottom the Weaver in the New Amsterdam's opening production, Shakespeare's *A Midsummer Night's Dream*. Klaw and Erlanger thought that casting the popular comedian would make the production a sure-fire success.

more serious pursuits. While working there, Flo, Jr., became convinced that vaudeville was the route to money and fame. From his Chicago base, he created a touring troupe featuring the novelty act Sandow, billed as the strongest man in the world. Adding attractions as he found them, the young producer built a thirty-two city itinerary of theatres from New York to Kansas City. By his thirtieth birthday he had earned $250,000 (millions by today's accounting) but soon gambled his fortune away. That was to be his lifelong pattern: earn a million, lose a million.

Ziegfeld's first Broadway venture was the revival of *A Parlor Match,* coproduced with the playwright-producer Charles Evans. In 1895, the men went to London in search of a fresh talent to play the lead and were advised to catch a performance by a beauteous singer named Anna Held. Ziegfeld not only signed the coquettish Held under his exclusive management but fell madly in love with her. (Falling for his leading ladies was another lifelong pattern.) Ziegfeld brought Held back to New York, where she divorced her European husband to live openly with the producer. (Witnessed by Diamond Jim Brady and Lillian Russell, the Ziegfeld-Held informal "marriage ceremony" performed in 1897 was never considered legal.) Although Held's charm outshone her theatrical talents, Ziegfeld's audacious promotion lifted her to stardom, and he featured her in lavish Broadway productions supported by innovative press campaigns. This string of shows filled Ziegfeld's bank account, but his weakness for the gambling tables rendered him nearly penniless by 1905.

Nothing is known of the first encounter between Klaw, Erlanger, and Ziegfeld, but the meeting must have had a kind of inevitability: sooner or later, these entrepreneurial dynamos were bound to collaborate. Initially, however, Klaw and Erlanger offered Ziegfeld a measly $200 per week to stage some vaudeville acts. Eventually, they offered him a contract to produce entertainments at the Jardin de Paris, atop the New York Theatre. (The New York Theatre was half of the Olympia, the complex on Broadway between Forty-fourth and Forty-fifth streets that Oscar Hammerstein I had opened in 1895 and that Klaw and Erlanger had bought and rebuilt.) There, from 1907 to 1911, Ziegfeld produced an annual revue that he called the *Follies,* a name suggested by Held and apparently borrowed from a newspaper column of the time by Harry B. Smith: "The Follies of the Day." (Smith claimed direct credit for the suggestion.)

Ziegfeld was not the inventor of the revue form, but he breathed new life into it. In contrast with American vaudeville—a concoction of unrelated acts comprising everything from equines to arias—the Parisian-style revue that Ziegfeld adapted, following Held's advice, was built around a single topical subject. The original 1907 *Follies* had no stars and poked fun at contemporary politicians and people in the news, who were also sometimes members of the audience. It actually became a mark of fame to be satirized in the *Follies;* Teddy Roosevelt, to his delight, saw himself spoofed in one of the acts. Held had also advised that the shows emphasize pretty girls—probably her best suggestion and the one that Ziegfeld turned into the hallmark of his shows.

The early *Follies* were not particularly popular with the critics, but they appealed to audiences and soon played to full houses. This trend did not go unnoticed by Klaw and Erlanger, who then moved Ziegfeld's revues to the New Amsterdam, where this flamboyant impresario could take advantage of the theatre's magnificent production facilities. The *Ziegfeld Follies of 1913* ushered in the most brilliant chapter in the New Amsterdam's history and was the making of the theatrical legend named Flo Ziegfeld.

Ziegfeld came to epitomize the new breed of twentieth-century producer who controlled every aspect of a show. This modern producer raised the capital for a production, chose the stars, the director, and the designers; made the major decisions regarding writers, composers, lyricists, and choreographers; and presided over every detail of the production. In Ziegfeld's case, he assembled a production group that did his bidding, and many remained with him for a long time.

Klaw and Erlanger also entrusted the fate of the New Amsterdam's roof theatre to Ziegfeld. He called upon designer Joseph Urban, whom he had lured into his fold in 1915, to redesign the space and convert it into an after-show nightclub. The audience sat at tables, enjoying overpriced food and drink, along with the amenities of noisemakers and telephones, and the Ziegfeld girls were encouraged to mingle with patrons after the show. The roof theatre and its productions, known as the *Frolics,* were snuffed out by the long arm of the law in 1918, when the pall of Prohibition settled over the land. But Ziegfeld, undaunted, reconfigured the space as a showcase for developing talent and for trying out new acts with his established stars, until these intermittent *Midnight* (also *Nine O'Clock*) *Frolics* were discontinued permanently in 1928.

Between runs of the *Follies*, Klaw and Erlanger continued to produce plays and musicals at the New Amsterdam, sometimes alone and sometimes with other Broadway stalwarts like Charles Dillingham or George C. Tyler. Ziegfeld also presented non-revue musical fare that helped keep the playhouse lighted, sometimes for entire seasons. In 1920, the Ziegfeld-produced *Sally*, a Jerome Kern and Victor Herbert musical starring Marilyn Miller, was an instant success that ran for 561 performances.

By 1920, Marc Klaw's name was no longer appearing in the New Amsterdam programs. The partnership that had formed the Theatrical Syndicate and built Forty-second Street's grandest theatre had ended acrimoniously, and Klaw had gone out on his own, building a theatre on Forty-fifth Street and forming a production company. Indeed, the Syndicate itself had essentially dissolved, put out of business by negative attention from the federal government and by the aggressive Shubert brothers.

Klaw departed, but in 1920, Ziegfeld became part owner of the New Amsterdam with Erlanger and Charles Dillingham. With only two exceptions, they presented an annual edition of the *Follies* at "The House Beautiful" until 1927. That year, Ziegfeld, backed by money from newspaper czar William Randolph Hearst, opened his own theatre at Sixth Avenue and Fifty-fourth Street (named the Ziegfeld, naturally). He produced one edition of the *Follies* at the Ziegfeld, but mostly he presented musicals, including what is now hailed as the bedrock work of the American musical: Jerome Kern's *Show Boat*. After Ziegfeld died in 1932, the Shuberts bought the rights to the title *Follies*, but although a few editions followed, they never approached the glory of the Ziegfeld years. A master of self-promotion who spent money (usually someone else's) as if he had his own passbook to the U.S. Treasury, Ziegfeld had dominated Broadway during the heyday of the teens and 1920s with a brilliant, if temperamental, hand.

The fortunes of the New Amsterdam turned around significantly when Klaw and Erlanger brought in Florenz Ziegfeld, and Ziegfeld brought in the *Follies*.

THE END OF AN ERA

Perhaps W. C. Fields, who might have remained only a masterful vaudeville juggler had not Ziegfeld showcased his comedic talents in the *Follies of 1915,* should have the final word on his boss: "Nothing or anyone could compare with him," he recalled after the producer died. "Ziegfeld was a genius."

As for the presiding genius of the once-powerful Syndicate, Abe Erlanger, he sold his interest in the New Amsterdam but continued producing on Broadway. It was assumed he had amassed a fortune during his lifetime, but at his death in 1930, said fortune was dismantled to pay his creditors.

Like a few other banks in the early days of the Great Depression, Dry Dock Savings Bank was surprised to find itself in show business. Still, as principal mortgagor of the New Amsterdam Theatre, Dry Dock leased the venue intermittently until 1937 and did not do too badly. The theatre hosted several interesting productions during this period, including the stylish Howard Dietz and Arthur Schwartz musical revue *The Band Wagon,* which starred Fred and Adele Astaire in their last joint appearance on Broadway (Adele retired from the stage after the show closed) and gave the world the memorable song "Dancing in the Dark." *Murder at the Vanities,* a combination murder mystery and musical revue by Earl Carroll, also did well at the theatre in 1933.

But the New Amsterdam's illustrious history ended on January 6, 1937, with a production of Shakespeare's *Othello* starring Walter Huston as the jealous Moor. It was a case of the audience and the critics hailing Robert Edmond Jones's sets and lighting but hating Huston and the production, which was withdrawn after a mere twenty-one performances.

Eager to rid itself of the House of Ziegfeld, the bank put it up for auction. In 1937, a buyer finally appeared in the person of Max A. Cohen, a film-house operator who intended to add it to a collection that already included the old Candler and the former Lew Fields. The price for the New Amsterdam was $1.5 million—almost the sum that Klaw and Erlanger had spent to build it.

Although Cohen kept the door open for legitimate productions, he immediately began to renovate the building for showing films. The façade was stripped of its sculptural groupings, and a tall art deco shaft bearing the theatre's name went up instead. A box office placed near the entrance posted new prices: from 10 to 25 cents. On July 3, 1937, the New Amsterdam became a second-run movie house; ironically, its first motion picture, like its opening stage production, was *A Midsummer Night's Dream,* with a bevy of Hollywood stars and a script that had been refined by a team of Hollywood writers. Whether this selection was just an absurd coincidence or a deliberate choice by the owner will never be known.

Chafing at his inability to present first-run movies because of Hollywood's strictures—and warned by Dry Dock that it would take back the house if he ever put burlesque on the stage—Cohen continued his policy of offering second-run features. After the war, he made more changes to the house, in an attempt to compete with the movie palaces then dotting the theatre district, but to no avail. In the late 1960s, Cohen retired, and his longtime business manager, Mark Finkelstein, became owner of the New Amsterdam. From time to time, the owners would rent out the rooftop space for use as a radio studio, a theatre, or a rehearsal hall.

In 1979, the New Amsterdam was designated a city landmark—effectively saving it from the wrecking ball, and subsequently the Nederlander Organization, which owns and operates legitimate theatres around the country, purchased the house and made plans to use it for staging musicals. The company proposed to open the roof theatre first, however, and announced that the opening production would be a one-act version of Bizet's *Carmen,* adapted and staged by the avant-garde director Peter Brook. But when the Nederlanders discovered grave structural faults in the building, they halted the renovation and opened the production elsewhere. In 1992, New York City and the State Urban Development Corporation (UDC) purchased the New Amsterdam for $247,000.

Unfortunately, the Nederlanders had not securely covered the areas where their workers had made openings and tapped into the theatre's structure. Over the next few years, rain, snow, and the city's famous black soot poured through holes in the roof. By 1994, The House Beautiful was a ruin: the auditorium reeked of decay; cracked plaster and broken ornamentation littered the floor and stairwells; fungi had sprung up from the rain-soaked, moldy rugs; and murals had decayed and ripped, left hanging in pieces from the walls. It seemed as though the UDC had bought itself a disaster.

Ziegfeld presented yearly editions of the *Follies* almost without interruption. "Hello, Frisco!" was one of many *Follies* songs that became a hit.

During the late nineteenth century and well into the twentieth, comedians came in pairs: Weber and Fields, Savoy and Brennan, Laurel and Hardy, and Ziegfeld favorites Gallagher and Shean.

A NEW BEGINNING

In the early 1990s, it was no secret that the Walt Disney Company was seeking a permanent venue in the theatre district as a home for its musical productions. Although the first Disney musical to be staged on Broadway would not open until April 1994—*Beauty and the Beast*, at the Palace Theatre—in April 1993, Michael Eisner, then head of Disney, had flown into New York to look over the New Amsterdam with an eye to its acquisition. It fell to Cora Cahan, president of The New 42nd Street Inc., to lead the tour. Into the morass of detritus that once was the theatre, Cahan shepherded Eisner, guiding him up the stairs, into dressing rooms, onto the stage, and behind the stage—into all the nooks and crannies of the dilapidated theatre space. Perhaps he envisioned what the playhouse could look like after reclamation. Whatever prompted his decision, Eisner instructed his staff to begin negotiations with the City and State to acquire the house.

In December 1993, the Disney Development Company signed a "memorandum of understanding" with the 42nd Street Development Project. Reasoning that the presence of Disney on Forty-second Street would spur the redevelopment of the area, New York Governor Mario Cuomo and New York City Mayor Ed Koch announced that restoration would commence immediately. Cultural critics feared that Mickey Mouse would take over the street. At the conclusion of protracted, sometimes contentious, negotiations, Disney agreed to put up $8 million, and the State agreed to lend $21 million toward the reconstruction costs. (Of course, following New York tradition, the cost overruns were spectacular, and the further reclamation costs proved to be more than $10 million above what had been budgeted.)

The internationally renowned architect Hugh Hardy, who had an impressive record of resurrecting old theatres, was engaged to perform a small miracle by bringing the New Amsterdam back to life. First, he had to stabilize the building by repairing the roof and the windows to prevent more moisture from leaking into the house. Then temporary heaters were brought in to dry out the interior. To work with Hardy, Disney hired Theatre Projects Consultants, an international design firm that prepared the building program and collaborated on the design of the stage and auditorium,

as well as the integration of state-of-the-art equipment. Hardy asked the difficult questions: When the job is done, should the old house look as it did in 1903, or like one of the later versions, with the "improvements" that successive owners and managers had made? Should the elaborate 1903 façade be re-created, or should the art deco marquee survive as a record of a later era?

The final decision, according to Hugh Hardy, was to "honor [the New Amsterdam's] layers of history by undertaking 'an interpretive' restoration" whereby the old theatre could meet contemporary standards both in front of and behind the curtain and yet "acknowledge the passage of time."

Since much of the original décor had been destroyed, Hardy and his team of experts salvaged all they could, then made molds of the recognizable shards of plaster, recasting them to create reproductions for terra-cotta balustrades, bas reliefs, carved wood paneling, and art nouveau details. The boxes, removed during the movie years, were replaced, and each was adorned with a different flower motif. The reconstruction team restored the decorative murals where they could, and used imagination and ingenuity to fill in the many missing depictions. All the historical and illustrative documentation they could unearth guided their work, supplemented by techniques such as paint analysis and computer-generated design, which coordinated the myriad details. Recognizing the danger of imparting a "too new" look to the restored theatre, the team created special painting and glazing effects to "age" its work.

At the same time, according to Hardy, "new amenities, such as air-conditioning, lobby space on the mezzanine and balcony levels, new men's and women's lounges, together with elevator access [had] been subtly added." Theatre Projects, addressing Disney's requirement of an additional one hundred and fifty seats, had extended the orchestra seating. "Stage lighting, rigging, sound systems, and all the other technology required for modern performance [had] also been carefully and unobtrusively inserted," Hardy noted. The Walt Disney Company opted not to reinstate the roof garden, deeming its problems of vertical access too expensive to solve.

All was made ready for the grand opening of the new-old New Amsterdam. But Disney executives chose to reopen the theatre not with Shakespeare or a classic, or even a spectacular musical, but with an oratorio called *King David*, composed by Alan Menken (the composer and lyrist for Disney's *Beauty and the Beast*), with book and lyrics by Tim Rice. Performed largely before invited audiences—including the press—the production introduced the theatre community to the House that Disney Rebuilt.

What can be considered the *real* opening of the renovated New Amsterdam occurred on November 13, 1997, when a spectacular Disney production became the artistic and commercial hit of the season. *The Lion King,* based on one of Disney's most popular animated films and directed by Julie Taymor, proved an auspicious beginning to a new chapter in the story of this grand old theatre. The extraordinary production made its home at the New Amsterdam until June 13, 2006, when it moved to the Minskoff to make way for Disney's stage musical version of *Mary Poppins.*

LIBERTY

THEATRE

42ND STREET
West of Broadway

THE LIBERTY

1904

The Forty-second Street façade of the Liberty Theatre, with its American eagle proudly decorating the building's summit.

Marc Alonzo Klaw and Abraham Lincoln Erlanger were as different as two men could be. Klaw was slim (some might have said skinny) and his face was long and lean; Erlanger was rotund of body and full of face. Klaw, born in Paducah, Kentucky, in 1858, had trained as a lawyer, while Erlanger, born in Buffalo, possibly in 1860, seems to have begun life as a theatrical booking agent. According to later newspaper accounts, Klaw was seen as "a diplomat" and "sane," but Erlanger "prefer[ed] to be likened to Napoleon." Or as one journalist put it, "The keynote of [Erlanger's] character is an articulate appreciation of himself."

Different though they may have been physically and temperamentally, the men became business partners, and from 1896 to 1916 ran the Theatrical Syndicate, which booked productions in New York City on tours to theatres around the nation. Their methods may have been brutal, but their entrepreneurship benefited the city's theatre district. In 1903, Klaw and Erlanger had elevated the atmosphere of Forty-second Street by opening the sumptuous New Amsterdam Theatre near the southwest corner of Seventh Avenue. In 1904, they opened the more modest Liberty up the block, intending it as a home for the comedy team of Gus and Max Rogers, who were billed as the Rogers Brothers. As with the New Amsterdam, Klaw and Erlanger turned to the architects Henry B. Herts and Hugh Tallant, and to interior designer F. Richard Anderson.

The plot of land that the theatrical partners wished to build upon was oddly shaped. One section, a long narrow strip that was 80 feet deep and 20 feet wide, fronted on Forty-second Street; the property's main area, which was 99 feet deep and 100 feet wide, backed onto Forty-first Street. The funnel-like strip became the new theatre's entranceway, at 234 West Forty-second Street, and the larger, nearly square portion housed the theatre itself. Ultimately, the auditorium was made 72 feet wide, and the distance from the footlights to the back wall of the house a mere 60 feet—considerably smaller than the lavishly spacious New Amsterdam. The Liberty accommodated only fifteen rows of orchestra seats and, even with two balconies and eight boxes, sat only about 1,200. In that small house, however, every audience member undoubtedly had a good view of the stage, even those seated up in the astonishingly steep second balcony, or gallery.

The theatre was built to present musicals as well as comedies, so the architects accommodated the need for many scene changes. The stage was more than 35 feet deep and 72 feet wide, and the height from the deck to the top of the rigging loft was approximately 70 feet. At 36 feet wide and 32 feet high, the proscenium arch left a good deal of wing and fly space for storing scenery. But there was no sounding board between the top of the proscenium and the auditorium's ceiling, which meant that the Liberty lacked a structural component that would have helped reflect sound back into the house.

Klaw and Erlanger invested less money in the Liberty than in the New Amsterdam, which had been constructed to support a ten-story office building. Still, at first glance, the façades resembled each other. Like the New Amsterdam's, the Liberty's entrance doors were set within an archway and flanked on each side by an announcement board, while above the arch a sign rimmed with electric lights proclaimed the current attraction. There the resemblance ended, however.

The Liberty's design culminated in a recessed arch at the building's third story. This feature was topped by a stone shield bearing a relief sculpture of Philadelphia's famous Liberty Bell, capped proudly in its turn by a sculpted eagle, wings raised and outspread as though it had just landed atop the building.

Inside, beyond the entranceway with its gold- and aluminum-domed ceiling, an audience member found himself in a spacious ivory and white foyer, with a grand staircase leading to the balconies and other stairs going down to the lounges: one with weathered oak paneling and weighty furniture upholstered in Spanish leather for the men, the other decorated with apple green, ivory, and gold pansies for the women. Ivory and gold also predominated inside the auditorium, where the walls for the eight cantilevered boxes were decorated with an ornamental arch surmounted by the Liberty Bell and eagle motif. One contemporary journalist described the interior as "designed in the style of Francis I." Noting that "this style flourished in the times of the later troubadours," the writer considered it "appropriate in character for a theatre devoted to light music and comedy."

Klaw and Erlanger may have built the Liberty at half the cost of the New Amsterdam, but they apparently spared no expense on fireproof exits. There were twenty-one fireproof escape routes inside for the audience, and exterior fire

The interior of the Liberty Theatre, showing its unusually shallow auditorium, a feature that made the Liberty an intimate house with excellent sightlines.

escape galleries were constructed outside the actors' dressing rooms. Supposedly, the theatre could be emptied, from top to bottom, in two minutes, which was undoubtedly reassuring for both audiences and performers. The previous year, on December 30, 1903, a fire had started above the stage at Chicago's new, reportedly fireproof Iroquois Theatre. More than six hundred people died—mostly women and children who had been watching a matinee of an entertainment called *Mr. Blue Beard*. Klaw and Erlanger had not only produced the show in New York before sending it on tour; they were also two of the six proprietors of the Iroquois. Clearly, they needed to improve their public image.

Adding to the audience's protection was the Liberty's asbestos curtain, which was raised before a show began and would drop during a performance only in case of fire. When down, it offered a striking view of Henry Hudson's ship *The Half Moon* sailing past Manhattan Island.

THE LIBERTY'S PRODUCTIONS

As Klaw and Erlanger had intended, the Liberty proved kinder to musical and light entertainment than to the melodramas that the managers periodically booked. Between 1904 and 1920, musicals, operettas, and comedies kept the Liberty vital. *The Rogers Brothers in Paris,* which had been running at the New Amsterdam, inaugurated the Liberty on October 10, 1904, and departed soon after. George M. Cohan's first major musical, *Little Johnny Jones,* produced by Cohan and Sam H. Harris, moved into the house on November 7, 1904. The show was a family enterprise from first to last: Cohan wrote the book, music and lyrics; his parents, Jerry J. Cohan and Helen F. Cohan, were in the cast, and so was his first wife, Ethel Levey. George himself starred as Johnny Jones, the honest, patriotic American jockey who travels to England to win the Derby. Blessed with two signature Cohan tunes, "The Yankee Doodle Dandy" and "Give My Regards to Broadway," as well as massive sets and an exuberant company of seventy-five, *Little Johnny Jones* was a critical success. And although it remained at the Liberty for only fifty-two performances, Cohan toured it to great acclaim and returned with it to New York (for presentation in other theatres) in 1905 and 1907.

In 1905, *The Rogers Brothers in Ireland* filled the Liberty for 106 performances, but other entries enjoyed even longer runs. A sentimental item called *Polly of the Circus,* by Margaret Mayo, ran for 160 performances in 1907. One of its attractions was beauteous, twenty-year-old Mabel Taliaferro as Polly, who gives up the circus life for the love of a minister. (Taliaferro would move on to a substantial career in silent films.) Additional draws were the circus artists who provided realistic color for the production: Mr. Peter Barlow and His Equine Paradox; Miss Elsie St. Leon, Queen of Equestriennes; and the Famous St. Leon Family of European Acrobats, among others.

A so-called comedy-drama titled *The Clansman* opened on January 8, 1906, and played fifty-one performances. Adapted by the Reverend Thomas Dixon, Jr., from his white-supremacist novels *The Clansman* and *The Leopard's Spots,* this melodrama takes place after the Civil War and presents four acts about the supposedly dangerous effects of Recon-

struction on white men and women. In a self-aggrandizing pamphlet called "The Clansman," Dixon had written that "the future of this nation depends on the strength and purity of our white racial stock." In Act I, a black man reenacts the rape of a white girl; Act IV required actors to be costumed in white robes to look like members of the Ku Klux Klan.

Only forty-one years had elapsed since the end of the War Between the States, and in the South—where *The Clansman* first played in 1905—the play had drawn sympathetic white audiences over objections from African Americans. Perhaps scenting controversy, Klaw and Erlanger booked the production into the Liberty, with policemen on hand on Forty-second Street for opening night. But aside from a claque of partisan white Southerners, there was little drama in the audience that evening. A few New York critics praised the acting and the script; most did not, calling the play "wild and somewhat splotchy' (*The Evening Sun*), "tawdry and innocuous" (*The World*), and "coarse and crude" (*The New York Herald*).

The play might have disappeared into the annals of New York theatre history, except that pioneering filmmaker D. W. Griffith largely based his 1915 movie *The Birth of a Nation* on Dixon's melodrama. On film, the positive portrait of the Ku Klux Klan and the negative portrait of African Americans roused the outspoken ire of both white liberals and African Americans.

Interestingly, Klaw and Erlanger had a love-hate relationship with the young film medium. Instinctively recognizing that movies would threaten legitimate theatre and vaudeville, they were by 1909 forbidding the Syndicate's contracted actors to appear in moving pictures. That defensive attitude, however, gave way to greed as Klaw and Erlanger soon realized they could make money from the new entertainment form. In 1913, the partners contracted with the Biograph Company to produce two feature productions per week from among their theatrical properties, and during the summer of 1915 they presented the New York premiere of *The Birth of a Nation* at the Liberty. Erlanger, in fact, arranged with Metro Pictures to make a film of the play *Ben Hur,* which the producer owned. In 1926, that successful stage melodrama would become an equally successful movie.

The Clansman may not have been the New York success that Klaw and Erlanger had hoped for, but generally, the first two decades of the Liberty's theatrical life were banner

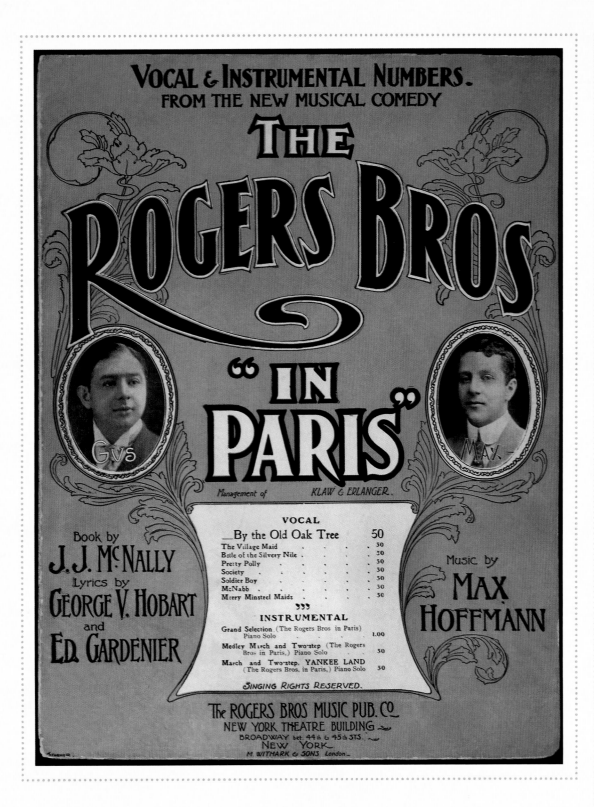

A poster for the hit comedy *The Rogers Brothers in Paris*—Klaw and
Erlanger's answer to the comedy team of Weber and Fields, who had gone
their separate ways in 1904.

THE ROGERS BROTHERS

Gus Rogers was fat, Max was lean. Together they were the Rogers Brothers, a song-and-dance team that one reviewer called "human Gatling guns of talk" and another described as "little more than overgrown school boys."

They were indeed brothers—two of eleven children born to Morris Solomon, a Jewish tailor downtown on Varick Street, and his wife, Hannah, both of whom had come to the United States from Newcastle, England. Gus had been born in 1869, Max in 1873. Determined to go on the stage, the brothers tried all manner of comic routines before settling on German dialect and patter, known in the trade as a Dutch act (from a mispronunciation of *Deutsch,* meaning German). Their competition in this line was the successful comedy team of Weber and Lew Fields, who also talked and sang in German dialect and whom the Rogers Brothers at one point imitated bit for comic bit, routine for routine. But they were never as inventive as Weber and Fields.

The Rogers Brothers enjoyed their first hit, *A Round of Pleasure,* at the Knickerbocker Theatre at Broadway and Thirty-eighth Street, in 1897, under Klaw and Erlanger's management. Two years later, they opened in the first of the musical shows portraying them in various places and parts of the world. They went to Harvard, Wall Street,

Central Park, London—a different locale and a new show almost each year. No matter where they went, they looked comically out of place, their pants either too baggy or too short, their jackets and vests loudly checked or striped. In their daily lives, the brothers were rather dapper; onstage they looked and behaved like clowns.

On October 10, 1904, the pair opened the new house with *The Rogers Brothers in Paris,* which had been playing at Klaw and Erlanger's other Forty-second Street theatre, the New Amsterdam. Sporting a goatee, Gus portrayed a character named Rudolph Khan, and Max played one Adolph Finkleleiner. (Despite the show's title, the siblings ended up in St. Louis.)

To Klaw and Erlanger, the timing must have seemed fortuitous; earlier that year, in May 1904, Weber and Fields had dissolved their legendary partnership, incidentally making way for rivals. But in truth, the popularity of the Rogers Brothers was in decline, and in 1909 Gus died of typhoid, leaving Max to perform on his own until around 1914. Max died on December 26, 1932, at the age of fifty-nine.

The Rogers Brothers dressed sharply while offstage, but onstage they played characters that looked and sounded foolish, to the delight of their fans.

In Margaret Mayo's 1907 romance *Polly of the Circus*, the charming star
Mabel Taliaferro played an orphan who becomes a bareback rider.

Edith Day and Frank Craven in "Going Up," a musical play at the Liberty

Klaw and Erlanger anticipated that the racist *The Clansman* would cause a political stir when it opened at the Liberty in 1906, but audiences were unimpressed. It is remembered today as the source for D. W. Griffith's pioneering film, *The Birth of a Nation*.

That fascinating phenomenon, the airplane, helped make a 1917 musical farce called *Going Up* one of the most popular shows ever to play the Liberty.

years. *The Spring Maid*, with book and lyrics by Harry B. Smith and Robert B. Smith, and music by the Austrian composer Heinrich Reinhardt, satisfied the public's craving for operettas for at least six months in 1911. *Have a Heart*, Jerome Kern's first musical with book writers and lyricists P. G. Wodehouse and Guy Bolton, opened in January 1917. On December 25

of that year, George M. Cohan and Sam H. Harris produced the Liberty's longest-running production: a musical about an aviator called *Going Up*, with book and lyrics by Otto Harbach and music by Louis A. Hirsch. Starring Frank Craven (who would later make theatre history creating the role of the Stage Manager in *Our Town*), it ran for 351 performances.

Klaw and Erlanger had brought Florenz Ziegfeld's *Follies* to the New Amsterdam and profited mightily. On June 2, 1919, they presented a similar, if less lavish, entry at the Liberty: *George White's Scandals*. As with subsequent editions of the *Scandals*, White produced and staged this first outing, a revue in two acts and eighteen scenes. The book and lyrics were written by White and Arthur Jackson, the music by Richard Whiting. The show included specialty acts; skits involving relative unknowns such as Lou Holtz and the blackface comedy duo Moran and Mack; and "An Operatic Fan Fan" with George White, the dancer Ann Pennington (famous for her dimpled knees), and lots of girls. The reviews were mixed—one suggested that White go back to the *Follies*—but audiences liked what they saw.

The Liberty sailed into the 1920s on a tide of change. In 1910, Klaw and Erlanger had finally received a challenge to their monopolizing Syndicate. The Shubert brothers and John Cort, an independent producer who owned theatres in Seattle, had formed the Independent National Theatre Owners' Association, which brokered an agreement with Klaw and Erlanger to allow both Syndicate and independent artists to perform at the Association's theatres. By 1916, the Association had cracked the Syndicate's monopoly—and had begun to establish its own.

Three years later, Klaw and Erlanger officially dissolved their partnership. According to a newspaper account, the men had not spoken since Erlanger fired Klaw's son Joseph in 1918. But money matters were also at issue, and for the next several years the men would take each other to court. Erlanger continued to produce shows, by himself or in partnership with others; Klaw built the Klaw Theatre (later the Avon) at 251 West Forty-fifth Street and became an independent producing manager. He died in 1936.

The Liberty saw its share of stars during those first decades. Tyrone Power, Sr. (the father of the film actor) wore a stern expression and a feathered headdress to play the blind Lonawanda, Chief of the Ockotchees, in a terrible 1906 melodrama called *The Redskin*. In 1907, dark-haired Eleanor Robson won praise for her performance in a romance called *Salomy Jane*; three years later Robson would leave the stage and marry the wealthy financier August Belmont, eventually using her money and social position to found the Metropolitan Opera Guild.

That epitome of gilded-age femininity, Lillian Russell,

appeared for a brief run at the Liberty in 1908, in George Broadhurst's comedy *Wildfire*, with which she had toured the country. Laurette Taylor, who would later originate the role of Amanda Wingfield in Tennessee Williams' *The Glass Menagerie*, appeared on the Liberty's stage in 1917, in the short-lived comedy *The Wooing of Eve*, by Taylor's husband, J. Hartley Manners. Onstage with Taylor was a comparatively unknown young actress named Lynn Fontanne.

The commercial theatre responded to the boom mentality of the early 1920s, and for a time the Liberty thrived. Jerome Kern's musical *The Night Boat* opened in 1920 for a lengthy run, followed soon by George White's *Scandals of 1921* and, also in 1921, another Otto Harbach musical, *The O'Brien Girl*. Twenty-one-year-old Helen Hayes, already on her way to being a star, opened at the Liberty on February 20, 1922, in George S. Kaufman and Marc Connelly's *To the Ladies*. With the delicate Hayes as Elsie Beebe, a young wife who helps further the career of her spendthrift husband, the comedy ran for 128 performances and then traveled to George M. Cohan's Grand Opera House in Chicago. One critic called Hayes "Maude Adams' successor." Sheppard Butler of the *New York Tribune* wrote, "Miss Helen Hayes—the demure mite of the glowing face and tilted nose whom we liked so well in 'Bab' . . . is wistful and eager and appealing, given to droll rushes of tumbling words and lovely little moments of tenderness. Without any flamboyancy of acting, she easily dominates the play."

The New York theatre world was flooded with talented actors and singers, and a number of them performed at the Liberty during the 1920s. Jeanette MacDonald, who would later find stardom singing in films with Nelson Eddy, appeared in 1923 in *The Magic Ring*, although she was overshadowed by the show's beloved star, who went by one name: Mitzi. Leo Carrillo, a dialect comedian on the vaudeville stage who would also journey to Hollywood to work in movies and then in television on *The Cisco Kid*, played a pacifist turned fighter in Booth Tarkington's comedy *Magnolia*, in 1923.

But during the early years of the decade, possibly the biggest coming together of talent on the Liberty's stage occurred on December 1, 1924, with the opening of the musical *Lady, Be Good!* The music was by George Gershwin, the lyrics by his brother Ira. This was their first Broadway collaboration and their most successful musical of the 1920s—it ran for 330 performances. The prolific Guy Bolton

On largely white Broadway, revues such as Lew Leslie's *Blackbirds of 1928*,
featuring African-American performers, suddenly became popular during
the 1920s when Broadway producers capitalized on the popularity of
Harlem's nightclub entertainers.

BILL "BOJANGLES" ROBINSON

Luther Robinson was born in Richmond, Virginia, on May 25, 1878, to Maxwell Robinson, a machine-shop worker, and Maria Robinson, a choir singer. According to legend (probably one spread by Robinson himself), he didn't like the name Luther and strongly suggested to his younger brother, Bill, that they switch names. When Bill refused, Luther persuaded him to do so with his fists, and the switch was on. That eagerness to fight—he reportedly had a quick temper—probably earned Robinson his nickname, Bojangles: from "jangler," meaning contentious.

Robinson's parents died in 1885, and a grandmother took charge of the boys. But the elder sibling didn't stay around Richmond for long. At age six, he was already dancing in local beer gardens, and by age eight he was in Washington, D.C., appearing in the chorus of a minstrel show called *The South Before the War*. Arriving in New York in 1900, the twelve year old challenged tap dancer Harry Swinton to a buck-dancing contest and won. Two years later, adhering to what was known in white vaudeville as the "two-colored" rule, which required that African Americans perform in pairs, Robinson teamed up with dancer George W. Cooper and toured on the Keith and Orpheum circuits. The two danced together until 1915, when they had a falling out. Apparently charismatic and popular enough to make his own rules, Robinson went solo until 1927.

Described in vaudeville programs as "The Dark Cloud of Joy," Robinson charmed audiences; his tapping mesmerized them. He wore what was known as split clog shoes—ordinary shoes with a wooden half-sole attached from the toe to the ball of the foot, and left loose to give him greater flexibility and make a bigger sound. According to one description of his style, he inserted "Buck or Time Steps . . . with skating steps or crossover steps on the balls of the feet that looked like a jig; all while he chatted and joked with the audience." When Robinson performed his famous stair dance, which he introduced in 1918, he made sure that each stair sounded at a different pitch.

After Robinson's first Broadway musical, *Blackbirds of 1928*, there was no stopping the man's fame, or the admiration of both white and black audiences. When the

Bill "Bojangles" Robinson was one of the most remarkable tap dancers in the history of American show business.

market for African-American revues evaporated during the 1930s, Robinson went to Hollywood, where he appeared in fourteen movies, including *Harlem Is Heaven* (1932), *The Little Colonel* (1935) with Shirley Temple, and *In Old Kentucky* (1935), playing the role that Harry Swinton had originated onstage.

Robinson's private behavior drew frowns in some quarters, for he liked to gamble and often carried a gun. But his popularity outran the naysayers. He was elected mayor of Harlem in 1933 and reportedly gave millions of dollars to needy friends and charities. Few could argue with Robinson's charisma, whether it surfaced in his distinctive way of talking (he coined the word "copasetic") or in his instinct for the theatrical gesture. He claimed to have invented his stair dance when he was receiving an honor from George V of England and, as Robinson told it, instinctively danced up the steps to meet the king. To celebrate his sixty-first birthday, in 1939, Robinson tap danced down Broadway from Columbus Circle to the Broadhurst Theatre on Forty-fourth Street, where, in his return to the New York stage, he was starring in *The Hot Mikado*, a swing musical based on Gilbert and Sullivan's operetta *The Mikado*.

After Robinson died on November 25, 1949, his body lay in state at an armory in Harlem. On the day of the funeral, schools closed, and the press estimated that thousands of mourners gathered along the sidewalks to watch the great dancer's funeral procession go by.

wrote the libretto with one of his frequent collaborators, Fred Thompson, and the show presented that luminous dancing team, Fred Astaire and his sister, Adele, in their first starring roles on Broadway. Felix Edwardes staged the book scenes, Sammy Lee the dances and ensemble scenes, and a young visionary named Norman Bel Geddes designed the sets.

The story of *Lady, Be Good!* was slight, but appropriate for the happy-go-lucky attitude of the first half of the 1920s. In Act One, dancers Dick Trevor and his sister, Susie, are thrown out of their home and forced to do their singing and dancing at the houses and parties of friends; in Act Two, the pair comes into a lot of money. But the score, written the same year that George Gershwin, then twenty-six, composed *Rhapsody in Blue,* contained entrancing music and lyrics, notably the seductive "Oh, Lady, Be Good!" and the lively, toe-tapping "Fascinating Rhythm." (Another glorious song, "The Man I Love," was dropped in Philadelphia.) With the Astaires dancing feverishly, and vaudevillian Cliff Edwards, otherwise known as "Ukulele Ike," playing the banjo, "Fascinating Rhythm" stopped the show at practically every performance.

Almost a year later, on December 28, 1925, the Gershwins, Bolton, and Thompson returned to the Liberty with the musical *Tip-Toes,* starring petite, blonde, blue-eyed Queenie Smith as "Tip-Toes" Kaye, a vaudeville dancer marooned in Palm Beach, Florida, with her two penniless uncles. Ira Gershwin thought that the score, which included a rhythmic ballad about love at first sight, "That Certain Feeling," and the jazzy "Sweet and Low-Down," was stronger than that of *Lady, Be Good! Tip-Toes* ran for an honorable but less than staggering 194 performances.

In 1921, a show called *Shuffle Along,* by Noble Sissle and Eubie Blake, opened at the Sixty-third Street Music Hall and made theatre history by becoming the longest-running book musical to have been produced, directed, written, and acted by African Americans. Commercial producers watched the show become popular with white theatregoers, and *Shuffle Along*—really more of a revue—became a model for the decade, particularly in the hands of a white producer and director named Lew Leslie. Leslie offered New York audiences productions such as *Plantation Revue* (1922), *Dixie to Broadway* (1924), and *Blackbirds* (1926), which starred the enticing Florence Mills.

Leslie's most successful experiment in this genre was *Blackbirds of 1928,* which opened at the Liberty on May 9,

1928, and outdid *Shuffle Along* (and anything that ever played the Liberty) by running for 518 performances. Jimmy McHugh wrote the music; Dorothy Fields, the daughter of producer and comedian Lew Fields (of Weber and Fields), penned the lyrics; and at least one of their songs, "I Can't Give You Anything but Love," became a standard.

The African-American cast included jazz singer and vaudeville star Adelaide Hall; the dancer Bill "Bojangles" Robinson, who once again stunned audiences with the stair tap routine that he had originated; Aida Ward, a stage, radio, and nightclub singer who later performed at the Cotton Club with the Duke Ellington and Cab Calloway orchestras; and comedian Tim Moore, who would one day play George "Kingfish" Stevens on the *Amos 'n' Andy* television program of the 1950s. On opening night, Allie Ross's Plantation Orchestra wore gray coats, red ties, and sported red boutonnieres. Theatre critics relished the production. "Bill Robinson," wrote the *New York Post's* Robert Littell, is "the only man who can actually make the ball and toe of his feet talk."

The long run of *Blackbirds of 1928* belied the erosion that had begun to eat away at the Broadway theatre. Only a few years earlier, during the 1925–26 season, it had seemed that the commercial theatre could do no wrong. An organization called the Broadway Association, which had formed in 1911, estimated in 1926 that 750,000 people passed through Times Square each night, to patronize the theatres, restaurants, and hotels that dominated the area. Given what seemed an endless supply of theatregoers, real estate speculators went about buying up lots in the theatre district, building theatres, and leasing them to long-term renters who would in turn rent them to theatrical producers of individual shows.

But this put pressure on producers to come up with long-running hits, always hard to come by in the theatre. At the same time, in the get-rich-quick atmosphere of the mid-1920s, investors who knew little about theatre were putting money behind a large number of lightweight vehicles, many of which quickly flopped. This dual track—the search for hits and the large turnover of short-lived productions—imparted to show business an aura of great activity but a weak foundation. When theatre lost much of its drawing power, these investors would prove more interested in erecting office buildings and movie houses than in supporting the stage.

It might have been better for the Liberty's fortunes if

Erlanger had kept *Blackbirds of 1928* running there, but in the week of October 15, 1928, he moved *Blackbirds* to the Eltinge, to make room for a comedy called *Mr. Moneypenny.* Lasting for a mere sixty-one performances, *Mr. Moneypenny* is notable today for having been directed by Richard Boleslavsky, an original member of the Moscow Art Theatre and co-founder with Maria Ouspenskaya of the American Laboratory Theatre; and for featuring the Broadway debut of an eighteen year old named Evan Heflin, later known to film audiences as Van Heflin.

As it turned out, the Liberty would host only one more hit show during its lifetime: *Subway Express,* a drama of murder on the New York subway, by Eva Kay Flint and Martha Madison, which opened on October 24, 1929. The production entertained audiences with what Brooks Atkinson called "a murder more ingenious than most" and "a picturesque set showing the interior of a moving subway train," and ran for 270 performances. (It then moved across Forty-second Street to the Theatre Republic.) A musical called *Brown Buddies,* about African-American men in uniform, reunited Bill "Bojangles" Robinson and Adelaide Hall at the Liberty on October 7, 1930, but even this charismatic pair could not extend the run for more than 113 performances. Perhaps the surprisingly serious plot discouraged audiences; more likely, the production was simply a casualty of the Great Depression.

On March 7, 1930, Abraham Erlanger died. Whether one liked him or detested him, Erlanger had been a force in the theatre for over forty years and apparently had won the respect of New York politicos and fellow producers. In fact, for one fleeting moment in 1909, the Democratic Party even considered running Erlanger for mayor of New York City. At his funeral, at Temple Emanu-El on Fifth Avenue and Sixty-fifth Street, pallbearers included Governor Alfred E. Smith, Mayor James J. Walker, and theatrical producers Florenz Ziegfeld, Charles H. Dillingham, Daniel Frohman, and Sam H. Harris. After the service, a squad of motorcycle police led the funeral procession to Beth-El Cemetery in Brooklyn.

Initially it was reported that Erlanger had amassed a personal fortune of $75 million. In fact, the sum was closer to $3 million, and with debts, and claims by an actress who asserted she was his common-law wife, Erlanger's estate ultimately dwindled to nearly nothing.

THE DOWNFALL

Without Erlanger, the Liberty was rudderless. Max Rudnick, a producer who had begun his career by owning motion picture theatres in Brooklyn (and would soon bring burlesque to the Eltinge, which he was operating), leased the house, and the venue struggled on for three more years. Rudnick screened movies during part of the 1931–32 season; the Liberty went dark for practically the entirety of 1932–33. Burns Mantle, in his summary of that season for *The Best Plays of 1932–1933,* wrote, "This theatre season survived on half rations. No more than half the theatres in New York were in use, something less than half the actors were employed, and virtually all bankrolls were in hiding." The Liberty's last legitimate production was an item called *Masks and Faces,* a three-act comedy by one A. J. Minor about a woman in love with a phantom man who always takes her husband's place when they embrace. The play opened and closed on March 18, 1933. Soon after, the Liberty became a movie house.

In 1944, Brandt Theatres, a chain of film houses founded and owned by Bernard B. Brandt and his brothers Louis, William, and Harry, gained control of the Liberty. By the 1960s, the Liberty had become a third-run movie house.

When the idea of redeveloping Forty-second Street's "sin strip" began to gain ground, at the beginning of the 1980s, City at 42nd St., Inc. commissioned the New York architectural firm of Hardy Holzman Pfeiffer Associates to prepare a study of ten Forty-second Street theatres, including the Liberty. The architects found the building structurally sound and much of the original plasterwork in good shape, but two of the four boxes on each side of the house were missing, and the state of the "production facilities"—electrics, gridiron, and so forth—was "poor." The Liberty's façade had long since lost its liberty bell and eagle and had acquired an ugly marquee that jutted above the sidewalk on Forty-second Street. The study noted that the exterior was in poor condition and recommended a new façade. The estimated cost of renovation: at least $2 million.

Renovation almost became a moot point in 1990, when a fire broke out in the Liberty, wrecking the interior. Mel Gussow, writing in the *New York Times,* described the Liberty as "the most dilapidated of the theaters, with the orchestra almost entirely reduced to rubble," although the grand asbestos curtain was still hanging. Now it was estimated that a renovation would cost nearly $16 million.

Despite the challenge and the cost, a number of nonprofit companies and organizations submitted bids to operate the theatre, and as of August 1992, the *Times* was still describing the Liberty as the "most likely" to be renovated. In 1996, producer Jedediah Wheeler and the enterprising En Garde Arts Inc., a nonprofit theatre company that produced in unusual spaces in New York City, presented the Irish actress Fiona Shaw in a reading of T. S. Eliot's poem "The Waste Land" for a limited run, and eager theatregoers carefully wended their way into the Liberty's dimly lit, damp auditorium for the unique performance.

But eventually Tussaud's Group Ltd., in the United Kingdom, signed with Forest City Ratner (the block's developer) and The New 42nd Street Inc. to build an American version of London's legendary wax museum, Madame Tussaud's. Behind the walls of the wax museum, the Liberty's auditorium remains largely intact, although the stage has been modified. It awaits what theatre architect Craig Morrison calls "imaginative reuse."

The interior of the Liberty Theatre struck hard times in the years following its demise as a legitimate house, but its famous asbestos curtain, painted with a scene of the Half Moon sailing up the Hudson, survived until the end.

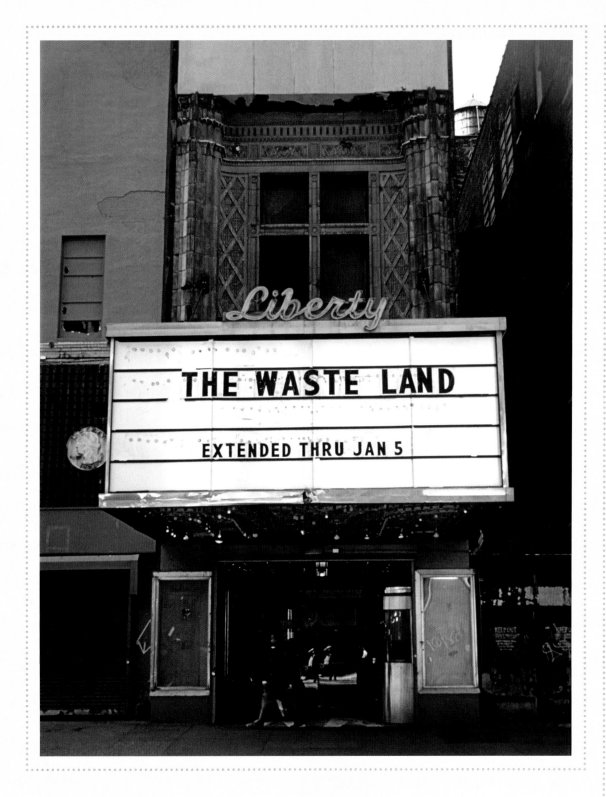

In 1996, in an effort to revive the Liberty as a legitimate theatre, producer Jedediah Wheeler and the nonprofit En Garde Arts company brought Irish actress Fiona Shaw to interpret T. S. Eliot's grand poem "The Waste Land."

Lew Fields Theatre

42ND ST. BET. B'WAY AND 8TH AVE.

HAMLIN, MITCHELL & FIELDS, MANAGERS.

OSCAR HAMMERSTEIN, OWNER.

THE LEW FIELDS

1904

Oscar Hammerstein I built the Lew Fields Theatre on the south side of
Forty-second Street, but the impresario would soon seek accommodations
with the Shuberts. Fulfilling the supposed jinx of being on the street's
unlucky side, this theatre was the venue for a series of flops.

The impresario Oscar Hammerstein I had an obsession to build theatres and opera houses. And so, in 1904, he built his eighth theatre, at 254–58 West Forty-second Street, on the south side of the street. This side of Forty-second was reputedly a jinx for theatres, but Hammerstein, with his customary hubris, ignored that superstition. Initially, he intended on calling his creation the National, but finally he named it the Lew Fields Theatre, after the popular vaudevillian and producer to whom he was leasing the new hall.

After nearly three decades of playing vaudeville and producing musicals with Joe Weber, Fields had ended their partnership and joined up with Fred R. Hamlin, who had produced the lavish first musicalization of Frank L. Baum's *The Wizard of Oz*, on Broadway. Julian Mitchell, who had staged the show, was an innovative director of musicals. The three would make up the creative team of the Lew Fields Stock Company, with the famous comedian acting as both star and manager.

WEBER AND FIELDS

Lew Moses Fields was undoubtedly one of the finest comedians that vaudeville produced. With his partner, Joe Weber, this tall, gangling entertainer amused audiences from 1877 to 1904, when the team officially broke up. (For years afterward they would reunite for special occasions and for several Hollywood turns.) On his own, as an actor and producer, Fields became a force in the legitimate theatre.

Although he would become famous playing a German immigrant who garbled the English language, Fields rarely talked about his own immigrant origins. His parents—Solomon Schoenfeld and Sarah Frank—were Orthodox Jews who had lived in a shtetl near Warsaw, Poland, where Solomon established a tailoring business. In 1872, fearful of pogroms and the prospect that their four sons might be conscripted into the Czar's army, Solomon and Sarah escaped to Germany with their children and boarded a ship for the arduous voyage to New York City. Moses Schoenfeld was five years old.

Solomon set up a tailor's shop on Manhattan's Lower East Side, and his sons attended public school. According to the definitive biography by Armond Fields, Lew Fields' great-nephew, and Armond's son, L. Marc Fields, Moses was "a born mimic": he learned English quickly and displayed an ability to imitate the numerous accents and dialects that surrounded him in the melting pot of Lower Manhattan.

Along the way, Moses met the boy who would become his best friend, Morris "Joe" Weber, the youngest of thirteen children and, like Moses, the child of Jewish immigrants. Apparently they became pals while watching a clog-dancing contest on the playground of the Henry Street School and vowing that they could do it better.

Weber and Fields in civilian dress. They grew up on the Lower East Side of Manhattan, became close friends, and entertained audiences wherever they could, evolving a sketch in which they played immigrants who fractured the English language.

The boys were inseparable. They hung around the Bowery, watching the daily parade of rich and poor, beggar and thief. Sundays they would dress up as street urchins and hawk home-baked gingersnaps, and Lew would affect a stutter to melt the hearts of charitable passersby. Presenting what the biographers call Weber and Fields' first nonprofessional performance, the team was a hit.

Perhaps it was the attraction of Manhattan's streets, with their seemingly endless variety of human types and dramas; maybe it was the discomfort of their families' airless tenement apartments, or the boredom of the classroom. Whatever the reasons, the two friends preferred the streets to home and school. They hustled and begged and worked odd jobs, and they paid or snuck their way into as many saloons and dime museums, minstrel shows, variety halls, and legitimate theatres as they could find below Fourteenth Street. In the fourth grade, they were expelled from school, apparently for entertaining (or distracting) their classmates with backflips and jokes. Though readmitted, they were never rehabilitated. In 1877, when they were only ten years old, Joe Weber and Lew Fields (for that was what he called himself) decided to create a variety act.

For the next ten years, the pair worked variety shows on the Bowery and on the road, painstakingly developing their signature characters, style, and patter. They fashioned what the trade called a "Dutch" act, because it poked affectionate fun at the Germans, or *Deutsch,* who had emigrated to America and who, like Weber and Fields and the immigrants they knew firsthand, struggled with the language and manners of their new world.

MIKE: I am delightfulness to met you.
MEYER: The disgust is all mine.

Tall Lew was Meyer, who often wore a cutaway and top hat, and carried a cane; short Joe, made wider by wearing a fat suit, was Mike. They expressed their affection in knockabout physicality that apparently was even more hilarious than their dialogue. As Fields' biographers noted, "The dialect distortions emphasized the frustration of all immigrants trying to communicate their humanity through the coarse filter of an unfamiliar language. The violence did not arise out of antagonism or hostility. . . . It was in the name of friendship and mutual understanding that the two 'Dutchmen' strangled, gouged, punched, and kicked each other around the stage."

Lew, it soon appeared, was the more creative of the two, while Joe possessed the tougher business sense. They formed their own company, operated a theatre, and by 1904 had not only risen to the top of their profession but helped raise the standards of variety entertainment.

Around 1904, however, their professional aims, which had merged artistically and profitably for so long, diverged. Fields, it seemed, wanted to make a mark in

JOSEPH M. WEBER

Short, well-padded Joe Weber was the put-upon half of Weber and Fields' comic turns. When the pair separated in 1904, Weber continued to perform, reuniting only on occasion with his former friend and partner.

the legitimate theatre. He envisioned a type of musical comedy that comprised more than simply songs and variety skits strung together by the thinnest of plots (or, more likely, no plot at all). He also loved spectacle and indulged artists whom he thought particularly talented, a modus operandi that, in Weber's opinion, jeopardized their business operation.

Had the pair remained performers only, perhaps they would have stayed together. Being producers as well as entertainers strained their partnership and their friendship, and early in the twentieth century, both dissolved, although the friendship would eventually be resurrected.

In private life, Fields was a happily married man, and at least three of his children were as stagestruck as their father: Herbert and Joseph became librettists; Dorothy became a librettist and lyricist. Fields had only one vice: gambling. In relation to vaudeville and the legitimate stage, his gambler's willingness to take artistic risks had served Weber and Fields well. But once Fields became a producer on his own, his dedication to excellence and his tendency toward extravagance outran his ability to keep him, his family, and his numerous projects afloat. A misjudged business arrangement with theatre owners Lee and Jacob J. Shubert, who cared more for the bottom line than for artistry or the well-being of artists, eventually brought Fields to bankruptcy. Still, he kept producing until 1930 and, periodically, for money and pleasure, reunited with Weber to entertain audiences who remembered Meyer and Mike in their heyday.

Lew Fields last performed onstage with Joe Weber in 1932 and acted with him for the final time in the 1940 movie *Lillian Russell*. He died on July 21, 1941. Weber died ten months later.

Tall, skinny Lew Fields was the bullying half of the comic duo of Weber and Fields. He was also a skilled director and producer who wanted the American musical to become more than an elaborate variety show.

Side boxes would eventually disappear from modern theatres, but Hammerstein I designed and built the Lew Fields in the tradition of the opera houses that he loved.

Their new theatre was situated on a plot of ground sixty-six feet wide and ninety-nine feet deep. Occupying the entire lot, the building stood shoulder-to-shoulder with the narrow entrance to the American Theatre and with a brownstone that housed dentists' offices.

As at the Theatre Republic, Hammerstein worked with the Philadelphia architect Albert E. Westover. But the impresario took the lead in the design. The four-story, red-brick and limestone façade followed a Neo-Baroque style favored at the time in England: round windows decorated the top floor, and two pairs of Ionic columns enhanced the façade's center expanse. The building code prohibited erecting a marquee over the sidewalk but, Hammerstein being Hammerstein, he hired carpenters to work at night, building an enclosed entrance and box office that jutted out across the sidewalk,

surmounted by a marquee that spelled out "Lew Fields Theatre" in dozens of white light bulbs.

Like the Theatre Republic that Hammerstein had built on Forty-second Street four years earlier, the Lew Fields was a small house. The raked orchestra sat fewer than five hundred people, the first balcony merely two hundred, and the steep second balcony, or gallery, another two hundred. Nine boxes, in three rows of three, adorned each wall, and a box was built into each side of the first balcony. The upper walls and boxes were white and gold; the lower walls, and the seats and carpeting, a soft shade of green.

That Hammerstein used every available inch of public space for seats left little room for an audience to mingle during intermissions. What's more, the tight entranceway made it difficult for audiences to enter at their leisure—or to exit quickly in case of fire.

Such a possible emergency did not bother him apparently, for this inveterate inventor boasted to the press that he had designed a unique fire protection system. *The New York Dramatic Mirror* reported that "hundreds of iron pipes comprising the gridiron," where the lights are hung, "are connected into an immense system of flood pipes, which from their height of 70 feet above the stage floor can be made to liberate a deluge of water. . . . Simply by pulling a chain on the stage the valves of the two roof tanks, each containing 5,000 gallons of water, are opened and the flood pours down the side walls of the house and thoroughly drenches every other portion of the stage." Luckily for Hammerstein and subsequent owners of the Lew Fields, this invention was never put to a test.

By comparison with most of the other theatres on Forty-second Street, the stage was small. The proscenium opening was only thirty feet wide; the height from the stage floor to the proscenium, thirty-five feet; and from the footlights to the back wall of the stage, a mere thirty-one feet: not a lot of room for the elaborate musicals that Fields wanted to mount. But the reporter from the *New York Dramatic Mirror* found no problem. "Mr. Hammerstein was forced to economize space as much as possible," noted this Broadway scribe, "but in spite of that he has turned out a building that is attractive and pretty and well adapted to the presentation of musical comedy. . . . The stage is not very large but is equipped with many improvements invented by the architect manager for the quick handling of scenery."

IT HAPPENED IN NORDLAND

The first show to try the equipment was a new musical called *It Happened in Nordland*. Originally titled *The American Ambassadress*, the show was commissioned by the Fields-Mitchell-Hamlin team, which hired the popular composer of operettas Victor Herbert; librettist and lyricist Glen MacDonough, who had scored a hit during the previous season by writing the book and lyrics for Herbert's *Babes in Toyland*; and a hefty leading lady named Marie Cahill, possessor of a strong voice and an even stronger temperament. Cahill was cast as Katherine Peepfogel, the American Ambassadress to the Court of Nordland, who, for reasons of diplomacy, agrees to masquerade as the missing Queen of Nordland. Along the way she encounters her long-lost brother (Fields) and saves him from a firing squad. Mitchell would direct.

Fields' biographers write that the comedian and his artistic colleagues aimed to create a show that integrated story, music, choreography, and scenery in a cogent and seamless way rarely intended by the musicals that saturated Broadway back then. However, Cahill, like most stars of that era, insisted on stopping the production to sing songs that showed off her voice but had absolutely nothing to do with the action. As a result, conflicts simmered during out-of-town rehearsals and performances.

Despite the friction, and the illness and death of Fred Hamlin, *It Happened in Nordland* inaugurated the Lew Fields Theatre on the snowy evening of December 5, 1904. The weather did not prevent celebrities such as Lillian Russell and Stanford White from attending, or critics from gushing. "Snow is not always a sign of frost," enthused the *Evening Sun*'s reviewer. "At all events it was not last evening, when Oscar Hammerstein and Lew Fields, like a brace of Sir Galahads, crossed Forty-second street and successfully slew the hoodoo which has been nestling on the downtown side of that thoroughfare for so long."

The *New York Times* endorsed the musical's book, Cahill, Fields, the costuming, and the female chorus, which the reviewer called "a beauty show. There wasn't an ugly face even in the last row." *The Tribune* praised Victor Herbert's

music "of gay marches, pretty little tunes that are not serious, and lively dances." The critic at the *World,* while averring that he did not know exactly what happened in Nordland, singled out Julian Mitchell's staging: "A tumult of color effects and groupings which, even in this day of high art in stage management, fairly dazed the first-nighters. . . . The jumble of events thrown on a stage none too large for a company of eighty-six showed a mastery of mechanical detail."

Lew M. Fields opened the Lew Fields Theatre in 1904 with the musical *It Happened in Nordland*, in which Fields, who directed, aimed to create a more unified show than the jumble of song and dance that usually filled Broadway musicals.

Irish-born composer Victor Herbert, who created the music for It *Happened in Nordland*, wrote some of the richest scores to be heard on Broadway, including the immensely popular *Naughty Marietta* in 1910.

But some reviewers sprinkled sharp-edged criticisms among their valentines. Several found the book wordy and overlong. (Fields would prune the libretto during the run.) Others found fault with Cahill's interpolated songs. The critics generally seemed to grasp that Fields and company were trying to formulate a more modern musical, with which Cahill's star turns interfered. In April 1905, right before the production was supposed to leave New York for a tour of Boston and Chicago, Cahill threatened to quit, and Fields, who believed that no star was more important than the music, replaced her with a talented unknown named "Billie" Norton, who agreeably sang the score as Herbert had written it. By the time the production returned to the Lew Fields, prior to another tour, it was a tighter show. All together, *It Happened in Nordland* ran for 254 performances, making it one of the longest-running productions to grace Hammerstein's new theatre.

THE SHUBERTS

That November, Lee and Jacob J. "Jake" Shubert took over the lease of the Lew Fields. Broadway gossipmongers had been suggesting for a while that Fields and Mitchell were tired of shouldering the management of their house. But Lew's biographers—his great-nephew Armond Fields and Armond's son, L. Marc Fields—suggest that the Shuberts seduced the comedian-producer into making what looked at the outset like a better deal: lease-sharing of the Shuberts' older but larger Herald Square Theatre on Thirty-fifth Street; sole artistic control of a company; and, always important to the spendthrift Fields, the backing of Shubert money.

If the comedian had remained on Forty-second Street, perhaps his taste and obsession with excellence might have kept the Lew Fields awash in long runs. As it was, the minute the Shuberts produced their first entry in 1906, a musical item called *The Press Agent* that lasted only forty performances, the "hoodoo" that Fields and Hammerstein had supposedly ousted returned to roost. The Shuberts stayed around for one more failed production, then, cutting their losses, sold their lease in March 1906 to the actor James K. Hackett, who promptly renamed the theatre the Hackett and staged his first production that August.

JAMES KETELTAS HACKETT

James Keteltas Hackett had been born in Ontario, Canada, in 1869, to a well-known theatrical family. His father, James Henry Hackett, was a celebrated American actor who died when his son was two years old; his mother, Clara C. Hackett, was a popular actress. The younger Hackett grew up in New York City. There his mother provided her young son with two rooms in their home; she built him a stage, for which he proceeded to write scripts, paint scenery, and charge 25 cents for his performances. At City College he distinguished himself playing football, baseball, and lacrosse. He also was founder and chief actor of the City College Dramatic Club and started the Dramatic Club of the Manhattan Athletic Club. He briefly

attended law school, but then, like his parents, the strapping, firm-jawed man with the matinee-idol looks turned to professional acting.

By 1906, Hackett was a respected leading man in romantic dramas and known, among other things, for having the best-looking legs in the business. "Mr. Hackett's legs in '[*Don Caesar's Return*],'" wrote one critic, "are the best things he has ever done. No sword-and-cloak drama can possibly fail when it has such lissome length of limb in the title role. . . ."

At the outset, Hackett fell victim to the theatre building's jinx. His opening salvo, a farce called *The Little Stranger* that debuted on August 27, 1906, closed after an embarrassing twenty-five performances. He brought in shows that he or others had produced with some success elsewhere, but at the Hackett, they folded.

An actor-turned-producer named James K. Hackett took over the Lew Fields in 1906 and promptly renamed the theatre after himself. But his only success during five years of management was a 1907 murder mystery called *The Witching Hour*.

Meantime, Oscar Hammerstein I was trying to sell the theatre. For the fifty-nine-year-old impresario, the enterprise had been nothing but a headache, seeing how the city's authorities regularly accused him of violating building codes. What is more, he had recently opened his (second) Manhattan Opera House, to compete with the Metropolitan Opera, and was planning to build an opera house in Philadelphia. He needed the cash. In February 1907, he sold the Hackett for $400,000 to the producer Henry B. Harris, who agreed to let Hackett ride out his lease.

The first production under Harris's management was a comedic drama called *Maggie Pepper* that starred forty-one year old hazel-eyed Rose Stahl as a salesgirl who marries her boss. It was the first entry in Harris's strategy to draw women into his theatre.

More than a year after Hackett had put his name on the marquee, the theatre hosted a drama called *The Witching Hour,* by the successful Missouri-born playwright Augustus Thomas. Involving murder and mental telepathy, "it proved," wrote the critic Burns Mantle, "one of those lucky dramas to which fascinated adherents returned again and again." Opening on November 18, 1907, it ran for 212 performances. When it finally departed, Hackett installed a four-week revival of the swashbuckling *The Prisoner of Zenda* and, undoubtedly showing lots of leg, re-created his performance of Rudolph Rassendyll, the heroic commoner who impersonates the King of Ruritania.

But *The Witching Hour* proved to be the Hackett's one and only hit. For the next four years, the theatre stumbled along, subleased periodically to various producers but with Hackett as manager to the bitter end. Occasionally, a production would draw moderate crowds. In 1909, petite, vivacious Grace George—who would later introduce several of George Bernard Shaw's plays to American audiences— filled the house for 112 performances of a comedy called *A Woman's Way.* But mostly the productions came and went all too quickly.

Interestingly, under Hackett's tenure, only two musicals moved into the theatre, suggesting that, contrary to Hammerstein and Lew Fields' original conception, Broadway's commercial producers found the house and its stage too small for their musical projects, and unlikely to turn a profit.

HENRY B. HARRIS

In spring of 1911, the theatre's owner, Henry B. Harris, who had patiently been waiting for Hackett's lease to run out, finally took over the theatre. Like Hackett, Harris came from a theatrical family. His father, William Harris, Sr., had been a theatrical manager and producer in Boston before joining Marc Klaw, Abraham Erlanger, and Charles Frohman when they formed the Theatrical Syndicate in 1895. But unlike Hackett, Henry Harris had a strong record as a producer, both in Boston and New York, where he had built and was operating the Hudson Theatre on West Forty-fourth Street.

One of Harris's first moves was to repair and renovate what he was now calling the Harris Theatre. Working with the architects Henry Beaumont Herts and Hugh Tallant, he removed the box office and the original entrance from Forty-second Street, to conform with the city's plan to widen the thoroughfare; built a new entrance and lobby; tore out most of the proscenium boxes; installed a new proscenium arch and ceiling; and redecorated the balcony. He altered the color scheme by incorporating soft shades of brown. In the foyer, Harris set up a bronze bust of his father, to whom he dedicated the theatre.

On August 31, 1911, when the newly outfitted Harris opened with Charles Klein's comedy-drama *Maggie Pepper,* one first-night critic approvingly wrote that "the boxes that

The canny theatrical producer Henry B. Harris took over the Lew Fields and changed its name yet again to the Harris in 1911. He was in the process of turning around this theatre's failing fortunes when he went down with the *Titanic* in 1912.

used to overhang the seats and interfere with the vision from some of the seats on the side have been removed and more orchestra seats have been put in. The whole interior has been redecorated in soft tones, with the chairs upholstered to harmonize with the walls."

Some critics, in fact, found the theatre more appealing than the play, which was about a struggling young woman who works in a department store and ends up marrying the store's owner. But everybody adored endearing, earnest Rose Stahl as Maggie. "There is drama in the life of every woman," Stahl later told *The Theatre* magazine about the character of Maggie Pepper. "Perhaps the plain lives have the most

drama. They have one element of it—sacrifice. I like to play such women. I will never play the character of a woman who has crossed the border. American audiences don't care for such women on the stage nor in life, and they are right. Why spend three hours at the theatre with a woman you couldn't invite into your home?"

Audiences spent 147 performances with Maggie at the Harris, and when the production exited to go on tour, Henry Harris opened *The Talker* in January 1912. Written and staged by Marion Fairfax, who averred that "Women can write just as good plays as men . . . but it's a difficult thing to make the public and the managers believe it," *The Talker* made a star of the subtle, powerful actress Pauline Lord and ran for 144 performances.

Perhaps Henry Harris had discovered the secret of making his theatre into a successful house: well-written dramas, contemporary themes that appealed to women, and stars (preferably female). "It behooves the producing manager to seriously consider the tastes of women," he told a reporter for a New York daily in 1911. "I have had caused to be kept a record of the attendance at the Hudson Theatre, . . . and found, to my surprise, that seventy percent of the audiences were made up of women. . . . And let me tell you right now, women as a class are better judges of the merits of a play than men. They have a finer sense of dramatic proportion, their views are not obscured by the logic of dollars, their sympathies are more susceptible to attack than the calloused, selfish, and wor[l]dly feelings of our American men . . ."

Harris, unfortunately, never got the chance to prove his theory. On April 15, 1912, he met his own dramatic end: aboard the sinking SS *Titanic* in the North Atlantic, the forty-five-year-old producer put his wife into one of the last lifeboats and went down with the ship.

There were no more hits for quite a while. Although Harris had left his business—and his considerable debt—to his wife, his father took charge of running the theatre. Perhaps because of the estate's poor financial outlook, William Harris, Sr.'s spur-of-the-moment solution was to lease it to other producers, such as Selwyn and Company and the New Era Producing Company, whose head, a self-taught lawyer named Joseph P. Bickerton, Jr., would one day bring Noel Coward to New York. Like many commercial producers at the time, Bickerton and the Selwyn brothers tended to use theatres as revolving doors. If one of their shows was failing, they'd close it and bring in one of their hits from another house. Often the transfer would be only for a couple of months, prior to sending the more successful production on the road. At the end of December 1913, New Era brought in the musical *Adele*, which had been enjoying a lengthy run at the Longacre Theatre, and in June 1915, Selwyn and Company transferred its hit farce *Twin Beds* from the Fulton Theatre on Forty-sixth Street to the Harris; *Adele* stayed on for only about six weeks—*Twin Beds* lasted slightly over two months.

In between, however, the Selwyns opened Henry Arthur Jones's drama *The Lie* at the Harris. In London, this dark play about two sisters' rivalry had titillated audiences, and in New York, the presence of Margaret Illington, whom some critics called "the American Sarah Bernhardt" (others gave that title to Mrs. Leslie Carter), led to a 176-performance run.

The transferring of successful shows, rather than the mounting of original productions, became the stock-in-trade at the Harris under the Selwyn management. On February 7, 1916, it brought in the George M. Cohan and Sam Harris production of Cohan's jolly farce *Hit-the-Trail Holliday*, a spirited comedy modeled on the baseball player-turned-evangelist William Ashley "Billy" Sunday. Cohan's brother-in-law, Fred Niblo, played Billy Holliday, a bartender who becomes a temperance preacher. Next, the Selwyns booked

Fair and Warmer, a popular light farce involving marital infidelity that starred sensuous, dark-haired Madge Kennedy.

Another stock-in-trade at the Harris was its flops, notable today only because of the stars—and would-be stars—that had the misfortune of appearing in them. On October 17, 1917, Alfred Lunt made his Broadway debut in a short-lived

In 1920 the Lew Fields passed to Harry Frazee, who also owned the Boston Red Sox. One year later, Frazee brought in *Dulcy*, a comedy by George S. Kaufman and Marc Connelly that made a star of Lynn Fontanne.

bit of silliness called *Romance and Arabella*, about a young widow, played by Laura Hope Crewes, who makes up for lost time by romancing several men. (In one of those coincidences so dear to the theatre world, Lynn Fontanne was playing a few doors east at the Liberty in *The Wooing of Eve*; however, Lunt and Fontanne would not meet for another two years.)

Then there was *Why Worry?* That was probably the question twenty-seven-year-old vaudeville comedienne Fanny Brice should have asked before taking the part of a waitress in a Jewish restaurant—one of her songs was about the experiences of a Yiddish vampire. The *New York Times* called this melodramatic farce "an unfortunate succession of incoherent situations." *Why Worry?* folded after twenty-seven performances.

It was all too much worry for the Selwyns, who had just opened their own theatre on Forty-second Street and were building two more. In 1918, they leased the Harris to Thomas Dixon, author of the racist play *The Clansman*, who soon rented it out to Harry Herbert Frazee for the drama *A Good Bad Woman* and then ran silent movies when *Woman* abruptly closed. The Selwyns did not abandon the Harris completely frustrated, however. On November 10, 1919, they opened a comedy by Salisbury Field called *Wedding Bells*, which the critic Burns Mantle considered one of the best plays of the 1919–20 season. In March 1920, the Harris passed to yet another owner when Mrs. Henry B. Harris sold the house to Frazee.

H. H. FRAZEE

Theatre historians see H. H. Frazee as the man who produced and directed the 1925 Broadway production of the hit musical *No, No, Nanette* (at the Globe Theatre, later the Lunt–Fontanne, on West Forty-sixth Street). The rest of the world came to know him as the Red Sox owner who sold Babe Ruth to the Yankees. Born in Peoria, Illinois, on June 29, 1880, Frazee appears to have been stagestruck from the time he could walk into a theatre. At a fairly young age he became assistant treasurer and advertising agent for Peoria's Grand Opera House, and in 1896, when he was sixteen, he went on the road as an advance man and stayed there, producing his first road show when he was only twenty-two.

By 1907, the hustling twenty-seven-year-old had amassed enough money to build the Cort Theatre in Chicago. Then he struck it rich by co-producing the hit musical *Madame Sherry*. Shortly before Jack Johnson's 1910 title bout with Jim Jeffries, Frazee took Jeffries and heavyweight wrestler Frank Gotch on an exhibition tour. All in all, the man with the porcine chin and the big cigar apparently made enough money to build the Longacre Theatre in New York City three years later.

For Frazee, everything was a great game, and he had the maxims to prove it, as demonstrated in some of his quotable quips: "No one ever made any money in this world unless he took a chance." "Ready Money—there is nothing like it." "I am a great believer in Luck—the only thing we know for sure about Luck is that it is going to change some time." One year after the Longacre opened, Frazee's luck hit a rough patch. A company that held a mortgage (one of three) on the Longacre sued the Frazee Realty Company for money owed on the loan. Frazee had to sell the Longacre to pay up.

But Harry Frazee was not one to be disheartened where financial enterprise was concerned. Soon he was indulging in a sport he loved nearly as much as theatre: baseball. In 1916, he signed his name to a note and bought the Boston Red Sox for $262,000. By this time, anybody who knew anything about Frazee should have anticipated that this purchase, too, would encounter problems. Sure enough, three years after buying into the game that he called "the greatest amusement in the world," Frazee was yearning to own another theatre and option the script that would one day become *No, No, Nanette*—and was about to default on that $262,000 note. To raise cash, he made sports history—and incurred the eternal enmity of Red Sox fans—by selling the team's star slugger on January 3, 1920, for $125,000 plus the promise of much-needed loans.

This was the man who had bought the Harris Theatre. But luck, or some kind of gut instinct, prevailed. He scored a hit at the newly dubbed Frazee on the first pitch. *The Woman of Bronze*, a drama starring the commanding Margaret Anglin, opened on September 7, 1920, and ran for 252 performances. After that, Eugene O'Neill's *Gold* held on for only thirteen (in addition to script problems, the production's lead actor, Willard Mack, could not learn his lines). Then on August 13, 1921, Frazee and the astute producer George C. Tyler presented George S. Kaufman and Marc Connelly's *Dulcy*—and hit a home run.

Kaufman had brought Connelly an idea. He wanted to base his comedy on a character named Dulcinea, a cliché-spouting young bride who often cropped up in humorist Franklin P. Adams' famous column "The Conning Tower" in the *New York Tribune*. Dulcinea, Howard Teichman writes in his biography of the playwright, was "the very stuff of pure Kaufman": an innocent, a zany, a person so silly that she effortlessly scuttles the plans of those more powerful and devious than she. In the play, the first collaboration between Kaufman and Connelly, Dulcy invites one of her husband's business associates for a weekend house party, an excursion that allows the dramatists to poke fun at corporate America, certainly a favorite Kaufman occupation. In the middle of August, the Frazee, like all the other theatres in New York, was appallingly hot. Lynn Fontanne, playing Dulcy, was dripping in sweat by the time the performance ended. But by the next morning, when the reviews came out, she was a star, and Kaufman and Connelly were being praised for writing an inventive American comedy. The Frazee at last had a true hit.

After that, the venue's luck turned again. The Frazee hosted several intriguing productions: the Theatre Guild's staging of the German Expressionist *From Morn to Midnight*; entries from the Ethiopian Art Theatre (a venture sponsored by Julius Rosenwald, the president of Sears Roebuck, and Joseph Schaffner of Hart, Schaffner and Marx); the nineteenth-century English melodrama *Sweeney Todd*. But nothing drew in audiences, not even Kaufman and Connelly's *The Deep Tangled Wildwood*, one of Kaufman's few failures.

By 1924, Harry Frazee had had enough. On October 29, the *New York Times* reported that Frazee had leased his theatre for ten years to one Samuel Breuer, who in turn sold the lease to Meister Builders, Inc., and the Chanin Construction Company for $60,000 per year. A week later, the *Times* reported that Meister Builders et al., in the kind of flip that was becoming all too common with theatrical real estate, had subleased the theatre to the producer John Cort for $75,000 a year.

Was the building jinxed? Theatre people believe some houses are lucky, others not. But more than superstition was at work here. By the mid-1920s, Forty-second Street had become less attractive to theatrical producers, and the Frazee, with its small orchestra and steep second balcony, was considered out-of-date. Still, New York had enough theatrical activity to keep the Frazee booked—although maybe not with the kind of hit that Harry Frazee desired. One suspects that, after *Dulcy,* Frazee simply turned his attention elsewhere.

WALLACK'S

John Cort had already named a theatre after himself, on West Forty-eighth Street. So when he leased the Frazee, he called it Wallack's, perhaps to honor an earlier dynasty of actor-managers, several of whom he probably had known.

Cort was a shrewd man of the theatre. Born in 1861, the first year of the Civil War, he grew up on the East Coast and gradually worked his way to Seattle, where he took over the Standard Theatre and operated it as a "box-house"—a saloon with a stage at one end—for lumbermen and miners. The spot became so popular, that in 1888 Cort built a new Standard and soon erected a twenty-two hundred seat Grand Opera House for the good people of Seattle. Disliking the Klaw-Erlanger syndicate, he helped organize a group of theatres that fashioned alternative circuits in the middle of the country and farther west. Eventually coming East, in 1912 he opened his Cort Theatre in Manhattan with J. Hartley Manners' *Peg o' My Heart,* which played an eminently satisfying 603 performances. The Cort was considered a "lucky" house.

At Wallack's, Cort's first selection was the unfortunately titled *Shipwrecked,* which sank in less than a month. The closest thing to a substantial run came from Barry Conners' 1925 comedy *Hell's Bells,* which starred a darkly handsome twenty-six-year-old named Humphrey Bogart and introduced Shirley Booth to Broadway. *Laff That Off,* produced by Earl Carroll, received glowing reviews in November 1925, but in December it moved, to continue its run somewhere else. If even a smart man like Cort couldn't make a go of it, maybe the theatre really was jinxed.

Cort was the last theatrical producer to give it a try. Real estate in the theatre district was proving a better investment than the theatre-owning business. In October 1926, the Schulte Realty Company bought Wallack's, and eight months later sold it to an investor, which promptly leased it to another company. During the next three years, one failing production after another trod Wallack's boards, until a farce called *Find the Fox* came in on June 20, 1930, virtually at the last minute. (It moved in on a Thursday and opened the next night.) The playbill listed a prologue in a Pullman car, but since the

scenery wasn't ready, the audience never saw the prologue, which was just as well, for none of the critics liked what the producers did manage to stage—scenes, it turned out, that were set in an asylum for demented actors. *Find the Fox* gave three performances and became the last legitimate entry to play the theatre that Oscar Hammerstein I had built twenty-six years earlier for Lew Fields.

Like nearly all the legitimate theatres on Forty-second Street, Wallack's was destined to show movies. In 1930, a company called Excello Estates, headed by Max A. Cohen, leased Wallack's, turning it into a second-run movie theatre, and a marquee advertising Hollywood stars such as Joan Crawford and Clark Gable hung over the Forty-second Street sidewalk. Cohen bought the land underneath Wallack's in 1940, intending to tear down the building. Instead, he tore out the second balcony, put stadium seating in the orchestra, and removed the limestone façade, replacing it with a windowless sheet of bland stucco. Renamed the Anco, after Cohen's wife, Anne, it briefly showed "old-time" films, but largely it was a grind house, running action and, eventually, pornographic movies almost twenty-four hours a day. In 1988, the building was gutted and outfitted for retail space; in 1997 it came down, and the former Eltinge Theatre was moved to its site.

Eltinge
THEATRE

42ND STREET WEST OF BROADWAY

A. H. WOODS
MANAGER

THE ELTINGE

1912

Al Woods, one of Broadway's most colorful producers, built the Eltinge Theatre in 1912 for the female impersonator Julian Eltinge. Ironically, Eltinge never played the theatre that bore his name.

A. H. Woods was the epitome of the Broadway producer, right down to his Havana cigar and his signature greeting: "Hello, sweetheart." Writing about Woods many years after his heyday, the actress Ruth Gordon remembered that on "Hot summer nights, Al sat out front of The Eltinge watching Forty-second Street go up and down and into his theater, his chair tilted back against it, a Panama to keep the electric lights out of his eyes, one of which was markedly cocked."

Born Aladore Herman in Budapest, Hungary, in 1870, Woods came to the United States with his parents when he was four months old. (He added the surname when he began working in theatre.) Like many Eastern European immigrants to the United States, he was raised on the Lower East Side of Manhattan, where his father was a dealer in woolens. Also like many immigrants, Woods escaped from the tenements, the dirt, and the poverty as soon as he could. At the age of fourteen, he ran away to join the circus.

Somewhere during his youthful ramblings he developed a love of legitimate theatre and a gut instinct for what would sell. By the first decade of the twentieth century he was producing theatre in New York, where he was known as a "plunger"—a producer who took chances. If a play of his failed, he'd have another one in rehearsal the next day. "Once," he told Alan Dale of the *Chicago Herald*, "I had twenty-three plays on the road. They were all the same thing with different titles."

The story he told about discovering the female impersonator Julian Eltinge was a favorite with Woods. As he wrote in *The American Magazine*:

"I was walking into Hammerstein's vaudeville theater one day when I heard a fine voice coming from the stage. The usher was bringing me to my seat and I asked her who this beautiful, stylishly gowned woman was. She began to giggle, and walked away without answering. I wondered why she had laughed, but I understood when Julian Eltinge, at the end of his performance, removed his wig and revealed himself as a sturdy, well-built masculine individual. 'Good lord!' I remember saying to myself. 'If Julian Eltinge can fool an old theatrical bird like myself, he can fool thousands of others around the country.'"

That was 1909. Woods signed Eltinge to a seven-year contract, a business agreement from which both producer and star would reap hundreds of thousands of dollars. On September 11, 1912, Woods, Eltinge, and the Bloom Theatre Company opened the Eltinge Theatre at 236 West Forty-second Street. Woods, however, would soon hold a controlling interest as both owner and manager. Asked why he hadn't named the playhouse after himself, as most other theatre owners were doing, Woods answered, "The name of Julian Eltinge is better, and not only better, but best." Eltinge, ironically, never performed in the theatre that bore his name.

The architect for the Eltinge was the Scottish-born Thomas White Lamb, who had emigrated with his family to the United States in 1883, when he was twelve years old. He had studied architecture at the Cooper Union Institute and would soon become respected around the world for designing theatres and other places of entertainment. (Among other buildings, he would design a "double-decker" theatre in Toronto for Marcus Loew and the Ziegfeld Theatre in New York.)

Lamb's design for the Eltinge was elegant and spare. The building's square, terra-cotta façade was dominated by

JULIAN ELTINGE

The man in whose honor A. H. Woods named his New York theatre was born William Dalton, in Newtonville, Massachusetts, on May 14, 1881, or 1883. (The exact year, like so much else in Eltinge's life, is unknown.) Information about his early years is spotty, possibly because "Bill," as close friends called him, told various stories about his upbringing. But it seems that his Irish-American parents, Julia and Joseph Dalton, moved around quite a bit, for Joseph was a mining engineer who liked his liquor and had difficulty keeping a job. The star told of attending schools in Boston, Los Angeles, San Francisco, and even Butte, Montana, where he remembered seeing the variety performer Al Emmett Fostell doing a bit of female impersonation and not liking him much. One story had it that Eltinge was first sighted performing in female drag in Butte saloons around the age of eleven and was promptly shipped back to Boston, to live with an aunt.

When not impersonating a woman, Julian Eltinge looked surprisingly unremarkable.

For *Cousin Lucy*, a musical comedy about a debtor who masquerades as a woman in order to collect life insurance, Eltinge, as was his custom, costumed himself impeccably in fashionable, feminine clothes.

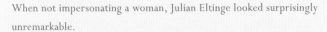

Over the years, Eltinge circulated several tales about the start of his career. One of the more inventive yarns had him attending Harvard and performing in a Hasty Pudding Club show. More likely to be true was that, in his early teens, he worked as a clerk in a Boston dry-goods store and in his spare time took dancing and singing lessons. By sixteen he was a member of a Boston cadet corps, an amateur all-male troupe that put on revues. As part of a cast of one hundred and fifty boys, he apparently stood out. He told one journalist, "Our director discovered that I could dance a little and handle my skirt with some grace, and by easy stages he inducted me into the front ranks of the chorus." The Cadets supposedly created a play called *Miss Simplicity* for him, but mostly he struggled. One day, however, the Broadway director and producer Edward E.

Rice spotted him in a show (the exact occasion is not clear) and cast him in a new musical called *Mr. Wix of Wickham*, which opened at New York's Bijou Theatre on September 19, 1904. By this time the performer was calling himself Julian Eltinge, to avoid embarrassing his family (the source of his stage name seems to be as much a mystery as the man himself).

"I played the tutor who does a girl part in the second act," he once told a reporter. "I got something like $13 per week—when I got it." *Mr. Wix* closed after forty-one performances, but Eltinge, now with a New York credit, began appearing around the country in vaudeville and in 1906 made his London debut at the Palace Theatre. While in London he gave a command performance for King Edward VII, who expressed his appreciation by giving

Eltinge a white bulldog.

By the time producer A. H. Woods first saw Eltinge onstage, the performer had acquired a reputation and a following. But it was Woods who took Eltinge out of vaudeville and gave him a Broadway musical in which he could star. *The Fascinating Widow,* for which Otto Hauerbach (later Harbach) wrote the book and lyrics, and Kerry Mills, Irving Berlin, and others composed the music, opened on September 11, 1911, at the Liberty Theatre on Forty-second Street and then moved to the Grand Opera House on Twenty-third Street. The show ran for only sixty-five performances, but Eltinge took *The Fascinating Widow* on tour, where it proved a hit and made money for both him and Woods. At the height of his stage career, Eltinge was drawing $12,000 each week.

Eltinge was by no means the only female impersonator in American entertainment at this time. Between 1900 and the middle of the 1930s, many of these performers appeared on vaudeville bills throughout the country. Everett Stuart was called "Stuart, the Male Patti," after the famous Italian opera singer Adelina Patti. In 1904, the *New York Dramati Mirror* hailed him as "the premier impersonator of the fair sex of the present day," and each year he toured Europe, wearing Paris gowns and sporting an ankle bracelet. Bothwell Browne entertained audiences with his impersonations of a showgirl, a suffragette, "The Pantaloon Girl," "The Fencing Girl," and Cleopatra of Egypt.

But Julian Eltinge surpassed the competition. His impersonations were never parodies of women but lovingly rendered transformations created in detail. As he apparently never tired of explaining to journalists, he studied the way that demure women sat, moved, and used their hands, although he never altered his voice—never attempted a false falsetto—when speaking or singing, and he never plucked the full, dark eyebrows that were naturally his. He did shave, however, and he always applied a white liquid to his shoulders and arms, then completed the effect by patting himself with large amounts of white powder. Eltinge estimated that, when he was in a show, he used five pounds of powder a week.

He paid close attention to hosiery and petticoats, fans, jewelry, wigs and hats, and a woman's underlying form. "The corset," Eltinge told a reporter for the *Cleveland Leader,* "is pretty much the instrument of my success." Supposedly he tried sixty different makes of corset before settling on the Norda, made by the Kenny Corset Company of Cleveland, which forced his five-foot eight-inch body into an hourglass shape, giving him a large, sloping bosom and a twenty-six-inch waist. The discomfort—and he admitted there was some—did not deter him. Offstage he wore a size 7 shoe; onstage he somehow pushed his feet into size 4½ heels, so that his feet would look small and dainty.

As for the gowns that completed the picture, they became increasingly lavish as the performer's earnings soared. Audiences, especially women, eagerly watched Eltinge's productions, waiting expectantly for each costume change as though attending a fashion show.

If Eltinge was dedicated to the minutiae of female apparel, he was just as committed to promoting himself. Realizing fairly early in his career that women were his primary audience, he reached them through the *Julian Eltinge Magazine,* in which he offered beauty hints, advice ("Julian Eltinge Advises Ladies to Learn Gentle Art of Boxing"), and secrets about his theatrical transformations. Before the Eltinge Theatre opened, the *New York Review* announced that the theatre would house a beauty parlor for demonstrating "complexion creams" and other beauty tools, including Julian Eltinge Cold Cream. The beauty parlor did not appear, but there was a Julian Eltinge Preparations Company on East Seventeenth Street, where women could order the cold cream, "Liquid Toilet Powder," and face powder, so that, the magazine's ads stated, they could "Be as Beautiful as Julian Eltinge."

Out of costume, Eltinge was a pleasant but bland-looking man, with large, almond-shaped eyes, a full face, and a tendency to put on weight. He dressed fairly nattily, but if one saw him on Manhattan's Upper West Side, where he owned a town house, or at the farm where his mother lived on Long Island's North Shore, one might not have given him more than a glance. Clearly the man really came to life when he was playing a woman.

He kept his private life, if he had one, a secret. To squelch suspicions that he was a homosexual, Eltinge and his press agents went to considerable efforts to market him as a man's man offstage. Periodically he would be photographed wearing overalls and standing on a ladder at his farm or paddling a canoe. When he played a new city, a heckler often was planted in the audience so that Eltinge could rough the man up later. If Eltinge was actively gay, he was successful in masking any liaisons.

In 1914, Eltinge starred in several silent pictures, and by 1917 he had settled in Hollywood, acting in films and producing a vaudeville group called The Julian Eltinge Players. His imposing Italianate home, Villa Capistrana, was located on a hill overlooking Silver Lake. Eltinge decorated the rooms with animal skins, tapestries, and massive furniture, and entertained Hollywood's silent-film stars.

Around 1925, Eltinge considered retiring from both the movies and the stage, supposedly to open a resort hotel in Alpine, California. But other motives may have been at work. For one thing, his brand of ladylike impersonation was now considered old-fashioned beside campy performers like Bert Savoy, whose hip-swinging walk and expressions such as "dearie" and "you *mussst*

come over" reportedly inspired Mae West's signature style of walking and talking. In addition, in 1923, during Prohibition, Eltinge had been arrested for smuggling liquor into the United States from Canada, and though he was acquitted, the embarrassing trial, excessive drinking, and his ballooning weight made it nearly impossible for Eltinge to find work. His hotel plan fell through, and the Depression eventually depleted his fortune.

Eltinge's last stage appearance took place in New York in 1941, when producer Billy Rose put him into a revue at the Diamond Horseshoe nightclub in the basement of the Paramount Hotel, off Times Square. There Eltinge's formerly triumphant impersonations fell flat, and one night, possibly feeling ill, perhaps acutely depressed, he stopped his performance and went home to his apartment on West Fifty-seventh Street. He died there ten days later, on May 7, apparently of natural causes.

One of Julian Eltinge's most famous roles was the title part in *The Fascinating Widow*. Here the fascinating widow takes a turn as a bathing beauty.

a multistory Roman arch that created a huge bay window, which unfortunately illuminated the rear of the house during the day and had to be blacked out with curtains for matinees. The view at night, however, was spectacular. The building's fourth and top story, where Woods and his brother, Martin, maintained their offices, looked from the street simply like a row of six slightly recessed windows. A steel and glass marquee jutted over the sidewalk, sheltering four sets of double doors beneath its canopy. Compared with other theatres of that time, the exterior of the Eltinge presented little ornamentation—a bit of architectural restraint that gave the building a certain grandeur.

The theatre was also one of the smallest on Forty-second Street. Despite two balconies, it sat only 889. Its proscenium was thirty-six feet wide, and from the footlights to the back wall of the stage was a mere twenty-eight-and-a-half feet. But it was all to Woods' taste. Unlike several of his Forty-second Street colleagues, he rarely produced musicals, lavish or otherwise. He loved bedroom farces and what were called "crook dramas," crime melodramas that enticed audiences into the theatre with their portrayals of gangsters and female victims—and action that usually took place within the walls of a box set.

Small though the theatre was, its interior decoration, by Paul B. LaVelle, made up for the embellishment that the exterior lacked. Ancient Egyptian and Greek motifs—a pair of plaster sphinxes above the proscenium arch, reclining maidens above the four pairs of boxes, dancing maidens adorning a mural on the sounding board—lent the Eltinge an exotic atmosphere. (When AMC Entertainment acquired the theatre during the 1990s, the mural was restored, revealing that the face of the central maiden, and possibly those of all the women on the sounding board, was actually a portrait of Julian Eltinge.) It was a theatre that audiences enjoyed stepping into, and once in their seats they found excellent sightlines and experienced an intimate relationship with the actors onstage.

The façade of Woods' beloved Eltinge Theatre was one of the more elegant on Forty-second Street.

SUCCESS AFTER SUCCESS

Woods certainly knew what audiences liked. For the theatre's opening production, on November 4, 1912, he booked a four-act crook drama called *Within the Law*, co-produced by Crosby Gaige and the Selwyn brothers and directed by Holbrook Blinn. Although it had suffered a difficult tryout in Chicago, Woods, who put money into the show, must have had a sense that it would run successfully.

Written by a Brooklyn newspaperman turned dramatist named Bayard Veiller, *Within the Law* presented a talented

Above the proscenium arch of the Eltinge Theatre were paintings depicting Julian Eltinge in the guise of mythological dancing maidens.

young actress named Jane Cowl as a department store salesgirl who becomes involved with an underworld gang. Arrested for a theft she did not commit, the handcuffed Mary Turner stands straight and tall in her employer's office and tells him that, if he wants to stop the stealing, he should pay his salesgirls more money. In prison she plots revenge, and when she gets out she follows through by seducing the employer's son and marrying him. Along the way, she gets caught up with a real group of thieves, a corrupt police inspector, and a murder, but in the end manages to prove her innocence.

The wood-paneled sets looked rich and appropriately foreboding. Dark-eyed Jane Cowl was languorous and seductive as Mary Turner. Crosby Gaige, nervously pacing up and down on the sidewalk on opening night, remembered

going back inside at the point when Mary turns vengefully on the department store owner. Cowl was supposed to say, "Four years ago you took away my name and gave me a number. Now I've given up that number and I have your name." Instead, the actress declared, "Four years ago you took away my number and gave me a name. Now I've given up that name and I've got your number!" During intermission, Cowl was in tears in her dressing room, terrified that she had ruined the play. But as Gaige reassured her, nothing could hurt the production: they already had a hit on their hands.

Burns Mantle, reviewing in the *New York Evening Mail*, wrote that *Within the Law* "is the liveliest crook drama, the best police play of its period." The *New York Times* critic called it "an exciting entertainment of the most vivid kind" and wrote that Cowl's "conquest was complete." The production ran for 541 performances and didn't close until December 1913. It made Cowl a star.

After *Within the Law* moved on, Woods' challenge as owner and manager of the Eltinge was to find another hit. When Michael Morton's *The Yellow Ticket* opened on January 20, 1914, the critic for the *Telegram* wrote, "Mr. Woods realized he must hit the high spots of playdom if the ghosts of 'Within the Law,' so long at home at the Eltinge, were to be chased out by the current reality. He rose nobly to the occasion with a constellation of players than which no brighter glitter in the theatrical firmament. He fell short just one act. There are two good acts in 'The Yellow Ticket' and a third act."

The play was of the kind Woods favored: melodrama. But the subject matter was unusually serious. The yellow ticket of the title referred to the badge of prostitution in Russia at that time. By holding a yellow ticket and prostituting themselves, Jewish women were permitted to live in St. Petersburg and other Russian cities from which they were ordinarily excluded. The heroine accepts a yellow ticket in order to be near her ailing father, but she refuses to become a prostitute, and when a member of the secret police tracks her down, she stabs him to death with a hatpin. On opening night, during the second intermission, the author told the audience that he had written the play to expose the infamy of the yellow ticket system.

The reviewer from the *Telegram* was right: Woods had assembled an excellent cast. Florence Reed played the

Al Woods was famous for producing melodramas that scared and comedies that titillated. But occasionally he produced a play with substance such as the socially conscious *The Yellow Ticket*, starring John Barrymore and Florence Reed.

Russian heroine, dashing John Barrymore the American newspaper correspondent who rescues her, and John Mason the evil emissary of the secret police. The performances apparently kept the production alive at the Eltinge through a respectable 183 performances, after which Woods produced Edward Sheldon's equally unusual *Song of Songs*, adapted from Hermann Sudermann's sexually suggestive novel; that, too, enjoyed a decent run.

But not until November 1915 would the Eltinge be host to another certified hit, once again produced by the Selwyns rather than by Woods himself: *Fair and Warmer*, a bedroom farce by Avery Hopwood.

Hopwood was a commercial producer's dream. Born in Cleveland, Ohio, he had come to New York shortly after graduating from the University of Michigan in 1905. From the time his drama *Clothes*, written with Channing Pollock, opened in 1906, until he died in 1928, almost every theatre season saw a play of his on Broadway, usually a sexually titillating comedy.

Hopwood was so successful that theatregoers would have been surprised to know the extent of the man's private unhappiness. Despite his having seen twenty-six of his works produced in New York, he was disappointed that he never attained the artistic excellence or recognition he sought. He drank heavily, and only his closest friends knew that he was homosexual—an orientation that, in the American theatre of the early twentieth century, Hopwood needed to disguise. When he was forty-six, he drowned while vacationing on the French Riviera, possibly the victim of a tryst gone sour.

Fair and Warmer, which opened at the Eltinge on November 6, 1915, was in the traditional Hopwood mold. In one critic's summary of the plot, "Billy Bartlett loves his wife Laura not wisely but too well . . . The brand of domestic bliss provided by Billy is so colorless that Laura turns to Philip Evans, a one-time fiancé, for excitement. She announces she will get a divorce and Billy is lowered into an avernus of despair."

Of course, everything turns out fine in the end, after the right people are discovered hiding underneath the wrong beds. As another reviewer wrote, "The plot of 'Fair and Warmer' is more than familiar. It is positively venerable."

But Hopwood's craft was formidable, and dark-haired Madge Kennedy was both enticing and funny as the woman with whom Billy dallies for a spell. "If the world seems gray and cold to you," wrote Charles Darnton in the *World*, "go

Madge Kennedy as Blanche Wheeler in "Fair and Warmer" seeks physical as well as moral support of Billy Bartlett (John Cumberland) in her efforts to be calm under stress.

White, N. Y.

In Fair and Warmer, one of Al Woods' most successful productions at the Eltinge, the adept comic actress Madge Kennedy finds herself in the wrong place at the wrong time.

and see 'Fair and Warmer' at the Eltinge Theatre, for this 'play of temperature and temperament' by Avery Hopwood is so bright and so capitally acted that it may be depended upon to drive away the blues, green devils or troubles of any other color." Heywood Broun at the *Tribune* dubbed it "among the most amusing plays New York has seen."

In July 1916, the Selwyns moved their success to the Harris, where it continued its 377-performance run. Woods barely paused before bringing in another hit. In August, he produced Max Marcin's *Cheating Cheaters,* leading Darnton to call Woods the "high priest of crook drama" and the Eltinge the "temple of crook drama." (Of the play's thirteen characters, ten were criminals.) Nobody out front seemed to mind, and *Cheating Cheaters* ran well into the spring of 1917, logging 286 performances.

By now the Eltinge had won the reputation of being a lucky house, and Woods' canny judgment largely kept it that way. Even if melodrama was his genre of choice, he was smart enough to produce or book the comedies that audiences also adored. After closing *Cheating Cheaters,* he opened the Eltinge's 1917–18 season with Barney Bernard and Alexander Carr playing Abe Potash and Mawruss Perlmutter in *Business Before Pleasure*. Bernard and Carr were comic performers in the vein of Joe Weber and Lew Fields, although their humor was more verbal than physical. Like Weber and Fields, Bernard and Carr had created an ethnic pair who fought most of the time but remained tight friends no matter what. Carr (Mawruss) was tall, Bernard (Abe) was short; Carr was irascible, Bernard was lovable. Bernard possessed a long, sad face that was born to do slow, comic takes.

In 1913 and 1915, Woods had produced the pair's first legitimate outings: the hit *Potash and Perlmutter,* and the slightly less successful *Abe and Mawruss,* in both of which the men played cloak-and-suiters (clothing manufacturers and sellers). Now Woods produced *Business Before Pleasure,* with a new script by Montague Glass, who had invented the characters and coauthored the first Potash and Perlmutter comedies, and Jules Eckert Goodman, one of the commercial theatre's strongest comic scribes. In it the two friends ditch the rag trade and go into the "fillum" business. "Once again," wrote Charles Darnton in the *World*, "Barney Bernard, as the senior member of the firm of Potash and Perlmutter, proved himself funnier than a pawnbroker at a picnic . . . Alexander Carr once more figured as the superior partner of the one and only Abe. The two comedians . . . made 'Business Before Pleasure' one long laugh." Once more, Woods had a hit.

In fact, as Woods and the Eltinge headed into the Roaring Twenties, it seemed that this producer and theatre owner could do no wrong. Even entries that were slightly experimental, such as *Under Orders,* a war drama in which two actors played numerous characters at a time when casts were usually twenty or more, drew audiences. In 1919, when Woods produced *Up in Mabel's Room*—a farce involving a pink chemise and starring the lovely Hazel Dawn—the witty critic for the *Morning Telegraph,* Rennold Wolf, wrote, "It is not likely that anyone save A. H. Woods, who has a leaning toward the lingerie style of art, would have presented the

comedy with equal success. To be sure, there are producers with greater sense of artistry and with equal facilities for stage directing, but there is none who gauges the spiciness of this sort of entertainment, its limitations and its possibilities, quite so accurately as Mr. Woods."

As if to prove his critics right, Woods opened the new decade at the Eltinge with *Ladies' Night,* a farce by the invincible Avery Hopwood and Charlton Andrews that filled the Eltinge for the entire 1920–21 season. The following season he brought in Hopwood's *The Demi-Virgin,* which he had opened at the Times Square Theatre across the street.

Ironically, despite the vital theatre economy of the early 1920s, after *The Demi-Virgin* the Eltinge was not awash in hits, perhaps because Woods was so busy producing all over Broadway and on the road. During the fall of 1920, he had opened four plays on the Great White Way. At the start of the 1925–26 season, he brought seven productions into town, including Michael Arlen's *The Green Hat* with Katharine Cornell and Leslie Howard, which he installed at the Broadhurst on West Forty-fourth Street.

The Broadhurst contained many more seats than the Eltinge and was located above Forty-second Street. Much as Woods loved the Eltinge, he was a practical man of the theatre and probably realized that the Street of Dreams was slightly losing its draw with New York audiences. During the 1926–27 season, Woods rented the Martin Beck Theatre on West Forty-fifth Street for what would be his biggest success of the decade: John Colton's melodrama of love, racism, and revenge, *The Shanghai Gesture*.

Still, Woods' critics were not really doing him justice. His affection for bedroom farce and melodrama did not mean that he did not know a stirring play when he read one, and he told reporters that he read several plays a day. But New York reviewers, famished for good, new American plays, were tired of the commercial diet of risqué comedy and maudlin drama. At the Eltinge, they panned popular fiction writer Fannie Hurst's first play, *Back Pay,* about a poor working girl gone wrong, for being "sentimental, false and rather meretricious." Reviewers also trounced the production of W. Somerset Maugham's London hit *East of Suez,* which starred Florence Reed as what was then called "a half-caste" woman. Alexander Woollcott in the *New York Times* opined that Maugham "would be considerably surprised if he could see the piece he wrote as it has now been condensed, retouched

Up in Mabel's Room was a farce involving a pink chemise and lovely Hazel Dawn (center), an actress and singer who would go on to act in silent films, marry a millionaire, and then retire early.

and generally softened and sentimentalized under the management of A. H. Woods."

After *Demi-Virgin* closed at the end of the 1921–22 season, most of the productions at the Eltinge didn't reach that goal, and only two passed the two hundred performance mark. One of those was *Spring Cleaning*, a comedy of manners by the English playwright Frederick Lonsdale that

opened on November 9, 1923. Produced by Arch and Edgar Selwyn and directed by Edgar, it starred Violet Heming as a wife whose husband shames her into discarding her degenerate associates by inviting a prostitute to one of her dinner parties. The other crowd-pleaser was *Blackbirds of 1928*, produced by Lew Leslie, which transferred from the Liberty in the fall of 1928.

The critics were not always right, of course. In January 1925, Lionel Barrymore opened at the Eltinge in *The Piker*, a play by a young British dramatist named Leon Gordon, who had already written a steamy drama called *White Cargo* and would go on to become a Hollywood screenwriter. In Barrymore's words, *The Piker* was a study of "a pathetic and pitiable weakling who is born licked." The plot evokes Georg Kaiser's expressionist *From Morn to Midnight.* Bernie Kaplan, a lowly bank clerk, falls in love with an actress and steals what he thinks is a small amount of cash, so that he can buy a good suit and impress the woman. It turns out that he's stolen more money than he intended and is now rich. But the actress discards him; the police, who have arrested someone else for the crime, don't want to hear his admission of guilt, so Bernie goes mad.

Critics hated the play, and Barrymore wrote in a New York daily, "I am constrained to believe that to the local play reviewer the only dramatic possibilities inherent in contemporary New York and its inhabitants are glorifiable girls and glamourous (*sic*) crooks and 'dicks' of the nonexistent variety." Barrymore went to Hollywood permanently and hardly ever appeared onstage again.

At the end of August 1925, Woods sold the Shubert brothers a 50 percent interest in his lease at the Eltinge, probably to raise cash to finance his extensive producing elsewhere. In exchange, any touring shows that started at the Eltinge were to be booked into Shubert houses on the road. If he couldn't find runaway hits for the Eltinge, Woods at least could present talented young performers: blonde, demure Ann Harding as an unmarried schoolmistress searching for the grave of her dead child in *Stolen Fruit*; Claudette Colbert in an elaborately produced English thriller called *The Ghost Train*; and a slip of a girl with a heart-shaped face and sad eyes—Sylvia Sidney—in *Crime.* As Woods and other producers knew, shows that drew lukewarm reviews in New York could often perform well on the road or in stock.

At the beginning of the 1927–28 season, when Woods was busy mounting *The Trial of Mary Dugan* at the National (now the Nederlander) on Forty-first Street, he leased the Eltinge to an entity called the Lambert Theatre Corporation, which booked and managed the venue. They set a kind of record for the house: seven flops in eight months, including a so-called comedy by Lawrence Langner, *These Modern Women.* Langner, a lawyer who had formed the Theatre Guild in 1918 and would one day found the American Shakespeare Festival in Stratford, Connecticut, was many things—but a good playwright was not one of them. Despite the efforts of director Rouben Mamoulian and set designer Cleon

Throckmorton, this send-up of the modern woman's supposed desire for extramarital love affairs proved earthbound. Somewhere during the Lambert tenancy, Woods must have decided that it would be a good idea to take the Eltinge back. By the time *Blackbirds of 1928* was ensconced, the Lambert Theatre Corporation was gone, and Woods, sitting in his office, tilting back in his chair, and smoking cigars, once again was managing his house.

Still, Woods knew that the theatre business had expanded beyond audiences' ability to sustain it. In September 1929, one month before the stock market crashed, he told the *New York Times* that there were too many theatres in New York and that at least thirty of the playhouses around Times Square had gone dark at some point during the 1928–29 season. For a time after the Crash, Woods hung on. The Eltinge did not. Ever "a plunger," Woods produced *Murder on the Second Floor,* a British thriller by Frank Vosper that starred a smoldering, dark-eyed twenty-two-year-old named Laurence Olivier; an item called *Love, Honor and Betray* with an appealing actor named Clark Gable; and even the Theatre Guild's production of *A Month in the Country* starring Alla Nazimova. They all failed. The last show Woods produced at the Eltinge, in August 1930, was *The Ninth Guest* by Owen Davis, whose plays he had presented consistently since 1906.

Ironically, Woods did not produce the final legitimate show that played the Eltinge. That honor was left to Richard G. Herndon, who mounted a drama set in Sing-Sing Prison, called *First Night.* This ran for eighty-six performances and closed in February 1931.

By now, Woods, like most of his producer colleagues, was struggling financially. After the failure of *First Night,* he leased the Eltinge to Max Rudnick, who operated movie houses in Brooklyn, for $45,000 a year, and Rudnick turned the theatre into a burlesque house. Sometime early in 1933, Rudnick took control of the entire building, and Woods vacated his office, with its walnut paneling, green carpets, and long-time secretary, Miss Levy, and moved his headquarters to the New Amsterdam. Eventually he also moved out of his luxurious suite at the Hotel Marguery on Park Avenue and into one room at the Hotel Alamac on Columbus. He would continue to produce legitimate theatre until 1943, but would have only one more hit: Ayn Rand's melodrama *The Night of January 16,* at the Ambassador. He got older and went broke, thus ending his colorful career.

Remembering Woods fondly, Ruth Gordon wrote about his last years: "He read scripts, drank coffee. Read *Variety*, drank coffee. Delivered scripts, drank coffee. Thought about things, drank coffee. But when you don't have a place to tilt your chair, or a show that could fracture 'em, 24 hours are a lot of hours. And one day in 1951 he died. He was 81."

CHEAP THRILLS

During most of the 1930s, the playhouse Woods loved offered up cheap talkies and strip shows. One of the headliners was Billie Shaw, who undressed to the tune of "If You Want to See a Little More of Me, Clap Your Hands, Clap Clap" and soon became Mrs. Max Rudnick. Local businessmen complained periodically about the burlesque houses that threatened to engulf the Broadway area, particularly Forty-second Street. The police would raid the Eltinge and close it, but indecency charges never seemed to stick. Even though New York City's new mayor, Fiorello H. La Guardia, was a reform-minded man, Tammany Hall corruption lingered on. In 1934, Rudnick, his assistant, and seven strippers were arrested, but when they came before the judge, the only evidence against them was the testimony of a two hundred-pound arresting officer giving his version of a "hootchy-kootchy" dance, "a swaying motion suggesting a tanker in a gale," wrote one amused reporter.

Finally, after years of issuing short-term licenses, in 1942 License Commissioner Paul Moss denied licenses to the Eltinge and the Republic, the two remaining burlesque emporiums on Forty-second Street. By the spring of 1944, the Brandt organization had acquired the Eltinge (as well as six other playhouses on the block), turned it into a movie house, renamed it the Laffmovie Theatre, and was running comedies. The Brandt chain rechristened it the Empire in 1954.

As the block deteriorated, so did the Empire's movies, which tended to favor the martial arts. Finally, in 1986, the Brandts decided to get out of the Forty-second Street movie business and sublet its seven houses to Leonard Clark's Cine 42nd Street Theatre Corporation, which in turn sublet the Empire to Sweetheart Theatres, Inc., a company that specialized in pornographic films.

When the redevelopment of Forty-second Street got under way, the old Eltinge was not considered a good candidate for restoration as a commercial legitimate theatre, mostly because the house seated fewer than one thousand people. The plasterwork was still in fairly good condition, but the boxes had been destroyed, and most of the murals had either been removed or covered over. The public spaces and the backstage areas would have required an expensive overhaul.

The ceiling and proscenium of the Eltinge were designated as landmarks, however, and thus Forest City Ratner, the block's developer, was required to preserve them. When part of the block on the south side of Forty-second Street was allotted to AMC Entertainment—one of the nation's largest movie chains—to build a multiplex, Forest City Ratner literally moved the former Eltinge 170 feet west toward Eighth Avenue, at a cost of $1.2 million, or $588 an inch.

On the morning of Sunday, March 1, 1998, a crowd of about six hundred witnessed an astounding sight, even for a city accustomed to the unusual. On that day the old Eltinge, weighing 7.4 million pounds, was being inched along steel rails to the site of its new home, which AMC Entertainment would open in 2000. The façade of A. H. Woods' beloved theatre remains the only part of the original structure visible on Forty-second Street, for the rest is surrounded by glass and concrete buildings. Within, escalators rise up through what used to be the Eltinge's proscenium arch, past the painted images of Julian Eltinge, to transport audiences to AMC's twenty-five-screen movie mall.

By the time Forty-second Street was reclaimed, the Eltinge had become
the Empire movie house. One Sunday morning in 1998, the theatre was
literally dragged toward Eighth Avenue by Laurel and Hardy, where it
became the core of an AMC multiplex cinema.

THE
CANDLER
THEATRE

THE CANDLER

1914

The Candler Theatre stood in the shadow
of the twenty-three story Candler office
building, both of them named after
Asa Candler, founder of the Coca-Cola
Company. The Eltinge is in the lower
right corner of the photograph.

Asa Griggs Candler was born on a farm in Carroll County, Georgia, in 1851, the eighth child of Samuel Candler, a thriving planter and merchant, and his wife, Martha. The Civil War interrupted the son's schooling, but the hard-working, religious young man learned to be a "prescriptionist," as a druggist was known back then, and he went into the pharmacy business, manufacturing patent medicines in nearby Atlanta. There he encountered one John Styth Pemberton, owner of a chemical company and inventor of a syrup that was the primary ingredient for what Pemberton called "Coca-Cola, the Brain Tonic and Intellectual Soda Fountain Beverage."

Noting that people liked the new beverage, but that Pemberton, whose health had deteriorated, was not marketing his invention very well, Candler slowly acquired the right to manufacture the drink (which, in some correspondence, he referred to as "Coco-Cola") and eventually he also purchased the formula—for $2,300, or so the story goes. In 1891 Asa Candler founded the Coca-Cola Company. By 1920 he was a millionaire.

But Candler was more than a calculating businessman. He possessed a sense of civic responsibility and a talent for self promotion. He wanted Atlanta to become an alluring, fiscally sound city. (Eventually he would be elected mayor.) So in 1906 he erected the seventeen-story Candler Building— Atlanta's tallest building at the time—to house the bank and headquarters of the Coca-Cola Company. After that, he built parks and playing fields in Atlanta and invested in real estate in a number of cities along the East Coast, often bestowing his name on the structures left in his wake.

In 1912, on a site formerly occupied by the Central Baptist Church, Candler bought a piece of Manhattan property at 220–24 West Forty-first Street that extended to Forty-second, and there he built a twenty-three-story, marble and terra-cotta mate to Coca-Cola's Atlanta landmark. Rising 341 feet, it was definitely the tallest building on Forty-second Street between Seventh and Eighth avenues.

This new Candler Building would not ordinarily have affected the theatrical growth of the block, except perhaps to lend it a sort of grandness. But to protect the views and the light enjoyed by the skyscraper, Candler constructed a five-story extension to the east of the tower and bought a piece

of property immediately to the west—the George Bruce Library—on which to erect another five-story extension, at 226 West Forty-second Street. There the theatrical producer Sam H. Harris, real estate investor Sol Bloom, and film distributor George Kleine carved out the ninth legitimate theatre to open on the Street of Dreams: the Candler Theatre.

Designed by the Scottish architect Thomas White Lamb, the Candler offered a marble vestibule that the theatregoer entered from Forty-second Street. The vestibule led to a foyer, then to a lobby, and finally to the auditorium, which was really on the Forty-first Street side of the building. A detailed account of the Candler Theatre's interior, in the May 16, 1914, issue of *Dramatic News*, describes a vestibule ceiling "beautifully stenciled in gold"; a spacious lobby that was more like a wide hall, for which the American painter Alfred Herter had woven six wall tapestries depicting scenes from several of Shakespeare's plays; and passageways and staircases "of a magnitude that shows no attempt at economizing in space."

As with the Booth Theatre on West Forty-fifth Street, which had opened the previous year, the Candler's auditorium contained only one balcony. Theatre historian and architect Craig Morrison called this the final step in the evolution from the multitiered horseshoe of the nineteenth-century American theatre. But even without a second balcony, the Candler accommodated 1,200 people: 625 in the orchestra and 575 upstairs. Designed for showing motion pictures as well as live performances, the Candler reduced the number of boxes to a single pair on each side, so that people in the balcony would have an unimpeded view of the large movie screen. Boxes, for decades the most sought-after seats in an American theatre, would soon be replaced on the desirability scale by the first five rows of the center orchestra.

The unusually wide proscenium and high ceiling made the house feel spacious; the décor and the lighting provided a sense of intimacy. Journalists wrote about the "harmonious color scheme" of Arthur Brounet's interior design—what Victor Watson in the *New York American* described as "mouse color and orange." (Perhaps he meant gray and orange.) "The ceiling is a thing of impressive beauty," wrote Watson of its curving, sweeping lines: no mammoth crystal chandeliers or glass globes to obtrude upon one's vision. Instead, a ring of delicate metallic chandeliers dangled unobtrusively, providing soft illumination.

The theatre's sweeping ceiling helped make this auditorium one of the most stylish on Forty-second Street.

Candler Theatre.

The Candler opened on the evening of May 7, 1914, with the film *Antony and Cleopatra,* which was produced by Societa Italiana Cines, filmed in Rome and Alexandria, Egypt, and imported by George Kleine. This silent "photo-drama," as it was called in the reviews, starred Anthony Novelli as Marc Antony, Gianna Terribili-Gonzales as Cleopatra, and supposedly a cast of thousands. An orchestra at the Candler played during all the scenes, and film historians have concluded that Signorina Terribili-Gonzales portrayed a fairly erotic Cleopatra. Still, reviews were mixed, and the day after the picture opened, the *New York Telegraph* reported that the Candler would switch to "spoken drama" the following season, under the aegis of George M. Cohan and Sam Harris.

GEORGE M. COHAN AND SAM HARRIS

In 1904, when Cohan and Harris solidified their partnership with a legendary handshake, Cohan, aged twenty-eight, already possessed a considerable reputation. The man who would later boast in song and story that he was born on the Fourth of July had been performing with his parents and older sister since he was seven. The "Four Cohans" had played variety shows all over New England, and one-night stands from Boston to San Francisco. "I can still smell those stuffy red plush cars in which we traveled," Cohan told a *New York Times* interviewer in 1933. "I remember punk boarding-houses from here to California and barns which were called opera houses. Still, it was a happy life." Young George Michael Cohan played the violin, composed and sold songs, danced (supposedly without ever taking a lesson), wrote farce sketches, and by the time he met Harris had written the music, books, and lyrics for two musicals in which he also starred—one on Broadway.

Cohan grew up among limelights and greasepaint. Samuel Henry Harris grew up on the tough Manhattan Bowery. There, in 1883, at age eleven, he hustled for pennies, delivering hats, telegrams—anything for which a messenger boy could be hired. If he had the nickel, he went to the theatres on the Bowery and sometimes worked as a stagehand. At seventeen, he met a man who had a

languishing towel-supply business; Harris made it turn a profit. At twenty, a friend took him to Greenpoint, Brooklyn, to see lightweight boxer "Terrible Terry" McGovern. Harris became the fighter's manager and carefully, shrewdly, crafted his client into the champion lightweight of the world. He even got McGovern into a play, which is how Harris got into the theatre business. He once told the journalist Mary B. Mullett, "You make a business man, a successful doctor or lawyer, a great actor or artist, just the way you make a champion prize-fighter. The great danger is in trying to go too fast. . . . Match yourself against a little harder job, and then a little harder one, and keep learning all the time!"

Sam H. Harris, one of Broadway's most astute and admired producers, managed the Candler from 1914 to 1919 with his business partner, George M. Cohan. They called their theatre the Cohan and Harris.

Cohan was a performer; Harris was a businessman. Still, in 1904, when they first met, the men had several things in common: they both possessed a sixth sense about what made good theatre, they both liked to work hard, and they both were broke.

There are several versions of how Cohan and Harris became a team. One has them meeting on a Staten Island Ferry, on their way to a Sunday outing of the Words and Music Club, an informal songwriters' group. Another story (Cohan's recollection) has them meeting *at* the picnic. Still another (also Cohan's recollection) has them introduced to each other in the offices of the H. C. Miner Lithographing Company—a popular source for Broadway's playbills and posters—having dinner, and *then* going to the picnic.

However they met, the slim, gregarious man of Irish descent and the small, wiry son of the Bowery took to each other and formed a partnership that would bring artistic and financial success the first time out—with Cohan's musical *Little Johnny Jones*—and for fifteen years afterward. They already owned one theatre—George M. Cohan's Theatre at Broadway and Forty-third Street—and in 1912 they subleased the Astor Theatre at Broadway and Forty-fifth Street. (They would sell the first in 1915 and sublease the second a year later.) Now they were trying to put their stamp on Forty-second Street. Their first theatrical production at the Candler, in 1914, proved notable.

George M. Cohan was undoubtedly one of the most imaginative, as well as one of the most driven, men ever to dazzle Broadway.

ELMER L. REIZENSTEIN

The journey to Broadway of Elmer L. Reizenstein's drama *On Trial* was the kind of story that Broadway denizens, from producers to journalists, loved to tell. As the playwright himself recounted in an autobiography, he was a skinny, nearsighted, red-haired kid who loved to read and loved theatre. Despite a checkered education, he had managed to enter New York Law School at the age of eighteen, and three years later had qualified for the bar. But clearly law did not excite him as much as literature. He had collaborated on a play with another young attorney, but now that friend was starting a firm, and Reizenstein, who had quit his job and was

waiting to hear if he had passed teaching and proofreading examinations, decided to write a play by himself. It took him two months to write *According to the Evidence*, a courtroom drama with flashbacks, a murder reenacted from more than one point of view, and at its center a Kentucky feud. "No subject," the author later mused, "could have been further outside the range of my experience and knowledge."

Reizenstein did not know anybody in the theatre, but he did know the names of a few producers. So he left badly typed scripts with Selwyn and Company and with Arthur Hopkins. He received a typed note back from Crosby Gaige at the Selwyn office and a handwritten note from Hopkins, both inviting him to come around. But when Reizenstein showed up at Gaige's door, the man was out to lunch, so the young playwright took himself to Hopkins' office. "Is the play original with you?" Hopkins asked. Reizenstein said it was.

"What are your terms?" Hopkins asked next. Reizenstein had no idea. So Hopkins drew up a fair contract, and two days later Reizenstein signed it.

Many years later, in the article "Playwrights I Have Known," Hopkins wrote that "Elmer had a splendid idea and a confused story. After I bought the play, I told him that we would have to begin by throwing away the story."

They worked on the script together, Reizenstein rewriting and every morning meeting with Hopkins to pore over the changes. When a final draft emerged, the structure remained, as did the murder. But the Kentucky feud was gone, and in its place were new plot twists involving a disreputable married man (the murder victim), a woman with whom he had once tried to have an affair, and her husband—the accused. And there was a new title: On Trial. Hopkins, it turned out, did not have the money to produce the show, but Cohan and Harris did, so they bought an interest in the production. In fact, after the successful Stamford, Connecticut, tryout, Cohan offered Reizenstein $30,000 for the rights. But Elmer, though young, was not stupid. He politely, but firmly, declined. His royalties from that first production and subsequent tours would later amount to around $100,000.

Today, On Trial feels melodramatic, and its flashback technique, while adeptly integrated into the whole, is familiar. But when the play opened at the Candler on August 19, 1914, the courtroom sequences, and the scene in which twelve male jurors decide the fate of the accused, sounded unusually realistic in comparison with the exaggerated language and strained plots of most American melodramas of that time. What's more, to cut back and forth between present and past, with its hint of an editing technique borrowed from the young medium of film, impressed and delighted theatregoers. The critic in the highly regarded Theatre Magazine called it "a talking moving picture as graphic and absorbing as any detective story."

"The opening night," wrote the critic Burns Mantle, in the Best Plays of 1909–1919, "was one of those rare occasions in the theatre when the very air trembles with the joy of an audience that has discovered a hit. The young author, his face flushed to match his red hair, was sitting in a stage box. Forced to acknowledge the ovation, he rose dazedly and stumbled through a little speech that was as much like a condemned man's thanks to a jury for his acquittal as a speech could be."

The endorsements from Hopkins, Cohan and Harris, the critics, and the public were well placed. Reizenstein, who within five years would change his last name to Rice, became one of a new breed: the serious, modern American dramatist. The experimentation with form, and the interest in justice, would continue in his later plays such as the expressionist The Adding Machine, Street Scene (which won the 1928–29 Pulitzer Prize for Drama), and the agitprop vehicle We, the People.

Elmer Rice was barely in his twenties when he wrote On Trial, the first play produced by Harris and Cohan at the Candler, in 1914. Rice would go on to win the 1929 Pulitzer Prize for his passionate drama Street Scene.

MORE SUCCESS

On Trial settled into the Candler for a 365-performance run, to the delight of Cohan and Harris, who forged ahead while many of their colleagues struggled to keep afloat. The 1914–15 season was not kind to Broadway, and the following season was mixed. In Europe, war had broken out at the end of July 1914, and although the United States was not involved, the inability of the Allies to win a quick victory had a depressing effect on markets everywhere.

Still, on September 1, 1915, Cohan and Harris opened Max Marcin's drama *The House of Glass*, which ran for seven months. When that closed, they mounted John Galsworthy's ironic drama *Justice*, staged by the up-and-coming British director Ben Iden Payne and starring John Barrymore as the piteous, imprisoned hero. Although the production barely passed the one hundred performance mark, it was a critical success, and Barrymore, who often played light comedy, demonstrated that he could immerse himself in a challenging, serious role.

All the chorus girls adored comedian Raymond Hitchcock, the star of the 1917 revue *Hitchy-Koo*.

RAYMOND HITCHCOCK AS HE MEETS A CLA

Success led Cohan and Harris to buy out Sol Bloom's and George Kleine's interests in the Candler, move their own offices to the theatre building's top floor, and change the venue's name. "The general public couldn't pronounce the old name," Leo M. Marsh wrote somewhat wryly in the *New York Telegraph,* "insisting on calling it 'Chandler' and other perversions of its true patronymic, so the producers have cut the Gordion knot." As of August 4, 1916, the theatre was known as the Cohan and Harris.

Luckily for the two friends, they both possessed a gambling spirit. Not until June 1917 did the Cohan and Harris present another hit: the musical revue *Hitchy-Koo*. The title's silliness reflected what Charles Darnton in the *Evening World*

called "a hodge-podge of entertaining nonsense." Produced by the comedian Raymond Hitchcock and E. Ray Goetz, and starring Hitchcock, or "Hitchy," *Hitchy-Koo* was a collection of skits and songs, helped along by pretty, if unglamorous, chorus girls.

What distinguished this revue was the particular talent of its star, a rail of a man with a shock of blond hair, a pointy face, and large ears, whom Darnton believed to be "the funniest man on the musical comedy stage." Audiences loved his "curtain talks," particularly a routine about the evangelist Billy Sunday, whom Hitchcock labeled "the P. T. Barnum of the hymnal." Wearing a suit and a straw hat, Hitchcock would sit in the orchestra, and before the curtain rose he'd stand

ROOM OF SCHOOL GIRLS IN "HITCHY-KOO." White.

up and greet his friends, assuring them that, even if the show went a little long, they'd see the "Finale," because the "Finale" was going to come first. He said hello to latecomers and called everyone—friend or stranger—by their first name, including the ambassador to Germany, who was apparently in the audience on opening night.

The Tribune critic opined that the show had been put together to give Hitchcock something to do until he was needed elsewhere. True or not, *Hitchy-Koo* filled the Cohan and Harris for about two months, then departed at the end of August to continue its 220-performance run at a different theatre and allow Cohan and Harris to bring in another hit.

For the next two years, from the start of the 1917–18 season until the beginning of the 1919–20 season, Cohan and Harris produced one runaway success after another at their theatre. First came the comedy *A Tailor-Made Man* (by Harry James Smith, with rewrites by Cohan), about a poor man who invents an imaginative if dishonest scheme for bettering himself—and does. Then there was Anthony Paul Kelly's romantic adventure about the Secret Service, *Three Faces East* (also with rewrites by Cohan), and finally *The Royal Vagabond,* subtitled "A Cohanized Opéra Comique."

Cohan had a formula for turning mediocre plays and musicals into hits. The critic George Jean Nathan once described it as "prefixing to each of the author's original speeches such phrases as 'By Gosh,' 'Gee whiz,' 'I say, kid' . . . and 'You said a mouthful,' of adding a wealth of back-slapping and thigh-slapping to the stage business, of writing in at least one mention of a million dollars and at least one cheer for the United States . . ." Cohan, in other words, cannily applied the art of appealing to middle-brow, patriotic America's love of a good show.

The music publisher Isidore Witmark had brought Cohan the script for an operetta called *Cherry Blossoms,* with a book by Stephen Ivor-Szinney and William Cary Duncan, lyrics by Duncan, and music by Anselm Goetzel. According to Cohan's biographer John McCabe, "the man who owned Broadway" thought it was the worst script he had ever read. Intentionally or not, *Blossoms* was a bad parody of all those European operettas set in fictional kingdoms with fictional Germanic names. Cohan decided to turn the piece into a complete send-up, and so he rewrote the script, added new songs and rewrote others, and brought forth *The Royal Vagabond.* Under Cohan's deft if predictable ministrations, the new show was

now about a barber from Hoboken, New Jersey, who returns to "Bargravia" to become king, abdicates to marry a milliner, and finally becomes president of the country, which is now a republic.

When *Vagabond* opened on February 17, 1919, the reviewer for the *Globe* called it the "nicest bit of satire on a dry and musty yarn," and Alan Dale of the *American* wrote that "the injection of the serum of Cohanization into what must have been a singularly deadly, old-fashioned and sinister 'opera comique'—gave us a jolly entertainment." The *Times* critic enthused that the original "has been brought startlingly down to date here and there by Mr. Cohan by the insertion of syncopated numbers, some flip patter, or a reference to Prohibition." *The Royal Vagabond* amused audiences for 348 performances, with a few interruptions now and then to accommodate an actors' strike.

Cohan also had his creative hand in *The Acquittal,* a three-act drama by Rita Weiman that Cohan and Harris opened on January 5, 1920, for a moderate run. But that would be the team's last co-production at its Forty-second Street theatre. In June 1920, the partnership that had brought so much pleasure to audiences, and so many rewards to its two producers, dissolved.

So what caused the breakup between Cohan and Harris? The Actors' Equity strike of 1919. Actors' Equity Association (AEA) had been founded in 1913 by 122 actors who were tired of working for unscrupulous producers. The latter could fire actors at will, for no cause; actors usually rehearsed for free, for as many hours as a producer demanded; on the road, actors often had to pay for their own room and board; and if a show folded out of town, actors frequently had to pay their own way back to New York. Star player or unknown, an actor was at the mercy of a producer's personal ethics and generosity, or lack thereof. Under its first president, the singer and comedian Francis Wilson, the AEA fought for a standard agreement. But little had changed since 1913; actors were still the victims of greedy producers, and the producers were only getting richer.

In February 1919, the Erlanger and Shubert management organizations were proposing to merge, to create a single, all-powerful group: the Producing Managers' Association (PMA). The announcement was a red flag for Actors' Equity, which immediately understood that an enormous amount of power would now be placed in the hands of a small coterie

Frederic Santley and Robinson Newbold risked physical injury in the popular Cohan and Harris musical *The Royal Vagabond*, the last show that Cohan and Harris produced together at the theatre. Renaming the house the Sam H. Harris Theatre, Harris managed it alone until 1926.

who cared more about making money than about performers' well-being. On July 1, 1919, Equity's existing contract with producers expired, and Equity demanded better rehearsal pay, an eight-performance week, holiday and Sunday pay, and recognition as a professional union with which producers would have to negotiate.

Later that July, members of Actors' Equity agreed to give up their charter and become affiliated with the American Federation of Labor to create the Associated Actors and Artistes of America, commonly known as the 4As. At that point, vaudeville mogul E. F. Albee (father of dramatist Edward Albee) issued a call to producers to squelch the AEA once and for all. On August 7, following an afternoon meeting at the Hotel Astor on Times Square, AEA members, now more than two thousand strong, adopted a resolution that called for producers to agree to the new contract and AEA's new union status, or expect that no AEA actors would work for any PMA producer. That night, the casts of twelve New York shows refused to go on. The strike had begun in earnest.

Cohan and Harris both sided with the managers, but Cohan was especially rebellious. As John McCabe wrote in his Cohan biography, "No one deplored the practices more, no one demonstrated in action the rejection of such practices more than Cohan. Cohan's actors were always well paid, both for rehearsals and performance . . . But Cohan, great performer that he was, had not worked hundreds of tank towns in the grimy sweat of vaudeville and road shows to insure his own enlightened management just to abjure it." Somebody other than Cohan was telling him what he would have to do, and Cohan could not abide it. He famously asserted that "Before I will ever do business with the Actors' Equity Association, I will lose every dollar I have, even if I have to run an elevator to make a living." From his point of view, the actors had broken their contracts with him. He resigned from the Lambs and the Friars, two actors' clubs where he had been a dedicated member.

On September 6, 1919, the strike ended after thirty days, with thirty-seven closed productions in New York and other cities, along with sixteen productions that were prevented from opening—and after a loss to managers of approximately $3 million. Producers, including Sam Harris, signed a five-year contract granting the conditions and recognition that Equity had sought. Cohan never signed the contract. Equity, recognizing his unique contribution to the American theatre, graciously gave him a dispensation whenever he produced or performed. A journalist reported that, in the office of Cohan and Harris, Cohan picked up a blotter with his picture in one corner and Harris's in another, "tore the blotter in half, tossed Harris's picture to him, and said: 'Sam, we're through.'"

THE SAMUEL H. HARRIS THEATRE AND HAMLET

The men remained friends, but now Harris was an independent producer, and the sole lessee and manager—and eventual owner—of the Forty-second Street theatre. He renamed it the Samuel H. Harris Theatre, but it was always known as the Harris.

For the next six years, Harris would bring a variety of productions into his Forty-second Street domain. The comedy Six-Cylinder Love, about a young married couple that buys a secondhand car and goes into debt, was silly but enormously popular. These days the show's only historical interest is that the cast included an actress named Hedda Hopper, who would become one of Hollywood's most dreaded gossip columnists. At the opposite end of the literary spectrum was Shakespeare's iconic tragedy Hamlet, starring John Barrymore, which opened at the Harris on November 16, 1922.

Barrymore was forty years old in 1922 and already a Broadway legend. The descendent of an illustrious Anglo-American theatrical family, and the youngest brother of character actor Lionel and leading lady Ethel, John was an actor who seemed to detest acting. At the urging of relatives and friends he had gone on the stage, mostly performing light comedy, but he demonstrated little enthusiasm for the craft. He preferred to seduce women, a vocation at which this strikingly handsome man was especially skilled. And he had a penchant for drink, which amounted to a second vocation and often got him in trouble both onstage and off.

Then the English director Ben Iden Payne cast him in John Galsworthy's Justice in 1916, and Barrymore demonstrated that he possessed a wide emotional range.

This famous 1922 photograph of John Barrymore as Hamlet hints at the intensity which the handsome actor brought to the role of his lifetime.

Four years later, Arthur Hopkins, the perceptive producer and director who had brought Elmer Rice's *On Trial* to Broadway, approached Barrymore about playing the physically and emotionally deformed title character in Shakespeare's *Richard III*. After intense private study with the renowned voice and acting coach Margaret Carrington, Barrymore opened at the Plymouth Theatre and gave what most critics deemed the performance of his career.

But the actor was depressed and ill after playing Richard—possibly from the anxiety and effort connected with preparing for the role, and undoubtedly from complications in his private life. In June 1922, Ethel apparently gave him a copy of *Hamlet* to read, and Barrymore, suddenly galvanized, went to Hopkins with a proposal. Hopkins, who had directed *Richard III* and would also stage *Hamlet*, convened with his designer, the innovative Robert Edmond Jones, and once again Barrymore studied and trained with Carrington, this time for more than a month.

"Of all the actors I have known," Hopkins later wrote in his autobiography, *To a Lonely Boy*, "[John Barrymore] was the most conscientious and untiring in preparation. Nothing was too much trouble. He would go to the costumer, the bootmaker, the wigmaker, the armor maker, twenty times each, forty if necessary to get everything right. He was the first to know his part. He would rehearse each time as though it were a performance. He was never late, never made excuses. He would rehearse scenes with other actors as long as they wanted. He never grew tired. To him perfection was the aim, and its attainment could not be too much trouble. He loved creating a part, and once that excitement had passed, the part interested him no more. . . ."

The *Hamlet* production was visually striking. Robert Edmond Jones' set consisted of an imposing flight of steps flanked by two castle walls and leading up to a platform and a high arch; front drop curtains helped mold the space. Jones relied on lighting, designed by George Schaff, to create effects. The ghost of Hamlet's father was suggested by light playing on the slightly rippling curtains, while a voice offstage intoned the Ghost's words to his astonished son. Props were minimal, and costumes not elaborate. The production's look exemplified the New Stagecraft, which Jones had essentially introduced to the American theatre and continued to champion.

When at his best in the part, Barrymore was America's first modern Hamlet: human rather than high-flown. Heywood Broun in the *New York World* wrote that "John Barrymore is far and away the finest Hamlet we have ever seen. He excels all others we have known in grace, fire, wit and clarity. . . . Barrymore's most original contribution to the role probably lies in his amplification of the unconscious motives of the Prince. He plays the closet episode with the Queen exactly as if it were a love scene."

Other critics, such as John Corbin at the *Times*, thought that Barrymore, Hopkins, and Jones had "snuffed out this drama . . . Mr. Barrymore has actually achieved Prince Hamlet without the play, and that is by way of being a tragedy." Kenneth MacGowan, writing in *Theatre Arts Magazine*, thought Barrymore extraordinary but inconsistent. "Barrymore," he opined, "gives the most brilliant Prince of this generation of English speaking actors—sensitive, gracious, intellectual, lovely of voice, and poignant with emotion—but he is not yet the responsible and self-dominating artist who can hold his work to a single steady impression."

Nobody, not even the actor himself, knew better than Hopkins how unpredictable Barrymore could be during a run. The director believed that the best performance of *Hamlet* Barrymore ever gave was one at which Ethel was the only person in the audience. There was no scenery yet, no costumes, and Ethel sat in the balcony of the Harris by herself, while Barrymore played to her. As far as performances before a full house were concerned, Hopkins said that Barrymore's first performance was always his best. "Some of his later [performances] were embarrassingly bombastic," Hopkins wrote. "He did not have the gift of knowing when he was right. He was always a conscious actor. He lacked Lionel's submersion and Ethel's theater sense. Once he had successfully created a part he was given to embroidering, and his embroidering was not good . . . Occasionally, due to some relaxation, his first good performance would come back. In a hundred-and-one performances he played many different Hamlets."

There are several stories about how Barrymore came to play 101 performances of *Hamlet*—one more than the even more legendary nineteenth-century thespian Edwin Booth. The most entertaining version has a few elderly gentlemen visiting Barrymore backstage and imploring him not to destroy the record of "the great master." (In fact, the record had already been broken by John E. Kellerd, who gave 102 performances at the Henry B. Harris Theatre—originally the Lew Fields—during the 1912–13 season. But Barrymore's dressing-room visitors clearly did not know that.) The old men's regressive plea was all Barrymore needed. He told Hopkins that he would give 101 performances and no more. Finally, as the perceptive Hopkins wrote, John Barrymore was "a brilliant creator, an erratic repeater, and, rarest of all, an actor who hated to act."

After *Hamlet* closed, Sam Harris brought in Owen Davis's *Icebound*, an unsettling play about the spiritual coldness and isolation of a New England family. Critics levied mixed praise on Davis's personal attempt to break away from melodrama, and the production sustained only a moderate run. It did, however, win the Pulitzer Prize for Drama in 1923. Davis's comedy *The Nervous Wreck*, which came into the Harris in October 1923, had a lengthier stay.

THE SHUBERTS, YET AGAIN

On September 15, 1926, *Variety* announced that the Shuberts had purchased Harris's theatre, reportedly for $1.2 million.

The reasons for the sale were undoubtedly financial. In 1921, Harris and songwriter Irving Berlin had pooled nearly a million dollars to build the Music Box Theatre on West Forty-fifth Street, which was becoming the center of Broadway's theatre world. But Sam Harris, ever the canny businessman, had probably also sensed that Forty-second Street, with its aging theatres, was yielding ground to newer houses on other thoroughfares.

Under the Shuberts, the Harris meted out several failures, a few moderate hits, and two substantial wins. One, in 1930, was John Wexley's prison drama *The Last Mile*, about the final hours of a man on death row. Thirty-year-old Spencer Tracy, in the role of a hard-as-nails prisoner, gave a performance that led film director John Ford to bring him to Hollywood. The other hit, also in 1930, was Zoë Akins' *The Greeks Had a Word for It*, a comedy that Percy Hammond in the *Herald Tribune* described as "three deluxe strumpets who are operating in New York's easy-money circles." A throwback to the women-as-gold-diggers comedies of the 1920s, it contained enough pungent dialogue and alluring actresses to entice an audience trying to recover from the shock of Wall Street's debacle.

Fittingly, the last production at the Harris was written by, produced by, and starred, George M. Cohan. Called *Pigeons and People* and subtitled "A Comic State of Mind in Continuous Action" (there was no intermission), this odd but pleasant vehicle allowed Cohan to portray a homeless eccentric named Parker, who is rescued from his park bench and his pigeons by a socially responsible young man. In the comfort of the young man's home, Parker dances, plays the piano, sings, tells stories—and generally wreaks such havoc that the nice young man wants to get the derelict back to the park as soon as possible. But Parker will not go until he is ready—until it has been demonstrated that organized society as represented by the young man is not nearly as beneficial as living on a park bench and feeding the pigeons.

Pigeons opened on January 16, 1933, and ran for seventy performances. That year, the Shuberts declared bankruptcy and lost the Harris, and the theatre became the movie house that it was originally intended to be in 1914. What with one sale and another, by the time the 1970s came around, the Harris, situated next door to Forty-second Street's only all-male bathhouse (the New Barracks), had joined the ranks of the block's grind houses. Restoration was promised, but finally, during the street's redevelopment in the 1990s, the

entire theatre building, except for the Forty-second Street façade, came down to make way for Madame Tussaud's.

URIEL KIRKLAND, VERREE TEASDALE AND DOROTHY HALL in "The Greeks Had a Word For It," at the Sam H. Harris Theatre.

A number of Broadway playwrights during the 1920s were women, and one of the most respected and popular was Zoë Akins. Her 1929 comedy *The Greeks Had a Word for It*, about three gold-digging friends, was a fitting tribute to the end of the Roaring Twenties.

SELWYN THEATRE
42ND STREET WEST OF BROADWAY

THE SELWYNS Owner : Manager

THE SELWYN

1918

The theatrical producers who put down roots on Forty-second Street were adventurers, and none more so perhaps, than the Selwyn brothers, Edgar and Archibald. Edgar, the oldest, was born in Cincinnati, Ohio, in 1875, and Archibald, or "Arch," in 1877. Presumably there was a set of parents, whose last name was actually "Simon," because the brothers were known to tell stories about growing up in Toronto, Canada, and then in Selma, Alabama, until their parents died. But the good-looking, dark-haired siblings seem from the outset to have invented themselves.

When his parents died, penniless seventeen-year-old Edgar apparently took off for Chicago, where he was so broke that he tried to commit suicide by jumping off a bridge into the Chicago River. But fortune was against him, so to speak: the river was frozen, deterring his headlong dive. As Edgar later dramatized in his 1915 play *Rolling Stones*, a passing thug held him up with a gun while he was contemplating the ice and demanded "your money or your life." "My life," Edgar reportedly replied—an answer which so astounded the crook that the two men proceeded to a pawn shop, hocked the gun, and split the proceeds.

True or not, it was the kind of story that epitomized the wild, up-and-down careers of the Selwyn brothers. Eventually Edgar made his way to New York, where he sold neckties and ushered at the Herald Square Theatre, until actor-playwright William Gillette hired him in 1896 to play a Confederate soldier in *Secret Service*. By 1899 Edgar had appeared on Broadway, and by the middle of the twentieth century's first decade, he was both a star and a playwright.

Arch followed his brother to New York in the 1890s. Borrowing money from a literary agent, he and a partner invested in a penny-slot weighing machine at Coney Island. When that effort went bust, Arch decided theatre was a better bet, and by 1912 he and Edgar had become Broadway producers. That year they and newly minted theatrical producer Crosby Gaige brought Bayard Veiller's melodrama *Within the Law* to the Eltinge on Forty-second Street. The popular production netted about $1 million for the trio in those years before income tax, and in 1914 the three launched Selwyn and Company. They soon leased the Harris (originally the Lew Fields), which had been floundering since Henry B. Harris died on the *Titanic* in 1912. By 1914 the Selwyn brothers had also formed the All-Star Feature Films Company, which would merge in 1917 with a firm run by Samuel Goldfish (later Goldwyn), to become the Goldwyn Pictures Corporation, a forerunner of MGM.

In 1917, Arch and Edgar leased two plots of land on the north side of Forty-second Street, with options to buy. The site at 215 to 231 West Forty-second was to be the location of the Selwyn Theatre. (The other property would soon be the site of the Times Square and Apollo theatres.) Crosby Gaige oversaw the design and construction. Rumor had it that the building of the theatre was being financed by the gangster Arnold Rothstein, who in 1919 would fix baseball's World Se-

Entrepreneurial brothers Edgar and Archibald "Arch" Selwyn built three theatres on Forty-second Street; their first, the Selwyn, opened in 1918. By 1925, the two men had severed their partnership.

ries between the Cincinnati Reds and the Chicago White Sox.

The Forty-second Street façade, trimmed in terra-cotta and sporting a balustrade above the top floor, was a six-story office building for Selwyn and Company and one of the least theatrical playhouse entrances on the street. However, the building's first-floor entrance led to a commodious array of marble-floored lounges, restrooms, and mirrored foyers as extensive as any on the block. And it led to the Selwyn's auditorium, which was situated behind the office building, parallel to Forty-third Street.

Audiences that bought tickets for a production at the Selwyn entered through the first floor of the six-story Selwyn office building on the North side of Forty-second Street. In 1997, following extensive demolition on the block, the empty building collapsed.

Arthur Brounet, who had designed the auditorium for the Candler, designed the Selwyn's house along similar lines. Again, there was a shallow, fanned auditorium with a single balcony, and the same "stepped" pair of boxes on either side of a wide proscenium. The Selwyn, like the Candler, seated just over a thousand people, but the décor was more luxurious. The balustrades on the stairways leading from the foyer to the balcony were of carved, yellow marble. The auditorium, including the balcony, contained wainscoting of rare blue-veined marble, which melded with the velvety overall color scheme: antique Alps-green, highlighted with Old Italian blue and antique gold. Blue was the color of the curtains and the upholstered seats. Lofty, triangular panels above the boxes contained Brounet's murals portraying various performing arts. "The luxurious fittings of the theatre are so unobtrusively applied," wrote the critic for the *New York Telegraph*, "that the opulence is rather inviting than commanding . . . The lighting scheme of the auditorium dome, balconies and foyer is all of the indirect and evenly distributed sort, with the added novelty of changing colors, gradations of white, pink, rose and purple being at the discretion of the operator." No matter whose money the Selwyns were using, apparently no expense was spared. They even installed a "shower bath" in each dressing room.

A TOUGH BEGINNING

On October 2, 1918, the Selwyn Theatre opened with *Information, Please!*—a comedy by Jane Cowl and Jane Murfin in which Cowl starred; the same actress had helped the Selwyns to a hit when she appeared in *Within the Law* at the Eltinge six years earlier. The flags of the World War I Allies were festooned on the outside of the curtain, and the national anthem was played before the show began. Crosby Gaige had gone to great expense to have Tiffany's engrave sterling-silver tickets for the opening-night critics, an unusual tactic even for those extravagant days.

The gifts were only partially successful. The critics praised the new theatre but not the comedy. The *New York Times* reviewer thought the Selwyn was "beautiful," but he found the play to be "Farce comedy of the flimsiest." Alan Dale wrote, "The acoustics . . . were so good, that every word spoken

The Selwyn Theatre was designed in a modern vein, with a fanned auditorium, a single balcony, and only one pair of boxes on either side of the proscenium.

upon the stage last night was heard—which was a pity . . ." *Information, Please!* closed after forty-six performances.

The Selwyns, like so many producers at the time, had more success with musicals. The first musical comedy they brought into the new theatre, an item called *Tumble In* (subtitle: "A Comic Rhapsody in Two Raps and Four Taps"), coproduced with Arthur Hammerstein, was not a hit but at least leaped over the one hundred–performance hurdle. Perhaps even more importantly, it brought the inventive lyricist and musical comedy book writer Otto Harbach into the Selwyns' fold.

Not until the Selwyn Theatre's second season did the house book anything resembling a hit, which turned out to be a musical comedy called *Buddies*, about American soldiers

billeted in France during the Great War. This moderately entertaining show had music and lyrics by the British singer and composer B. C. Hilliam, and a book by the Canadian-born librettist George V. Hobart. But mostly it brought to the fore dark-haired, forty-four-year-old Donald Brian, whose dancing and tenor voice had garnered him Broadway fame at the New Amsterdam back in 1907, when he played Prince Danilo in Franz Lehar's operetta *The Merry Widow.* According to Brian's biographer, Charles Foster, Fred Astaire once said that Brian "was undoubtedly the most graceful and elegant dancer ever to appear on the Broadway stage." And during an interview for the *New York Post* in 1985, ballet dancer Rudolf Nureyev mentioned that he possessed six minutes of silent film of Brian dancing in *The Merry Widow* and that "in my entire career I have never seen a dancer so skilled." At his last performance of the operetta, Brian had danced its famous waltz up and down the set's stairs seven times, each time with a different partner.

An intriguing footnote to the production of *Buddies* concerns the out-of-town tryout in Boston, which opened on August 12, 1919, at the Park Square Theatre, five days after the young Actors' Equity Association, trying to establish itself as the only union representing stage actors, was calling on members to strike. In Boston, Brian and his two costars felt torn between the union's requests and their desire to open the musical. Arch Selwyn, of course, did not want his show to close, but neither did he want to sign an agreement with Actors' Equity that would require him to meet all its new, if legitimate, demands. Brian and his costars bought the show for one dollar apiece, agreed to give Selwyn a percentage of the weekly box office and, as the new owners of the production, signed the agreement with Equity. (They and their fellow cast members, however, joined a general strike on Labor Day that closed all of Boston's theatres.) *Buddies* opened in New York on October 27, lasted 269 performances, and apparently made money for all concerned. It was immediately followed by another hit at the Selwyn: *Tickle Me,* with music by Herbert Stothart and book and lyrics by Harbach, Oscar Hammerstein II, and Frank Mandel.

At the beginning of the 1921–22 season, the Selwyn hosted its first non-musical that could be called a popular success: W. Somerset Maugham's daring romantic comedy, *The Circle.* Set in an English country house, the play involves an elderly couple who, when young, left their respective

A 1919 musical comedy called *Buddies*, about American soldiers in France during the Great War, apparently appealed to New Yorkers' patriotic sentiments and became the Selwyn Theatre's first hit.

spouses, the woman's five-year-old son, and the man's career in Parliament, to live together in Italy without benefit of marriage (their deserted spouses had refused to divorce them). In the play, the couple returns to England at the invitation of the woman's son, now grown and married. But during the visit, the young daughter-in-law decides to leave her husband and run off with a houseguest, making "the circle" complete. Maugham apparently wished to show that adultery was acceptable if a married couple was incompatible, but that love was not necessarily a recipe for happiness.

The script's somewhat amoral outlook was cleaned up a bit for American consumption, but *The New York Evening Journal* still called it a "daring comedy," and Percy Hammond in the *Tribune* labeled it "a comedy of much sophisticated charm." The draw for audiences, however, was not so much Maugham's amorality or wit as much as the two actors playing the older, adulterous couple: red-haired, flamboyant Mrs. Leslie Carter, a former Belasco star who had not been on a Broadway stage for seven years; and elegant, sixty-eight-year-old John Drew, Jr., "First Gentleman of the American Stage" (and uncle to Ethel, Lionel, and John Barrymore). Crosby Gaige recalled that Carter and Drew had some trouble remembering their lines on opening night, but that didn't bother the adoring crowd. According to the *Evening*

177

Telegram, the first-night audience at the Selwyn "gave itself up to . . . [an] orgy of appreciation." Burns Mantle reported that Mrs. Carter was supposed to enter with Drew, but, whether out of generosity or desire for the bigger hand, she delayed her entrance until his applause had died down. After that, the audience applauded her every chance it got.

Mrs. Carter was only fifty-nine, but the *Evening Telegram's* critic wrote that "Her face lacks the marvelous plasticity that in the older days enabled her to make a lightning change of expression." He added, however, that "she was delightful in her lighter moments." *The Circle* would be her last stage success. Five years later she was fired by A. H. Woods during the New Jersey tryout of *The Shanghai Gesture* and retired to California. She died in 1937. Drew had died ten years earlier, onstage to the last.

After *The Circle* closed in December 1921, the Selwyn presented a motley assortment of musicals and plays for the remainder of that season and throughout 1922–23. The Russian-born actress Alla Nazimova, who had acted with the Moscow Art Theatre and, early in the century, had created a sensation by performing Ibsen in New York, returned to Broadway after a number of years spent making movies. Her vehicle of choice was an English adaptation of an overwrought Hungarian drama called *Dagmar,* in which she played a promiscuous woman at a European spa. This time, however, her dark eyes and expressive face did not seduce the critics. "'Dagmar,'" wrote one, "is the sort of drama to which Nazimova . . . is admirably suited. It is a glib and showy thing . . . cheap and tawdry." Percy Hammond in the *Tribune* lamented sarcastically that Dagmar had "only one husband and two lovers during all the six acts."

There seems to be no explanation for the Selwyn's fallow period, except that the brothers were now also involved with the Apollo and the Times Square theatres. Then again, Edgar's attention was always fixed on several things at once; at this time he was also writing and staging a comedy called *Anything Might Happen,* which opened at the Comedy Theatre in February 1923 (and folded shortly afterward).

Finally, on June 19, 1923, the producer Rufus LeMaire and a twenty-five-year-old vaudeville performer named George Jessel brought the musical comedy *Helen of Troy, New York* into the Selwyn. With a book by George S. Kaufman and Marc Connelly, and music and lyrics by Harry Ruby and Bert Kalmar (probably best remembered for the song "I Wanna Be Loved by You"), this show about women working in a collar factory in upstate New York combined light, Kaufmanesque satire of American business with un-Kaufmanesque romance. The real attraction, however, proved to be a pert, blonde, twenty-six-year-old singer and dancer named Queenie Smith, who played Maribel McGuffey, the worker that saves the factory from the predations of an efficiency expert. The show made the vivacious Smith a star and gave the Selwyn a hit, which Selwyn and Company soon moved to the Times Square to make room for an even bigger success: a musical called *Battling Buttler.* Starring the fine comedian and character actor Charles Ruggles as Alfred Buttler, a man who leads one life in the country and another in the city, where he is a champion boxer, *Battling Buttler* also moved to the Times Square, where it finished its 313-performance run.

EDDIE CANTOR

Occasionally, of course, the Selwyn was on the receiving end of a popular transfer. From the Earl Carroll Theatre up on Fiftieth Street, in September 1924, the Selwyn received Florenz Ziegfeld's production of *Kid Boots,* a musical featuring the unique comedian Eddie Cantor. Like so many of the performers and producers drawn to Broadway in the late nineteenth and early twentieth centuries, Cantor had begun life on the Lower East Side of Manhattan. There he was born Israel Iskowitz on January 31, 1892, to Russian-Jewish immigrants. His mother died during childbirth the next year, and his father, a fiddle player and a dreamer, died of sadness and pneumonia when the boy was two. But Israel was raised by his maternal grandmother, Esther Kantrowitz, from whom he adopted an Americanized version of her last name. He took his first name because his girlfriend Ida Tobias (later his wife) had always wanted to go out with a boy named Eddie; Cantor obliged.

By his own account, the small, slender boy with the heavy black eyebrows, large brown eyes, and prominent ears started singing and entertaining on the streets of the Lower East Side. In his teens, "Banjo Eyes," as he was nicknamed, was winning local talent contests and appearing onstage in the theatres that populated the Bowery; by 1907 he had made it to vaudeville. When Cantor was in his early twenties, Florenz

Two elderly stars beloved by New York audiences, John Drew, Jr. and
flame-haired Mrs. Leslie Carter, appeared in 1921 in the American
premier of Somerset Maugham's sophisticated romantic comedy *The Circle*.

Ziegfeld saw him in a revue and put him into the *Midnight Frolics*, and he made his Broadway debut in the *Ziegfeld Follies of 1917*.

It wasn't just Cantor's quirky looks, unique inflections, or comic instinct that brought him popularity. It was his whole persona. Onstage, often wearing a suit and a bowler hat, he was so full of energy that he would skip across the stage or put dance steps into scenes that didn't call for any. During a song he would usually jump up and down, clapping his hands, and his signature exit was to prance offstage waving a handkerchief.

Cantor's vehicle *Kid Boots* was a show with lavish sets and costumes, and a typically lush Ziegfeld chorus. There was a strong, funny book by Anthony McGuire and Otto Harbach, an entertaining score by Harry Tierney, and light-as-air lyrics from Joseph McCarthy. But the real draw was Cantor as a golf caddie master and bootlegger in the American South, wearing checked knickers, singing "If You Knew Susie," telling jokes just this side of ribald (and often not in the script), and tossing verbal barbs at the Ku Klux Klan, Calvin Coolidge, and civic virtue. The show toted up 489 performances.

One of Cantor's favorite bits from *Kid Boots* went like this:

> Kid Boots rushes in, jumping about as if to work off an
> attack of fits.
> "What's the matter, Boots?" someone asks, trying to calm
> the guy down. "What are you jumping around for?"
> "Let me alone, will you!" Kid Boots exclaims, excitedly. "I
> just bought a secondhand watch. If I don't do this, it
> won't go."

Cantor lost millions when the stock market crashed in 1929. But with the tenacity born of a youth spent on the Lower East Side, he recouped his losses by becoming a mainstay of radio, movies, and early television. He died in California of a heart attack in 1964.

After *Kid Boots*, the second half of the 1924–25 season brought one failure after another to the Selwyn, possibly reflecting the breakup of Selwyn and Company. But Arch Selwyn on his own was proving an intelligent producer. He had brought *André Charlot's Revue of 1924* to the Times Square, with Britons Beatrice Lillie, Gertrude Lawrence, Jack Buchanan, and Herbert Mundin, and now, on November 10,

1925, he opened *Charlot's Revue of 1926* at the Selwyn.

The returning quartet of Lillie and Lawrence, Buchanan and Mundin, was eagerly anticipated. By the beginning of November, the first week's performances had been sold out, and the "second night" critics—those who did not write for daily papers and thus covered the production after opening night—had to review a matinee for the first time in anyone's memory. "It was carnival night last evening at the Selwyn," wrote Percy Hammond in the *Herald Tribune*, "and all the neighborhood notables were there in flowering bib and tucker."

Outside the Selwyn, the sidewalk was jammed with people trying to get in and police trying to keep them back. A velvet carpet led into the Selwyn entrance for those very important persons who did have tickets, many of whom came late. The curtain was supposed to go up at 8:30 P.M., but the show did not start until after 9:00, and the second half did not begin until after 11:15, which meant that critics who had to meet deadlines for an early edition did not see the whole show.

That was not unusual; in those years, critics often raced up the aisle before the curtain came down, to file their reviews in time for the morning edition. Still, is it possible that the critics felt mistreated? Hammond did not find this second Charlot revue as funny or melodious as the first one, and Gilbert Seldes in *The New Republic* loathed it. The Broadway columnist Walter Winchell called it "overrated" and recommended extensive pruning. However, Alexander Woollcott, who had raved the first time around, believed that "more imagination, more care, more fun and more showmanship went into the brewing of the New 'Charlot Revue' than into the one which was torn from our embrace a year ago . . ." In his view, it was not a performance, but a "reunion." Despite Woollcott's rapturous response, the show played only 138 performances.

Perhaps American critics and audiences were just a mite tired of British imports, for a little over a year later, in December 1926, the Selwyn sponsored another entry that arrived trailing ecstatic London reviews, only to meet with middling success on Forty-second Street: *The Constant Nymph*.

Based on a well-loved British novel by Margaret Kennedy, and adapted by Kennedy and the British director Basil Dean, *Constant Nymph* dramatized the marriage between a bohemian composer and the rich woman who wants to

Kid Boots, a 1924 musical involving a caddie master at a golf course, starred the irrepressible Eddie Cantor, who would take his rolling eyes and physical hijinks to movies and then to the young medium of television.

Two of the most stylish and at times silliest comediennes to grace Forty-second Street were Gertrude Lawrence and Beatrice Lillie, who came from England to play the Selwyn in André *Charlot's Revue of 1926*.

bring order into his life—and the composer's subsequent love affair with the sickly daughter of a revered family of musicians. New York critics disagreed violently about the merits of this three-act drama, and about the right and wrong way to adapt a novel for the stage. And even though the cast included fine actors such as Glenn Anders, Claude Rains, and Leo Carroll, audiences kept the production afloat for only 148 performances. But the play continued to have a life in the United States long after the 1926 production, and it was the source for three movies, the last of which, in a 1943 Hollywood version, featured Charles Boyer, Joan Fontaine, Alexis Smith, and Peter Lorre.

EDNA FERBER AND GEORGE S. KAUFMAN'S
THE ROYAL FAMILY

Toward the end of 1927, in the waning days of Forty-second Street's glory as a site for legitimate theatre, the Selwyn finally housed a long-running show that was also adeptly crafted: Edna Ferber and George S. Kaufman's comedy *The Royal Family*.

Ferber was born in Kalamazoo, Michigan, in 1885, and had begun her writing career as an author of fiction. But she had collaborated in 1915 on adapting her short stories into a well-received play for Ethel Barrymore, *Our Mrs. McChesney,* and in 1924 she and Kaufman had worked well together to

pen their first mutual effort, the comedy *Minick,* adapted from Ferber's story *Old Man Minick.*

Kaufman, four years younger than Ferber, was born in Pittsburgh and had started his career as a journalist in New Jersey and Washington, D.C. In 1917 he had become drama editor for the *New York Times,* and a year later the producer George C. Tyler had asked Kaufman to patch up a Broadway-bound comedy. From then on, Kaufman had continued to write comedies, usually in collaboration with another dramatist.

The kernel of the play was Ferber's idea: she wanted to write about a theatrical family. So, early in 1927, the playwrights repaired first to Ferber's Central Park West apartment, until Kaufman complained there were too many interruptions.

One of the most entertaining comedies to play the Selwyn was Edna Ferber and George S. Kaufman's *The Royal Family*, with Haidee Wright and Otto Kruger as members of a theatrical dynasty much like the Drew-Barrymores.

Jed Harris, who presented *The Royal Family* at the Selwyn in 1927, was one producer whom theatre people loved to hate.

Then they sequestered themselves in separate rooms at the St. George Hotel in Brooklyn, although, unknown to Ferber, Kaufman made his escape from Brooklyn every night into Manhattan, where he was carrying on an affair. Despite what

must have been a tiring schedule for Kaufman, he and Ferber wrote a tight first act and gave it to a relatively new, twenty-seven-year-old producer named Jed Harris.

Harris would go down in theatrical history as a man people loved to hate. He had a habit of sleeping most of the day and showing up at rehearsals late, "fresh as poison ivy," Ferber once said, and then would insult the cast, the playwright, the director, or anybody else he could find. He also liked to phone people at four in the morning, when, given his odd schedule, he, of course, was wide awake. The respected director and playwright George Abbott called him "the Little Napoleon of Broadway." But on the basis of a couple of phenomenally successful productions, by the late 1920s Harris had won a reputation as a smart producer, so Ferber and Kaufman brought him their script, and Harris agreed to put it on.

For years afterward, both authors would deny publicly that the lively, erratic Cavendish clan in *The Royal Family* had been modeled on that Anglo-American theatrical family the Drew-Barrymores. But privately, Kaufman admitted that Fanny Cavendish, the comedy's actress-matriarch, was modeled on Mrs. John Drew; that Fanny's actress daughter Julie was based on Ethel Barrymore; and that the theatrical manager was drawn from Charles Frohman, who had been theatrical manager to John Drew, Sr., and Ethel. And clearly John Barrymore was the template for the dashing, sometimes careless, Tony Cavendish. As the critic Burns Mantle wrote in his *Best Plays of 1927–1928*, "…it is reasonable to assume that if there had been no Barrymores associated with the American theatre there is little likelihood that 'The Royal Family' would have been written."

Ferber suggested Ethel Barrymore for the role of Julie; having worked with Ethel during *Our Mrs. McChesney,* she believed they had a sturdy professional relationship. But to everyone's dismay, Ethel not only refused the offer, she asked her lawyer to stop the production (he told her it couldn't be done), and for many years refused to speak either to Ferber or Kaufman. After that, no actress wanted to play Julie. Jed Harris, for his part, disliked the first cast he assembled, and after nearly ten days of rehearsal fired the whole bunch. In his memoir *A Dance on the High Wire,* he recalled telling Kaufman that "to come to rehearsal with this delicious script and find myself confronted by these 'adequate' actors . . . is like entering the Taj Mahal and finding a very dead *Matjes Herring* on the floor." He particularly hated the English actress Haidee Wright, whom he had hired to play seventy-two-year-old Fanny. He decided to shelve the production.

Eventually the show did go on, opening on December 28, 1927, the day after the opening of the revolutionary Jerome Kern and Oscar Hammerstein II musical *Show Boat,* which was based on Edna Ferber's novel of the same name. A

competent, if uninspired, actress named Ann Andrews played Julie, and Harris again cast Wright, whom he continued to deplore despite the praise she had received from both critics and audiences. Otto Kruger acted Tony Cavendish, although Harris, with his customary rudeness, later described him as "entirely lacking in the distinction and elegance I thought the part required. . . . there was nobody else to be found."

The critics liked the show better than its producer did. Alexander Woollcott called it "one of the happiest evenings ever I spent in the theatre. This is a fond, hilarious, tender comedy."

"Another walloping success," crowed Walter Winchell in the *Evening Graphic.*

Writing in the *American*, Alan Dale enthused about "A family of maniacs, and all on the stage at the same time, talking, jabbering, reminiscing, laughing, sorrowing and running the gamut of racket and rampage . . . an orgy of theatrical family life—the life that exists only in the playhouse." Kaufman's comedic sense, and Ferber's skill for humanizing characters and relationships, had merged to create a valentine to the theatre.

Shortly after the production opened, Harris decided to close it. Despite the positive reviews, the show was not selling out, he announced. Kaufman, who had been tolerating Harris's difficult personality with the patience of a dramatist determined to see his play put on, could not control himself any longer. "Jed, listen to me," he told the producer. "If you close *The Royal Family* without giving it a chance to build, I promise you one thing. The night the show closes, I'm going to come over to your apartment and murder you." *The Royal Family* played 345 performances.

The cliché "nothing succeeds like success" holds true in the theatre, and after *The Royal Family* finally ended its run, Arch Selwyn brought in three musicals that broke the one hundred-performance mark—one of them a genuine hit. First there was *This Year of Grace* in November 1928, a British import and the first revue for which Noel Coward had written the book, music, lyrics—everything. (He also costarred, with Bea Lillie.) Then, in December 1929, Selwyn coproduced *Wake Up and Dream,* a British musical revue by Cole Porter that included the torch ballad "What Is This Thing Called Love?" sung by Frances Shelley and danced by Tillie Losch and Toni Birkmayer. And in October 1930, the Selwyn showcased *Three's a Crowd,* a musical revue produced by Max Gordon, with music by Arthur Schwartz and book and lyrics by Howard Dietz. The enticing cast included Fred Allen, Tamara Geva, Fred McMurray, Clifton Webb, and Libby Holman, whose languid, seductive rendition of "Something to Remember You By" inevitably stopped the show. *Three's a Crowd* had a run of 272 performances, lasting until June 1931.

MORE STRUGGLES

Faced with the commercial theatre's growing struggles—and with his own financial difficulties—Arch Selwyn was clearly doing everything he could to keep the Selwyn from going under, even booking entertainment on Sunday nights, when Broadway theatres were usually dark. In November and December 1928, the Selwyn advertised "Unique Sunday Night Divertissements," which humorist Robert Benchley, who made an introductory speech at the first performance, called "another blow at that noble institution, home life in America." The Sunday nights were a potpourri that included the Denishawn Dancers demonstrating Javanese rhythm; Helen Morgan singing "The Man I Love," "I Can't Help Lovin' Dat Man," and "My Bill"—all from *Show Boat;* and the actress Cornelia Otis Skinner performing character sketches that she had written.

The tall, lean Skinner, who had dark eyes and dark hair that she wore in a knot at the back of her head, was the daughter of the esteemed actor Otis Skinner, with whom she had made her Broadway debut in 1921 in the melodrama *Blood and Sand.* But by 1928 she had made a career of writing and performing monodramas about fictional women, much in the manner of monologist Ruth Draper, to whom she was often compared. On the Selwyn stage, bare except for a table and two chairs, Skinner portrayed a range of characters both amusing and pitiable, including a Southern girl visiting the Sistine Chapel for the first time and lying on her back to see Michelangelo's paintings at their best; a young lady of the gay 1890s taking her first ride in an automobile; and a dowager losing the remains of her fortune to the gambling tables in Monte Carlo. Skinner was so well received that one Sunday "Divertissement" was completely given over to her performances.

Edgar Selwyn gave up on theatrical producing long

before his younger brother did. By 1929 he was writing and directing movies for MGM, and in 1930 he disbanded his New York office. Arch Selwyn, with help from Crosby Gaige, tried to hold on to the Selwyns' flagship theatre. But after *Three's a Crowd* closed in June 1931, the dwindling crowds encountered only failed productions at the Selwyn. Drydock Savings, which held the first mortgage, specified that if Arch could produce a hit and meet the Selwyn Realty Corporation's financial obligations to the bank, it would not foreclose. With that in mind, in June 1933 Gaige produced *Shooting Star,* a drama about the celebrated actress Jeanne Eagels, who had died at the age of thirty-five from an overdose of heroin. The critic John Mason Brown wrote that the play seemed "longer than life itself." In January 1934 Gaige coproduced a drama called *A Hat, A Coat, A Glove,* but the show ran for only thirteen performances. Then in February he brought in something called *Ragged Army,* starring Lloyd Nolan, which Gaige called "the most unhappy production of my entire career." What with one catastrophe after another, Gaige closed the appropriately named *Ragged Army* two days after it had officially opened.

In April 1934 it was announced that the Selwyn would be extensively altered in order to show motion pictures, and Drydock leased the theatre for three years to movie-theatre owner Max A. Cohen. That May the Selwyn began operating as a continuous-run, or "grind," movie house, and in July the bank foreclosed on the mortgage and soon after bought the theatre at auction for $610,000. Three years later, when Cohen's lease ran out, the Brandt movie theatre organization took control of the Selwyn. The Selwyns never produced there again. Edgar died in 1944, Arch in 1959, both in Los Angeles.

In 1949, the Selwyn enjoyed a brief renaissance as a playhouse. A pioneering off-Broadway group called New Stages had produced Jean-Paul Sartre's one-act drama about racism in the American South, *The Respectful Prostitute.* Glowing notices and queues at the box office had motivated the young company to move its hit uptown to Forty-eighth Street, where the production enjoyed an eight-month run at the Cort Theatre. When *Prostitute* closed, George Brandt, the thirty-three-year-old son of movie theatre entrepreneur William Brandt, put the production on his "subway circuit" of five legitimate theatres—in Brooklyn, the Bronx, Long Island, and Passaic, New Jersey—and suggested it would be a fine idea to bring a condensed version to the Selwyn, a tab

Arch Selwyn tried to keep the Selwyn alive despite the Great Depression and personal bankruptcy. But the last hit to play the theatre was *Three's a Crowd*, a 1930 musical revue starring Clifton Webb, Libby Holman, and Fred Allen.

After extensive renovations to the Selwyn, on July 27, 2000, the
Roundabout Theatre Company opened its American Airlines Theatre with
George S. Kaufman and Moss Hart's riotous comedy *The Man Who Came to
Dinner*, starring Nathan Lane and Harriet Harris.

version, which would play five times a day and alternate with a movie. The idea never caught on, and he went back to producing only movies.

When George first came to his father with this idea, the elder Brandt reportedly said something along the lines of, "Stick to the movies. A can of film never got laryngitis." Still, George persisted, and for eight weeks the abbreviated production did excellent business at the Selwyn, although the regular audience, largely men who also came to see the feature *Flame of Youth,* talked during the performances, wandered in and out of the movie house, and laughed at the drama's rough language. Most of them had never seen a play before. The experiment went so well that George subsequently produced a thirty-two-minute version of Avery Hopwood's 1920 farce *Ladies' Night,* calling it *Ladies' Night in a Turkish Bath,* and ran it at the Selwyn with the movie *Jungle Jim.* He also wanted to bring in condensed versions of *A Streetcar Named Desire* and *Born Yesterday.* But those projects never came to fruition. Perhaps Forty-second Street audiences, drawn to the plays by their suggestive titles, were ultimately disappointed, or playwrights did not look fondly on foreshortened editions of their works—or maybe the older Brandt finally put his patriarchal foot down.

After 1950, the Selwyn deteriorated along with the rest of Forty-second Street. Still, during the 1990s, the street's redevelopment brought a variety of potential users for the Selwyn, and in 1997 the avant-garde Wooster Group actually did use the theatre for a revival of its unique version of Eugene O'Neill's *The Hairy Ape,* starring Willem Dafoe. Luckily, nobody was in the area on the morning of December 30, 1997, at 5:20 A.M., when the abandoned six-story Selwyn office building collapsed. Adjacent buildings that had helped prop it up for almost a century had been torn down, weakening the structure; heavy rain delivered the coup de grâce.

The inheritor of the Selwyn turned out to be the nonprofit Roundabout Theatre Company, which had lost its lease on the Criterion Center, a former movie theatre that had been built at Broadway and Forty-fifth Street, partially on the site of Oscar Hammerstein's Olympia.

The Selwyn's renovation reportedly cost at least $17 million, enough of which came from American Airlines for the venue to be named after that organization, a christening that did not sit well with many in the theatre community.

Even so, the renovation was a respectful one. The Selwyn's upper boxes had long since disappeared when the theatre was converted into a movie house. (Boxes impaired sightlines and fostered mischief.) So the renovation restored upper and lower boxes, put in new seating, preserved the plasterwork and the Brounet murals, updated dressing rooms and equipment, and built a penthouse lounge on top of the theatre, along with other additions.

Appropriately, for a theatre whose physical and spiritual forebear had first hosted George S. Kaufman and Edna Ferber's *The Royal Family,* the American Airlines Theatre opened on July 27, 2000, with a revival of *The Man Who Came to Dinner* by Kaufman and Moss Hart.

The sparkling proscenium and stage of the American
Airlines Theatre.

Revitalized, neon-lit Forty-second Street, with the exterior of the
American Airlines Theatre.

TIMES SQUARE
THEATRE

SELWYN & CO.
LESSEES AND
MANAGERS.

THE TIMES SQUARE

1920

In 1920 the Selwyn Brothers opened first the Times Square Theatre and
then the Apollo Theatre, which shared a dignified façade, replete with Ionic
columns, on the north side of Forty-second Street.

The Times Square Theatre, at 215–19 West Forty-second Street, opened on September 30, 1920, and the next day Alan Dale in the *American* wrote a sort of valentine to the playhouses along the Street of Dreams: "I would suggest a passageway cut through the first theatre, starting from Broadway and extending through every house on the way to Eighth Avenue, and a ticket that would permit one to stroll through the entire dozen, thus seeing as many shows as possible on one occasion." Indeed, when the Selwyn brothers opened the Times Square—the second of the three theatres they would build on Forty-second Street—the business of producing plays felt grander than ever, and the street still saw itself as at the heart of New York City's theatrical universe.

Anticipating continued financial success, Archibald ("Arch") and Edgar Selwyn had asked their partner and co-producer Crosby Gaige to find property for them, and so he had. On the north side of the street, the Selwyns bought midblock property that consisted of one 105-foot parcel with an extant movie house, the Bryant, on Forty-second Street, and another one-hundred-foot plot fronting on Forty-third Street. Built in 1910 by George Sturges to show movies and vaudeville, the Bryant Theatre did not prove itself a moneymaker, and was finally razed.

The architect Eugene DeRosa designed an imposing limestone façade that embraced both the Times Square and its sister theatre, the Apollo, which would open that November. On the second level of the façade, six Ionic columns divided a loggia into bays screened by massive wrought-iron gates. At ground level, there were paired entrances beneath a shared marquee. One entrance opened onto a corridor that led to the Apollo Theatre's lobby, the other onto the long lobby that led to the Times Square. Like the most commodious of the Forty-second Street theatres, the Times Square and the Apollo were designed so that their auditoriums and stages would be parallel to the street. In the case of the Times Square, however, this meant that scenery had to be loaded onto the stage directly from Forty-second Street, an arrangement that would be cited during the 1990s as a reason (some might have said an excuse) for not renovating the theatre.

But that problem was many years in the future. And in any case, when the theatre opened, it was not the façade so much as the interior of the Times Square that drew attention. The orchestra fanned out, and the broad but shallow seating configuration gave audiences the feeling they were sitting close to the stage; the house sat 1,053, but, in addition to the orchestra, there was only one balcony and a mere four boxes, each pair positioned beneath a high, hemispheric canopy. The theatre's most striking feature, however, was its color scheme. This, wrote a critic for *Art and Architecture* in 1920, was "very unusual . . . offering novelty as well as harmony. The interior of the Times Square is Empire in style, worked out in silver, green and black. The walls are silver gray. The touches are green so delicate in tone that they melt imperceptibly into the grays, and the tapestried orchestra seats continue the color harmony, all standing out in contrast to the background of the carpet, which is black, and the curtain in folds of black velvet."

At the rear of the orchestra, a grand staircase wound up to the balcony, where women found a smoking and "retiring" room. The men's smoking and drawing room was in the basement, a Tudor-style space paneled with oak wainscoting and, wrote the *Art and Architecture* critic, "extremely inviting to the masculine element."

Cars and trucks were less prevalent in 1920 than they would be at the end of the century. Still, street noise often obtruded upon performances taking place on Forty-second Street. At the Times Square, narrow vestibules were installed along the side of the building closest to the street, muffling the honking and the bustle and, according to a reporter for the *New York Tribune*, making the auditorium practically "soundproof."

A TOUGH BEGINNING

The opening-night critics had braved heavy rain to get to the Times Square, and as far as they were concerned, the stylish new theatre outdid the production they watched onstage. Edgar Selwyn's *The Mirage*, a melodrama about a country girl who comes to the big city and ends up being kept by a married man, reminded most reviewers of similarly plotted but better plays. *The American's* Alan Dale (the critic who'd liked all the Forty-second Street theatres so much) called *The Mirage* "a genuine antique." He wrote, "I detest

The green, black, and silver color scheme of the Times Square Theatre's
auditorium made it one of the most striking on Forty-second Street.

these whining, tear-drenched gells who lack all grace and conviction. Besides they have been so frequent. . . ."

But even if they disliked the play, the critics generally agreed that its star, Florence Reed, would ensure a substantial run. Raven-haired, dark-eyed, flamboyant Reed had been

Channing Pollock's The Fool, *a drama about a minister's faith, proved popular at the Times Square in 1922. The dark-haired actress kneeling in the lower-right corner of the photograph is Sara Sothern, who would one day give birth to another beautiful actress: Elizabeth Taylor.*

making silent films since 1915, and now attracted adoring movie fans who stood at the back of the Times Square and applauded every time their idol appeared onstage. They even applauded her fur coat. "Miss Reed is wonderful," gushed the reviewer for the *New York Journal American,* adding, "She has so much magnetism, this woman, that the mere sound of her voice, just her walk across the stage, stirs an audience." Burns Mantle praised her "remarkable force." *The Mirage* chalked up 192 performances.

After the Reed vehicle closed in the spring of 1921,

Henry Stephenson   Adrienne Morrison   Arthur Elliott   Sara Sothern

James Kirkwood

the Times Square housed four unsuccessful productions, including a musical revue called *The Broadway Whirl,* by George Gershwin and Harry Tierney, which moved to the Selwyn, and a "melody drama" called *Love Dreams,* with a book by Anne Nichols. If the Selwyns had had more faith in Nichols, they might have been the beneficiaries of her next play, which made Broadway history and turned its author into a millionaire. But Nichols herself would produce *Abie's Irish Rose* at the Fulton Theatre, on Forty-sixth Street, from which it would move to the Theatre Republic, down the block from the Times Square, and end up giving 2,327 performances.

The Times Square was having such a run of bad luck that the Selwyns probably didn't have much confidence in the play they produced there on October 23, 1922: a melodrama with the uninviting title of *The Fool,* by Channing Pollock. (The title came from Tennyson's lines "They called me in the public squares/The fool that wears a crown of thorns.")

Pollock had been a drama critic for the *Washington Post* and the *Washington Times* before becoming press representative for theatrical producer William A. Brady and the Shuberts. But he really wanted to be a playwright. Toward this end he had been writing plays since 1904, when *The Pit,* his adaptation of Frank Norris's naturalistic novel, opened on Broadway.

The Selwyn brothers' co-producer, Crosby Gaige, wrote in his autobiography, *Footlights and Highlights,* that it took Pollock ten years to get *The Fool* on paper and that it almost didn't have a life after that. "Few plays," Gaige wrote, "have ever survived the open hostility that greeted this four-act drama which dared to show what might happen to a man if he tried to live in our time as Christ had lived in His." Many a producer had turned the play down before the Selwyns bought it, and many of the Selwyns' colleagues thought the brothers were courting bankruptcy to stick with it, even though a Los Angeles production had fared well.

The plot revolved around a character named Daniel Gilchrist, played by the handsome stage and silent-film actor James Kirkwood, who had stepped into the part just ten days before the production opened "out-of-town," in Hempstead, Long Island. Gilchrist, assistant rector at the Church of the Nativity, has returned from the Great War a changed man. "What," he asks, "would happen to a man who really tried to live like Christ?" On Christmas Eve, Gilchrist would rather be helping the starving than trimming a tree

with the rich, beautifully dressed women who belong to his church. Accused of sexual assault by a church member's jealous husband, Gilchrist leaves to establish "Overcoat Hall," a mission house that serves the poor. There, too, trials await him, including attacks from a doubting mob. They dare him to prove he's like Christ, at which moment a crippled girl in the mission throws down her crutches and walks. (This role was played by Sara Sothern, probably better known as the mother of film star Elizabeth Taylor.) In time, the rich patrons who spurned the rector want him back in their fold, but the impoverished Gilchrist remains with his mission.

As Gaige recalled this theatrical adventure, "The critics, and apparently most of the hard-boiled first night audience, viewed the play coldly. . . . For three weeks *The Fool* teetered on the brink of disaster. People of high and low degree wrote to Pollock denouncing him for treating such a theme on the stage."

But Pollock, drawing on his determination, and his experience as a publicist, visited churches, preached in pulpits, and apparently persuaded church folk to do the same. Eventually, according to Gaige, he got "a different sort of audience" into the Times Square, and the production sold out, making money for both the author and Selwyn and Company. Fox Film Corporation bought the movie rights for $150,000. The Selwyns, who had originally billed *The Fool* as "Channing Pollock's New Play," now billed it as "Channing Pollock's Great Play." It ran for 272 performances.

Soon after *The Fool* closed, a well-received musical by George S. Kaufman and Marc Connelly, *Helen of Troy, New York,* transferred from the Selwyn, and then, in a serious (but momentary) lapse of commercial judgment, Selwyn and Company co-produced an adaptation of Maurice Maeterlinck's *Pelléas and Mélisande.* "Jane Cowl was hell-bent to play Mélisande," wrote Crosby Gaige, "and in spite of everybody's protests, she did it. I remember that one of her recurring lines was, 'Oh! Oh! I am not happy, I am not happy.' This line rather accurately described the mood of her producers, and of the audiences who suffered through thirteen performances of Belgian piffle."

ANDRÉ CHARLOT'S REVUE OF 1924

While Cowl was putting audiences to sleep with *Pelléas*, Arch Selwyn was in Europe making contacts and scouting for plays. In Monte Carlo he made the acquaintance of a potential backer named Daniel K. Weiskopf, who, before Prohibition had amassed a great deal of money in the distilling business. In London, Arch saw one of André Charlot's revues. In January 1924, courtesy of Weiskopf's money, the Selwyns and the Times Square hosted *André Charlot's Revue of 1924*, which introduced New York City and North America to the wondrous talents of Gertrude Lawrence and Beatrice Lillie.

André Charlot was born and grew up in France, but by the time Arch Selwyn encountered him, he was a British subject. In France he had developed a style of intimate revue that he then introduced to London, where the genre became enormously popular. Broadway revues tended toward stars, elaborate sets and costumes, and songs and variety acts linked up by no theme that anyone could decipher. Charlot favored talented unknowns, simplicity, and snappy, short sketches. Although the *Revue of 1924* contained a chorus of pretty dancing girls, its core comprised a mere quartet of performers: Lawrence, Lillie, handsome Jack Buchanan playing the quintessential Englishman, and a short, pudgy character actor named Herbert Mundin. Arch Selwyn urged Charlot to make the revue a bit less British for American audiences; the director refused.

The four performers were reportedly eager to come to the States. (Lillie had once visited, but not to act.) But by the time the SS *Aquitania* docked in Manhattan, Gertie Lawrence and Bea Lillie were feeling homesick and experiencing twinges of uncertainty. As Lawrence later told a reporter for the *New York Tribune*, "suddenly I found myself on Broadway—a dirty, crooked, uninspired thoroughfare in the daytime. I first saw this noted street at 3 o'clock in the afternoon. . . . There was only a rude crowd of people and impossible traffic."

A week's tryout in Atlantic City did not help much, because Selwyn again voiced his concern that the show was too English. According to Lillie's biographer, Bruce Laffey, Selwyn did not understand the actress's technique and thought she wasn't "giving her all" at rehearsals. He wanted to cut her number called "March with Me." Again, Charlot refused. As so often happens in the theatre, everybody's worries melted away with the ecstatic response of the audience on opening night, which took place in New York on January 9. "March with Me" stopped the show. Lillie, dressed as Britannia, led a line of Girl Scouts in an extremely dignified manner, but of course tripped over her own feet and desperately tried to hold onto her helmet, shield, and spear at the same time. The audience, hysterical with laughter, got to its feet and called for more.

As for Lawrence, one critic wrote that "[her] acting was full of subtle charm. She sang a naughty anecdote so deftly that she then and there established the success of the enterprise. The first nighters raved about her for ten minutes and she had to be summoned from her dressing room in her kimono to acknowledge the celebration." The "naughty anecdote" was probably Philip Braham and Douglas Furber's famous "Limehouse Blues," about London's down-at-the-heels Chinatown—a song that would be associated with Lawrence from then on. Afterward, the crowd outside the stage door on Forty-second Street was so thick that traffic came to a standstill.

For the next nine months, New York toasted Lawrence and Lillie, who cavorted together offstage as well as on. (They were known to engage in backstage pranks, to the dismay of some of their colleagues.) Now they were Broadway stars, even if they weren't being paid star salaries. Still, they rented a duplex apartment on Fifty-fourth Street near Sixth Avenue and threw a party there every night after the show. During the summer, they played on the beach with the rich and famous in Southampton, Long Island.

The show's final performance at the Times Square was even more tumultuous than its opening night. The critic Alexander Woollcott reported that "Miss Lillie and Miss Lawrence were overwhelmed with applause each time they emerged from the wings." (Some audience members had seen the show twelve times.) Happily losing any tinge of critical objectivity, Woollcott described how, during Lillie's song "Rough Stuff," it was "her custom to flee from an Apache lover, jump off the stage and regain it only after scrambling across the auditorium in the cluttered path between the first row and the orchestra rail. Each night she lingers for a moment en route on some lucky lap." At the last

A song that Gertrude Lawrence made famous in *André Charlot's Revue of 1924* was the suggestive number "Limehouse Blues."

performance, Woollcott confessed that Lillie "sat on the lap of your gratified correspondent."

When it was over, the audience tossed roses and cheered and, both onstage and in the house, people joined hands, arm over arm, and sang "Auld Lang Syne." Outside on Forty-second Street, admirers clambered onto the roofs of the cast's waiting taxis. Had there been a horse and carriage for the two actresses, Woollcott mused, people would have led it through the streets.

THE END OF SELWYN AND COMPANY

During the 1924–25 season, the producing team of Selwyn and Company was dissolved. "In a period of eight years," Crosby Gaige recalled, "Archie, Edgar and I had developed our own interests along special lines. With the best of good will, we decided to part company, each becoming an independent producer."

The men's freedom from each other soon resulted in two substantial and entertaining productions. In the fall of 1925, Gaige produced another challenging play by Channing Pollock. *The Enemy* took place in Austria before, during, and after the Great War and was essentially an antiwar drama. Burns Mantle, who included it among his *Best Plays of 1925–1926*, wrote in his preface to the play that "The first audience was politely encouraging . . . and the reviews reflected this attitude. None was unfavorable, but several were lukewarm and condescending . . . questioning the supreme importance of his restatement of the accepted truths: That hate is the real enemy of humanity; that wars are inspired by hate; that there is no real difference between peoples and that if hatred and greed are banished from the earth there will be no war." As with *The Fool*, however, *The Enemy* appealed to audiences more than to critics. Alhough it wasn't the commercial success of the earlier play, it still filled the Times Square for slightly over two hundred performances. The following season, Edgar Selwyn produced Anita Loos' and John Emerson's entertaining comedy *Gentlemen Prefer Blondes*.

Loos stood 4 feet 11 inches tall and weighed about 90 pounds, but she never let her size stop her. She liked to tell

the story of how film director D. W. Griffith was speechless when he met the diminutive would-be screenwriter who had been sending him all those movie plots. A journalist for *Photoplay* once called Loos a "split-pint soubrette" who was "mentally, 50 or 40 large stern men, crouching down behind a little silk gown and a little soprano voice."

Another story Loos liked to tell was how she came to write her best-selling novel *Gentlemen Prefer Blondes*.

A petite, spunky brunette named Anita Loos wrote the best-selling novel *Gentlemen Prefer Blondes* and then turned it into a successful stage comedy. Subsequently, the play was the source for a film, a musical, and a movie version of the latter starring Marilyn Monroe.

During the early 1920s she and her husband, writer and director John Emerson, were taking that glamorous train, the Twentieth Century Limited, from New York to Los Angeles, in company with several Hollywood movers and shakers and one "unnatural blonde" en route for a screen test. "That girl was a lot bigger than I was," Loos wrote, "but she was being waited on by every male in our troupe. If she happened to drop the magazine she was reading, several of them would jump to retrieve it, whereas I was allowed to tug heavy suitcases from their racks while those same men failed to note my efforts."

"Why did she so outdistance me in feminine allure?" Loos asked. "Could her power, like that of Samson, have something to do with her hair?"

During the train ride West, Loos wrote down her thoughts on a yellow pad (she never learned to type, she said, because her feet dangled sixteen inches from the floor) and created a character sketch about a not-so-dumb blonde gold-digger from Little Rock, Arkansas, named Lorelei Lee. Remembering that her journalist friend H. L. Mencken liked blonde dimwits, Loos sent him the piece as a joke, but he urged her to flesh out the story and publish it. *Harper's Bazaar* magazine serialized Lorelei's romantic adventures, and in 1925 Liveright published the stories as a novel, which sold out the day it hit the stores. Novelist Edith Wharton famously called it "the great American novel (at last!)." Not surprisingly, Broadway producers were falling over each other to bid for the stage rights. Edgar Selwyn held the winning hand.

According to Gary Carey's *Anita Loos: a Biography*, she was enamored neither of the script she wrote nor of June Walker's portrayal of Lorelei Lee. Loos believed that her play needed repairs and that Walker was "too cozy and sweet." She would end up preferring the first movie version, which was shot in 1928 with Ruth Taylor as Lorelei.

The critic Alan Dale concurred. He opined that there were "many hearty laughs" but also "many sagging episodes." He did not think the play lived up to the book, and that Walker was "admirable" but hard to hear. By contrast, Percy Hammond called the play a "sophisticated frolic," and Alexander Woollcott wrote "the sum total of hilarity in the piece is enormous." Audiences generally agreed, and although business fell off a bit as the run progressed, *Gentlemen* toted up an honorable 199 performances.

During the 1927–28 season, the Times Square offered up only silent films. The Selwyns' energy was being channeled elsewhere during the last years of the 1920s, and they turned the Times Square over to a gifted if ornery theatrical-director producer named Jed Harris. In August 1928, Harris brought in a funny, hard-edged play about the newspaper racket by two men who had been in that business: Ben Hecht and Charles MacArthur. The play was aptly called, *The Front Page.*

"I don't believe many people realize the importance of *The Front Page*," opined Alexander Woollcott a number of years after the Broadway run. "The two geniuses who wrote that *magnum opus* literally turned Broadway around. It was a new kind of realism. After its opening night the theatre was never the same again. Thank God." Tennessee Williams, who was seventeen when *The Front Page* came to Broadway, once said that it "took the corsets off the American theatre and made it possible for one to write my kind of play."

The language had the brash, sometimes profane flavor of the pressroom in a big-city criminal court. The characters, particularly managing editor Walter Burns, played by Osgood Perkins (father of film star Tony Perkins), were ruthless and viciously funny. At the Times Square on opening night, the audience was looking at a scruffy set that contained only a few chairs, a table, and an enormous rolltop desk (essential to the plot): there, the reporters spoke intensely into the phones, or lounged around, smoking and drinking, their hats pushed back on their heads, scraps of paper at their feet. George S. Kaufman was the astute director, even though he didn't always get along with Hecht and MacArthur, who, in Kaufman's opinion, spent too much time in the local bars. Raymond Sovey designed the atmospheric set. Except for an occasional puritanical comment about the language, critics praised the play. Atkinson at the *New York Times* called it "scorching." Burns Mantle included it in his *Best Plays* of the 1927–28 season. It ran for 276 performances.

Soon the Times Square, like most of the theatres on Forty-second Street, would be fighting for its life. But before the final exit, it would host two unique productions: George and Ira Gershwin's satiric political musical *Strike Up the Band* (1930) and, one year later, Noel Coward's *Private Lives*, with Coward, Gertrude Lawrence, and a youthful Laurence Olivier.

The Gershwin brothers wrote their first score for *Strike Up the Band* in 1927, to a book by George S. Kaufman. As George Gershwin's biographer Edward Jablonski describes it, "Kaufman's libretto . . . gave the Gershwins, for the first time, the opportunity to produce a fully integrated score. It

One of the most innovative and laugh-filled plays to open at the Times Square, in 1928, was *The Front Page*, a satiric valentine to the no-holds-barred world of yellow journalism.

NEW YORK HERALD TRIBUNE, SUNDAY, APRIL 5, 1931

Scene From "Private Lives"

Visiting English stars Gertrude Lawrence and Noel Coward recline urbanely in Coward's *Private Lives*, an unrepentant comedy about the woes of marriage.

was literate, at times scathing, not at all typical of the musical designed for the tired businessman." Gone at last were songs dropped willy-nilly into the action, so that a star could sing a hit tune. The music, and the dances, were now integral to the story. The title song—a march, yes, but a parody also—had apparently come to Gershwin in a dream.

In June 1927, producer Edgar Selwyn tried the show out in Long Branch, New Jersey, and then took it to Philadelphia, where it was supposed to play six weeks before coming into New York. Selwyn closed it after two weeks and decided not to bring it in. Audiences and critics hated the production— mostly, he decided, because of Kaufman's book, which criticized the greed underlying a country's reasons for going to war.

In 1930, Selwyn gave the musical another try. This time he hired Morrie Ryskind, who had written the books for two Marx Brothers musicals, to delete some of the cynicism

from Kaufman's work. In the original, the United States goes to war with Switzerland over cheese and prepares at the end to battle the U.S.S.R. over caviar. Ryskind framed the action within a dream and simply had the U.S. fighting Switzerland over imported chocolate, apparently a more light-hearted commodity. The Gershwins wrote thirteen new songs, including "Mademoiselle from New Rochelle" and "Soon." Less biting than the first version, it still satirized politicians and statesmen who go to war. The Boston tryout for this version proved a success, as did the opening at the Times Square on January 14, 1930, with George Gershwin conducting the overture.

Private Lives once again brought Gertrude Lawrence

to New York, along with Coward, Olivier, and Jill Esmond, whom Olivier had recently married. The Broadway of the 1920s had offered up any number of sexually titillating comedies, including *Sex* by Mae West. But never had there been a comedy as erotically sophisticated as *Private Lives,* in which once-married Elyot (Coward) and Amanda (Lawrence) reconnect amid humorous mayhem, leaving their respective second spouses to make the best of a chaotic situation. Rarely had American audiences heard such true wit, or seen it deployed onstage with such apparently effortless grace. Somewhere beyond Forty-second Street, Americans were already feeling the harshness of the Depression, but at the Times Square there was nothing but glamour.

For several of the theatres along Forty-second Street, the final legitimate productions made a paltry showing. Not at the Times Square. In March 1933, Arch Selwyn produced a play by Edward Roberts and Frank Cavett called *Forsaking All Others,* which brought gravelly voiced Tallulah Bankhead back to New York after nine years in London and a stopover in Hollywood. (The cast also contained a restrained but noteworthy actor named Henry Fonda, in a walk-on role.) True, the play wasn't much. Based on a novel in verse by Alice Duer Miller, *Forsaking* centered around a woman (Bankhead) who has been jilted on her wedding day and lives to love again. But the opening-night audience, which included Sophie Tucker, Amelia Earhart, Helen Menken, and the playwright Philip Barry saw a better actress than the flamboyant twenty-two-year-old who had departed almost a decade earlier. She kept the play running until June 3, 1933.

THE DECLINE

The Times Square went dark for the 1933–34 season, most likely because the financially strapped Selwyn brothers were struggling to hold on to their three Forty-second Street houses. But on April 13, 1934, the *New York Times* announced that Harry and William Brandt had taken a five-year lease on the Times Square for continuous showings of second-run films. That June, Arch Selwyn filed for bankruptcy; he had less than six thousand dollars in assets.

And so began this theatre's decline. A photograph from 1935 shows the marquee advertising a film of the Joe

Louis–Max Baer fight, in which Louis demolished the former heavyweight champion by knocking him out in the fourth round, and of a B movie called *Hot off the Press* with Jack LaRue. Banners above the façade's pillars advertised "The Tops Movie Entertainment" and "Midnite Show Every Nite," and banners hanging between the pillars let the public know that seats cost fifteen cents for matinee and evening showings, but only ten pennies in the mornings.

In August 1939, a masonry wall was built to fill the proscenium, so that the stage behind it could be transformed into a haberdashery, with the load-in entrance on Forty-second Street serving as the storefront—apparently the first time a backstage space had been converted in this way. During the 1950s and 1960s, the Times Square mostly screened B Westerns, and the theatre's interior became increasingly decrepit. Then in 1986 the Brandt chain, perhaps impatient with the continuing demise of the thoroughfare—or the continuing confusion besetting renewal plans—subleased all its Forty-second Street movie houses, including the Times Square, to the Cine 42nd Street Theatre Corporation.

After that, the Times Square suffered the vicissitudes of New York State's redevelopment project. Time went by, and The New 42nd Street Inc., the nonprofit entity that New York State had set up to oversee the renovation of the block's theatres, held the lease on the Times Square. In August 1998, the Canadian entertainment company Livent, which had replaced the Apollo and Lyric with the Ford Center for the Performing Arts, was the winning bidder on the Times Square Theatre. Livent then planned to construct a new five hundred seat Broadway house, a theatre-related retail business, and ten thousand square feet of office space, all by the year 2000.

This turned out to be as close as the historic Times Square Theatre would come to being renovated as a performance space. By November 1998, Livent was overwhelmed by financial and legal problems and had exited from the deal. In 2004, The New 42nd Street Inc. announced that it finally had found a tenant: Eckō Unlimited, a hip-hop clothing and lifestyle company that was the brainchild of New York fashion designer Marc Eckō. According to the *New York Times*, the company intended to "transform the theater into a four-level, $25 million supermarket of what is cool and fashionable in clothing, art, video games, electronics and collectible sneakers for the urban youth market."

In the decades after World War II, the Times Square Theatre became a "grind house" that ran movies almost twenty-four hours a day.

APOLLO

GEORGE WHITE
LESSEE AND MANAGER

THE APOLLO

1920

The Apollo shared its marquee, as well as its façade, with the Times Square Theatre.

In the late teens, riding the crest of their success as Broadway producers, Archibald "Arch" and Edgar Selwyn were both busy men. Possibly for this reason, they left the negotiations for the acquisition of property on Forty-second Street to their partner and co-producer Crosby Gaige. The Selwyns would spend some $2 million for a site and the construction of two playhouses, the last that would rise on this famed street in that era. As architect and designer, the brothers engaged Eugene DeRosa of the firm DeRosa and Pereira.

DeRosa and Pereira had both served in the architectural firm of Thomas W. Lamb, a Scottish-born architect who had designed the Eltinge and the Candler theatres on the south side of Forty-second Street. DeRosa and Pereira's work for the Selwyns shows their mentor's influence. Lamb had derived his decorative style from Robert and James Adam, eighteenth-century Scottish architects whose light, elegant work incorporated ancient Roman, Palladian, and late

Underneath the shared marquee were paired entrances, one of which was a long corridor that led to the Apollo Theatre's lobby.

Renaissance motifs with supreme delicacy. The façade that the two theatres shared on Forty-second Street was a model of elegant restraint. An awning suspended from the building covered a first story of masonry, and a colonnade—six Ionic columns—was centered on the second story and rose to the third. Between the columns were decorative wrought-iron gates, and within was a *sgraffito* frieze. To the right and left of the colonnade, two projecting bays contained two tall rectangular windows in arches that, like the columns, rose to the third story. A straight entablature ran across the entire façade and was capped by four urns. On Forty-third Street, the Apollo's façade was a similarly restrained composition in red brick.

Entering from Forty-second Street, patrons would step into a long lobby that was divided into two sections. The walls of the first section were clad with a combination of rose and red marble, and topped by an ornate plaster ceiling and a frieze decorated in the Adam style. The lobby's walls and floor of the inner section were inlaid with black and white marble. Indoor stairways between the auditorium and the Forty-third Street wall replaced exterior fire escapes, a convenience for patrons that also provided a barrier against street noise.

The interior of the Apollo was considered advanced for its time. Intended primarily for musical presentations, its broad, shallow auditorium contained 1,194 seats divided among the orchestra, one balcony, and four boxes. The proscenium, forty-one feet wide by twenty-five feet high, was Adamesque in ornamental detail, and the boxes, lighted by crystal chandeliers, were set into elegant Palladian arches on either side of the proscenium and joined by a vaulted sounding board. The flat ceiling of the auditorium was crowned by a shallow dome decorated with low-relief plaster in a conservative, late Renaissance style, as interpreted by the Adam brothers.

Throughout the house, the color scheme comprised subtle shades of tan, rose, and blue, while the main curtain and drapes were fashioned of peacock-blue brocaded velvet. A mural by William Colton adorned the wall at the back of the auditorium, from whence patrons could take a flight of stairs down to a well-appointed and comfortable lounge that accommodated both men's and women's restrooms.

The single, cantilevered balcony was reached by a stairway at either end of the main foyer, and once there, the spectator was greeted by a carpeted, eighty-foot-long promenade that itself was furnished as a lounge (complete with fireplace) and spanned the entire rear area of the balcony. An aisle divided the balcony above the fourth row, making seats in the upper and lower sections easily accessible from side entrances and a center aisle.

IN NEED OF A HIT

The new venue opened its doors on November 17, 1920, with a frothy musical called *Jimmie*, produced by Oscar Hammerstein's son Arthur and co-written by Oscar's grandson, Oscar Hammerstein II. *Jimmie* was tailored to the talents of Frances White, a graduate of vaudeville and Ziegfeld's

New Amsterdam roof shows. Burdened by an unwieldy plot, it nevertheless gave White, who was cast as a cabaret performer, an opportunity to sing and dance and generally present her comedic talents. The Herbert Stothart score was pleasant, but *Jimmie* could not eke out more than sixty-nine performances.

The second offering at the Apollo was an abrupt mood change for any unsuspecting theatregoer who had attended *Jimmie*. The playhouse, originally intended for musicals, now served up Shakespeare's tragedy *Macbeth*, produced and directed by Arthur Hopkins. Lionel Barrymore, who was the star, suffered the indignity of having his performance described as tedious and compared unfavorably with Robert Edmond Jones's stunning settings and costumes. Critic Alexander Woollcott of the *New York Times* considered Jones's work "the star of a *Macbeth* that will be talked of till the cows come home."

For the next few years, the Apollo's stage could count few successes. Unmemorable musicals and plays were shuttled in and out of the theatre in short order, and whenever there was a lull in legitimate activity, the Selwyns lowered the movie screen to present films. One of the more interesting productions during this time was Sholom Asch's *God of Vengeance*. A drama about a brothel owner who seeks redemption and discovers that his daughter loves one of the prostitutes, the 1922 play proved too strong for contemporary tastes. The producer and cast were charged with obscenity and jailed, and a jury later decided that the play was "vicious and immoral."

Not until W. C. Fields arrived to open the new season in September 1923 did the Apollo have its first real hit: the musical *Poppy*. Long a star of the *Ziegfeld Follies* and the vaudeville stage, Fields, one critic wrote, "came out of pantomime and into a long and intricate speaking-role which he handles with all the ease and skill that he has in the past bestowed on billiard balls and cigar boxes." As that ultimate con man, Eustace McGargle, Fields created a persona that would last the rest of his career (and beyond). Appearing opposite Fields was Madge Kennedy, who revealed singing

After three years devoid of hits, the Apollo marked its first success with *Poppy*, starring W. C. Fields and Madge Kennedy. As Professor Eustace McGargle, Fields created the character that stuck to him for the rest of his career: the cane-carrying, cigar-chomping con artist.

SISTERS Gale quadruplets, Joan, Jane, June and Jean, in George White's new musical comedy, "Flying High," which will follow "Scandals" at Apollo Theater

and dancing talents that her delighted fans had never known she possessed. Audiences kept the show running for 346 performances.

In 1924, the dancer and producer George White arrived with his sixth edition of *George White's Scandals* and sent the fortunes of the Apollo rocketing upward. White's rollicking revues, which had first emerged in 1919 at the Liberty, would dominate the Apollo for almost a decade, challenging the best of the *Follies* but without the acres of chiffon and overblown budgets that characterized the productions of Flo Ziegfeld. White hired talented comics, singers, and dancers, some remembered, some not: Ann Pennington, a diminutive and dynamic dancer, zigzagged from the *Follies* to the *Scandals* in the course of her career, but did not star in either revue. George Gershwin provided music for five *Scandals,* and for the 1924 edition composed the glorious melody "Somebody Loves Me." He quit only when White refused to give him a raise, a bit of tightfistedness that fortuitously sent Gershwin off to write his own book musicals.

The composing and writing team of B. G. "Buddy" DeSylva, Lew Brown, and Ray Henderson replaced Gershwin for the 1925 *Scandals*—the edition, White later claimed, that introduced Broadway to the Charleston, danced vigorously by one of White's stalwarts, Tom Patricola. A young torch singer named Helen Morgan, who would gain fame in *Show Boat* two years later, was also in the cast.

The 1926 *Scandals* was considered by some to be the best of the series. For this outstanding edition, DeSylva, Brown, and Henderson wrote "The Birth of the Blues," "Black Bottom," and "This Is My Lucky Day." Willie and Eugene Howard provided the comedy, and Ann Pennington and Tom Patricola executed the Black Bottom, another dance new to Broadway. "The Birth of the Blues," set at the Gates of Heaven, presented a battle between "the classics" and "jazz," and ended with Gershwin's startling "Rhapsody in Blue."

White took a year off to produce a book musical, but returned in 1928 with another *Scandals* and still another new dance, which he called "Pickin' Cotton." The next year, DeSylva, Brown, and Henderson having temporarily departed,

Inevitably the *Ziegfeld Follies* spawned imitations, one of the most popular being George White's *Scandals*. From 1924 to 1931, White produced his *Scandals* periodically at the Apollo, ushering in acts like the singing and dancing Gale Sisters.

White handled some of the composing and writing chores, with Cliff Friend also providing music and Irving Caesar writing additional lyrics.

In 1931, Lew Brown and Ray Henderson returned (without Buddy DeSylva), and Ethel Merman, Ray Bolger, Rudy Vallee, Everett Marshall, and Ethel Barrymore Colt augmented the cast of White regulars. Merman stopped the show with "Life Is Just a Bowl of Cherries," a bit of determined optimism plunked down to offset the cheerless Depression.

One of the other highlights of the 1931 *Scandals* was the inclusion of the Gale Quadruplets, a singing and dancing act from California. Ziegfeld and his colleagues had often featured sister acts in their revues, especially twins, whom audiences seemed to find irresistible. But the Gales—Jean, June, Jane, and Joan—were the first quadruplets to arrive on Broadway, complete with birth certificates to prove the validity of their claim.

For most of the *Scandals* at the Apollo, the costumes and decorative curtains—necessary components of any revue—were created by the famed French-Russian designer Erté. White had set up a workshop in Paris for Erté and made trips to commission costumes for each upcoming *Scandals*. Beginning in 1931, however, White used designer Charles LeMaire, who would shift his talents to Hollywood when the revues on Broadway started to peter out.

When not producing or staging revues, White tackled musicals, two of which, *Manhattan Mary* and *Flying High*, were produced at the Apollo in 1927 and 1930, respectively.

Critics noted that *Manhattan Mary* was not really a musical comedy and not really a revue, but a mixture of both. There was a plot, but it revolved around a young woman from Manhattan's Greenwich Village who aspires to join the chorus of the *Scandals*, thus giving White ample latitude to introduce revue-style numbers. The chorus girl, of course, stands in for the indisposed leading lady and becomes a star. A simpering, lisping Ed Wynn, billed in the program as Ed "The Perfect Fool" Wynn, provided the comedy. The program also advertised that the show was "Clean from Beginning to End." It ran for more than 260 performances.

The cast of *Flying High,* which spoofed Charles Lindbergh's 1927 solo flight across the Atlantic, included comedian Bert Lahr, singer Kate Smith, the Gale Quadruplets, Oscar Shaw and Grace Brinkley as the love interest, and lots of pretty chorines. Lahr played a mechanic who accidentally takes off in a plane and breaks a flight record by ten minutes, because he doesn't know how to bring the plane down. Shaw arrived onstage from a parachute, and Smith broke the sound barrier with her powerful voice. Enlivened by Lahr's slapstick and enhanced by Joseph Urban's scenery, *Flying High* broke no existing records but was a solid hit for White, enduring for 355 performances.

Aside from the success of *Flying High,* the Apollo struggled to keep its curtain up. In February 1929, Brooks Atkinson of the *New York Times* described a play called *Harlem* as a "rag-bag drama and high pressure blow-out all in one." What it had was a powerful cast of sixty black performers, wasted (except for a scene or two) in a gangster melodrama set in Harlem. One critic noted that the play had no message to impart, but that its depiction of a black family lured to New York from the South nonetheless contained ample material for the making of a morality tale.

If *Harlem* portrayed one type of ghetto, Channing Pollock's *The House Beautiful* depicted another: that of a middle-class garden community set in New Jersey. The design by Jo Mielziner, which included moving platforms, slide projections, and atmospheric lighting, received most of the critical honors; the play was a kind of *Pilgrim's Progress* of a too-good-to-be-true family. Deciding that honesty is the best policy, and that heaven awaits the pure in heart, the noble head of the family suffers all kinds of indignities before his untimely death. Sentimentalism on Broadway has sometimes been risky, and in this case it provoked an unforgettable line from critic Dorothy Parker: "*The House Beautiful* is the play lousy." In 1931, slightly more than one hundred performances qualified it as a moderate success.

In 1932, Buddy DeSylva and Laurence Schwab took over George White's sublease at the Apollo to put on their show *Take a Chance,* the last hit that would occupy the Apollo's stage for years. With a cast that included Ethel Merman, Jack Haley, Sid Silvers, and Jack Whiting performing to the music of Nacio Herb Brown, Richard Whiting, and Vincent Youmans, the show could hardly fail. Short on plot but long on verve, it had something to do with two con men (Haley and Silvers) promoting the career of a nightclub singer (Merman). The show-stopping numbers belonged to Merman: "Eadie Was a Lady," "Rise & Shine," and "You're an Old Smoothie," a duet with Haley. *Take a Chance* remained at the theatre for almost 250 performances, but the producers had to cut the admission prices to achieve that run.

Times were hard on Broadway. In 1932, even before *Take a Chance* closed, the Apollo's mortgage was transferred to a company headed by movie-theatre operators Bernard, Louis, William, and Harry Brandt. In 1933, the theatre was host to one more legitimate show, the Lew Leslie revue *Blackbirds of 1933–34.* Although it was salvaged in some measure by the "guest appearances" of the great tap dancer Bill "Bojangles" Robinson, it never achieved the popularity of its predecessors and closed after just a few weeks.

After that, the Brandts leased the Apollo to Max Wilner, who announced that he would be presenting burlesque. Mayor Fiorello H. La Guardia's license commissioner, Paul Moss, withheld the license, but in October 1934, Wilner triumphed in the courts and began a policy of "glorified burlesque" at the Apollo, sometimes in tandem with movies.

For the next four years, Wilner withstood steady pressure by the city and the morals police, but finally Wilner relinquished his lease to the Brandts, who turned the Apollo into a movie house in 1938 (its sister theatre, the Times Square, was already showing motion pictures). Some time later, the Brandts' manager booked a foreign film called *The Lives and Loves of Beethoven* into the theatre and accidentally transformed the Apollo into a profitable, second-run art film house. Low box office prices kept its devoted patrons coming for years.

A NEW BEGINNING

Forty-second Street evolved into the street of grind movie houses and remained that way for almost half a century. As public desire for change grew stronger, the Brandt Organization decided to act unilaterally and turn a few of its select playhouses back into legitimate theatres, beginning with the Apollo. The Brandts poured $350,000 into the rejuvenation, switched the main entrance from Forty-second Street to Forty-third Street, renamed the house the New Apollo, and announced that it would reopen in February 1979 with *On Golden Pond,* by Ernest Thompson.

Previews began on February 21, but the play's official opening came seven days later, and an audience studded with stars such as Lillian Gish, Celeste Holm, and June Havoc

The Apollo degenerated into a burlesque house until Mayor La Guardia cleaned up Forty-second Street. Under the Brandts, the theatre became a home for second-run art and foreign films, but then joined the pack of grind houses and began showing horror movies.

celebrated both Thompson's drama and the Apollo's return to the legitimate fold. *On Golden Pond,* a bittersweet elegy exploring the human reluctance to accept old age and decay, succeeded with the critics and the public. It ran for 156 performances and was later made into a well-received motion picture with Henry Fonda and Katharine Hepburn.

On December 2, 1979, Martin Sherman's *Bent* had its premiere in the refurbished theatre. Harrowing in its detail, this drama depicted the horrific effects of Nazi persecution on homosexuals, particularly on one man (played by Richard Gere) who opts for survival amid the brutality that engulfs him.

Bent was not an easy play to sit through, but the approving critics urged audiences to see it as a sobering commentary on the eternal quandary of man's inhumanity to his fellow man. It enjoyed a decent run of 240 performances, which did not qualify as a hit in the late 1970s, when production costs were escalating at an alarming rate.

The next dramatic vehicle presented in the New Apollo, Lanford Wilson's *Fifth of July,* did rank as a hit. After opening at Circle Repertory Company, it moved to the refurbished theatre, opening there on November 5, 1980, and residing there for more than five hundred performances. Both amusing and touching, *Fifth of July* delicately dramatized the harrowing emotional ups and downs experienced by a group of former student activists, particularly a paraplegic Vietnam War veteran (acted by Christopher Reeve), who after much soul-searching eventually regains his faith in life. Described by critics as Chekhovian, the play ambles almost effortlessly through the trials and idiosyncratic behavior of the reunited friends. But the impact is haunting.

Fifth of July was followed by one final play at the New Apollo: *The Guys in the Truck,* which lasted all of one performance.

The doldrums along Broadway during the 1980s did not allow opportunities for the New Apollo to present live productions. Musicals became the main fare in the theatre district at this time, but the musical was unsuited to a playhouse with a small seating capacity. The Brandt Organization fell back on movies to fill the venue, until it was taken over by the State following condemnation proceedings. For a short period, the theatre was rented out to accommodate cable television and other projects. Finally, in 1987, while it was sitting idle awaiting its next incarnation, the City and State agreed to lease the New Apollo for jazz concerts. Renamed once again (this time it was called the Academy), the venerable playhouse was transformed into a cabaret by removing the orchestra seats and leveling the floor. A year later, as the Alcazar Theater, it was host to a short-lived nightclub revue, *Alcazar de Paris in New York.*

In 1990, the fate of the theatre fell into the hands of the

new organization created to guide its fortunes, The New 42nd Street Inc. Although it booked the venue sporadically in the early 1990s for popular music entertainments, the organization began to seek a permanent role for the theatre along a reshaped and re-ascendant Forty-second Street. The New 42nd Street Inc. hoped to preserve the Apollo, but there would be no happy ending for this venue. Like the Lyric, it had apparently outlived its usefulness as an entertainment hall, and like the Lyric, the Apollo was destroyed to make way for the Ford Center for the Performing Arts—now the Hilton Theatre.

During the Apollo's brief come-back as a legitimate house, Christopher Reeve, Swoosie Kurtz, and Amy Wright were featured in Lanford Wilson's delicate drama *The Fifth of July*, which moved in 1980 from Circle Repertory Company's Greenwich Village theatre to the "new" Apollo.

George White once told a reporter that he had learned to dance at around the age of eight—maybe earlier. He was born in 1890 or perhaps 1892, possibly to a wealthy manufacturer who lived on Manhattan's Upper East Side, more plausibly to an improvident Jewish garment manufacturer named Weitz who lived on Manhattan's Lower East Side. When George was six, his father went broke, and the family moved to Toronto. There the youngster sold newspapers on the street to bring in a few coins, and every free minute he had, George would sneak into burlesque houses and watch the shows; that, he used to tell, was how he learned buck dancing.

True or not—and George White, one feels, liked to embroider the fabric of his life—the dark-haired, wiry young man with the small frame found his way back to the States, where he apparently jigged for money at brothels in New York City's Tenderloin, danced in the *Follies*, and eventually became producer, director, and book writer of musical revues featuring beautiful women.

Despite intermittent setbacks, usually of his own making—he often gambled away the money his shows earned—he produced the *Scandals* annually until 1926 and again in 1928, '29, '31, '36, and '39. His show *Music Hall Varieties* replaced the *Scandals* in 1932 and '33; and in 1934, '35, and '45 the *Scandals* were filmed in Hollywood. Filled with variety acts and lines of showgirls (with White usually at the center of the line), the *Scandals*, onstage and onscreen, provided showcases for many talented performers who later became stars, among them Ray Bolger, Ann Miller, Alice Faye, Bert Lahr, and Eleanor Powell. George Gershwin composed five *Scandals*, as did Ray Henderson, who wrote "The Birth of the Blues" for the *Scandals* of 1925.

On more than one occasion, White was the object of civil suits brought by women who accused him of manhandling them, and later in life he spent a year in a California jail for the hit-and-run deaths of two newlyweds. Long after the *Scandals* were history, White could be found putting shows together for venues in the Catskills and Las Vegas, but those ventures rarely worked out. He died in Hollywood on October 11, 1968.

Short, dapper George White made and lost a good deal of money bringing his *Scandals* revues to Broadway, but like many a theatrical producer from this period, ended his career in poverty.

THE NEW

FORTY-SECOND STREET

At the end of the nineteenth century, many signs pointed toward the creation of a new theatre district to be located in the area around Forty-second Street on the West Side of Manhattan.

The population of the thriving city was moving north, and a public transportation network of streetcars and elevated railways was following in its wake. Theatre followed the people. In 1893 Charles Frohman, at the time possibly the most respected producer on Broadway, moved his Empire Theatre Stock Company to Fortieth Street, within sight of Long Acre Square.

Long Acre (soon to be Times) Square had a dubious reputation. Nicknamed "Thieves' Lair," it had gone from being an area dominated by the horse-and-buggy trade to being a red-light district, home to pickpockets and prostitutes who worked out of the brownstones that lined the square and its surrounding streets.

But the time was ripe for the city's risk takers and dreamers to brave the area's reputation. Defying good sense, in 1895 Oscar Hammerstein I erected the Olympia, a block-long, turreted entertainment palace on Broadway between Forty-fourth and Forty-fifth streets. He ran out of money, as dreamers will, but the "Father of Times Square" turned his attention to Forty-second Street, and there he eventually constructed three theatres, one of which survives even today as the jewel-like New Victory.

Indeed, beginning in 1893, twelve theatres rose up along Forty-second Street between Seventh and Eighth avenues, and from then until shortly before the advent of the Great Depression, around 1930, Forty-second Street thrived as the nexus of a golden age of theatre. Legendary men and women of the American stage—George M. Cohan, Lew M. Fields, Bill "Bojangles" Robinson, Lillian Russell, and Tallulah Bankhead, to name five out of hundreds—performed there. Daring producers like Hammerstein, Al Woods, Florenz Ziegfeld, and Archibald and Edgar Selwyn made and lost fortunes there, offering up an array of entertainment: romantic comedies and bedroom farces; operettas, musicals and revues; melodramas; classics—and, once in a while, a forward-looking American play.

On opening nights, hansom cabs and (as the twentieth century progressed) automobiles lined Forty-second Street, discharging women in evening gowns and furs, and men in top hats and tails, their shirtfronts gleaming from the white light streaming from the bulbs that encircled the theatres' signs and marquees. Inside, audiences found wonderlands of marble and plaster, velvet and plush, boxes, balconies, domed ceilings, and ornate prosceniums—all a lush prologue to the entertainment they would soon see onstage. In other urban realms, the late nineteenth and early twentieth centuries saw the emergence of modern architecture. But on Forty-second Street, the theatres temporarily staunched the flow of time, echoing the Victorian era and the Gilded Age.

After a performance, couples repaired to Murray's Roman Gardens, on the south side of Forty-second Street (where Madame Tussaud's New York, the wax museum, now stands), to dine in mirrored splendor among replicas of ancient Roman columns, images of naked goddesses, a terraced fountain, and a resplendent Roman temple that rose up two stories to the restaurant's ceiling. In 1927, a restaurant operated by an Italian immigrant named Vincent Sardi opened in a building under construction by the Shubert brothers, at 234 West Forty-fourth Street, and soon producers and other theatre folk were making Sardi's their favorite late-night spot.

By 1937, legitimate theatre had vanished from the block. Hammerstein's Victoria had come down years earlier, replaced by the Rialto movie house. The American Theatre, victim of a fire, was razed the year after the stock market collapsed. One by one, the remaining venues installed movie screens—the Lew Fields was essentially rebuilt as a movie house—along with the new technology called air-conditioning, so that these motion picture houses could run during the summer months when legitimate theatres traditionally closed. The first movie theatre to be air-conditioned was the Rivoli movie palace on Broadway, in 1925.

In truth, the theatres' demise was almost inevitable, even before the Great Depression inflicted the coup de grâce. Newer, more comfortable and modern facilities had been built along other streets, north of Forty-second. The business of commercial theatre had lost ground to motion pictures and the ubiquitous real estate entrepreneurs who had no interest in the legitimate stage. Prohibition had killed the restaurants. Murray's closed, replaced in 1925 by Hubert's Museum. There, for a dime in the afternoon and fifteen cents in the evening, one could descend to the basement and watch Professor Heckler's Flea Circus or stare at Martha "the Armless Wonder," Chief Running Elk and Princess Beppa, and other sideshow curiosities that intrigued the masses of people who arrived at Forty-second Street by subway. The street's legitimate theatres might close, but Hubert's would remain in business until the late 1960s.

True to the developmental cycles that often affect (and afflict) cities, this thriving street decayed with a vengeance. By the 1960s, garish billboards defaced the limestone façades of the theatres, and ugly marquees advertising B Westerns jutted across the sidewalks, side by side with novelty shops. Prostitutes, hustlers, and drug dealers invaded the street; exploitation films played nearly twenty-four-hours a day in the "grind" movie houses; the novelty stores became peep shows; and a seedy jumble existed cheek-by-jowl with arcades, weapons stores, and adult bookstores catering to every lurid taste. The block became known as the Deuce, a street of grimy haunts for pickpockets, midnight cowboys, the sexually adventuresome, and the sexually mercenary. At night

the street still shimmered with the voluptuous white glare of the marquees, but most New Yorkers avoided the block whenever possible.

Cities are slow to retrieve their dilapidated neighborhoods. So much is needed: community leadership, money, the ability to navigate the maze of rules and policies with which urban government is burdened, and most of all, political will. Mayors John V. Lindsay (1966–73) and Edward Koch (1978–89) supported efforts to reclaim Forty-second Street and the Times Square area. But it took until 1980 for the City and New York State to create the 42nd Street Development Project, and it was only in 1984 that the City and State announced a plan to establish a thirteen-acre renewal site along the street from Broadway to Eighth Avenue. The long-awaited plan

A schematic drawing shows how the Apollo and the Lyric theatres stood near each other on Forty-second Street.

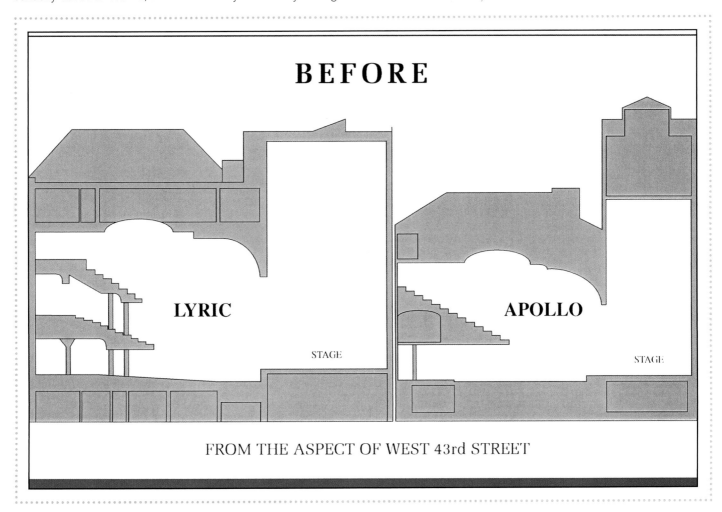

BEFORE

LYRIC

STAGE

APOLLO

STAGE

FROM THE ASPECT OF WEST 43rd STREET

described Forty-second Street's remaining theatres as "irreplaceable architectural and historical assets" that should be restored for cultural and entertainment purposes.

Irreplaceable the theatres may have been, but who should go about renovating them, and how, proved formidable obstacles. Equally challenging was the task of coming up with a vision for a new Forty-second Street that would both entice developers and please New Yorkers. For ten years, architects' studies, litigation, developers' bids made and withdrawn, and optimistic announcements were all noised about—but one saw little visible progress.

In 1990, the State, exercising its right of eminent domain, finally took ownership of two-thirds of the renewal site and created a nonprofit entity called The New 42nd Street Inc., which was charged with long-term oversight of the historic theatres, including their renovation and operation. One year later, The New 42nd Street voted to renovate the old Theatre Republic (known as the Victory movie house) and run it as a nonprofit theatre for young audiences. In 1992, The New 42nd Street signed a ninety-nine-year lease for the Victory, the Liberty, the Selwyn, the Apollo, the Times Square, and the Lyric. For the time being, the New Amsterdam, the Eltinge (known as the Empire movie theatre), and the Candler (better known as the Harris) would remain under State ownership.

Still, for Forty-second Street and its moribund theatres to be fully revived and made attractive to new, creative tenants, the block needed the help of an organization with money and a recognizable name—an organization with clout. An organization like the Walt Disney Company.

The renowned architect David Childs, of Skidmore, Owings & Merrill, designed the Bertelsman Tower in

A schematic drawing demonstrates how the Ford Center for the Performing Arts could fill the space vacated by the demolished theatres.

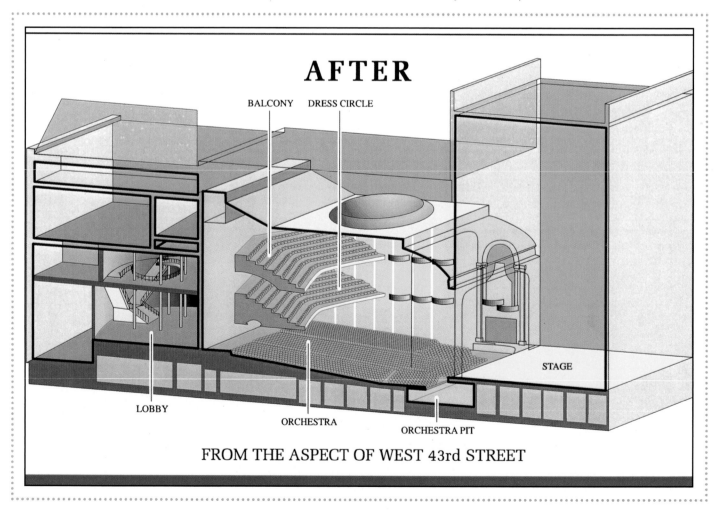

AFTER

BALCONY   DRESS CIRCLE

LOBBY

ORCHESTRA

ORCHESTRA PIT

STAGE

FROM THE ASPECT OF WEST 43rd STREET

Times Square, and is the current project architect for the Freedom Tower at Ground Zero. He believes that Disney's willingness to take up residence in the New Amsterdam was the turning point: "Michael Eisner, then Disney's CEO, really saw Times Square and became convinced about it. He saw an opportunity, and it took a great deal of vision, because that place was pretty seedy. [Disney] could have moved in there and spent a lot of money and not caused a chain reaction. But it did."

In 1995, Disney finalized its agreement to lease and renovate the New Amsterdam Theatre, and soon other developers and builders were playing variations on Disney's theme, with a fair measure of commercial and artistic success. Forest City Ratner eventually moved the old Eltinge toward Eighth Avenue, where it was subsumed into a multiscreen movie complex. All but the façade of the Candler was demolished, and parts of the Liberty were integrated within

the New York outpost of Madame Tussaud's wax museum. The Canadian producing company Livent scooped out the innards of the Apollo and the Lyric, to form a new Broadway house called the Ford Center for the Performing Arts, constructed of contemporary materials to impart to the theatre an early twentieth-century lushness. (Unfortunately, Livent went bankrupt, and Ford came close to it, and the building is now the Hilton Theatre.) The Selwyn eventually went to the nonprofit Roundabout Theatre Company, where, after the application of much care and money, it was reborn as the American Airlines Theatre.

The daring theatrical producers who confidently bestrode Forty-second Street one hundred years ago would barely recognize their thoroughfare today. For that matter, neither

An aerial view of the rubble-strewn lot where the Ford Center for the Performing Arts would eventually rise.

would anyone who grew up in New York City after World War II and before 1990. The exploitation movies and the peep shows are gone, all rousted out of existence during Mayor Rudolph Giuliani's administrations. Five legitimate theatres now play the street, including a "black box" space called the Duke on Forty-second Street. The New Amsterdam and the New Victory have been restored to their former glory. The crowds of New Yorkers and tourists that swarm the sidewalks, pushing into the theatres and movie houses, reflect the country's ethnic diversity, and one observes they are younger and less formal than the audiences that frequented the street a century ago. On an average weekday, half a million people commute to the Times Square area. In 2004 alone, 31.4 million people paid a visit to what has truly become the crossroads of the world.

Of course, if you stand on the northwest corner of Seventh Avenue and Forty-second Street, where Hammerstein's Victoria once stood, and fix your gaze toward Eighth Avenue, you behold a forest of unimaginative neon signs advertising not only theatres and cineplexes but also gigantic fast-food outlets and chain stores. The street in this respect is indistinguishable from the new Times Square and anathema to savvy urban critics. "For those who loathe the new Times Square," writes journalist and author James Traub, "this clean, shiny and hard-edged 42nd Street offers the textbook example of 'Disneyfication'—the methodical corporate engineering of the fun experience."

David Childs admits that he is nostalgic about the time when Times Square was really a theatre district. "Today," he agrees, "it's an entertainment district." He also laments that "unnatural laws" were imposed on the area during its reclamation—those, for instance, applying to a developer who must have "so much square footage of signage per building," with the unfortunate result that there are acres of signs competing for the onlooker's attention.

Still, Childs views the new Times Square and The New Forty-second Street as vital gathering points, no matter what may be their aesthetic shortcomings. "It's wonderful to see New York rejuvenating itself," he says. "The buildings need the patina of time, and that's already happening. A city like New York looks better and better when it gets these layers of compost. There was an enormous cleaning out—a sense of an area being completely redone—and the area needs this continuing mix of architecture and environment that

comes with a city over time. But it's the space between the buildings—the public realm—where people jostle and mix and argue, where there are honking cabs—that makes Times Square so different from any other part of New York."

Finally, perhaps, there is even a kind of poetry remaining in Forty-second Street's endlessly flashing neon, touting a mixture of high culture and honky-tonk that is emblematic of contemporary America and perhaps always characteristic of

Interior of the former Ford Center. When the Canadian theatre company that built the Ford Center encountered financial problems, Clear Channel Entertainment and the Hilton Hotels Corporation took over the building and renamed it the Hilton Theatre.

Exterior of what was formerly the Ford Center for the Performing Arts and which is now the Hilton Theatre.

New York City. As Traub writes in the *New York Times,* "On a warm weekend night. . . sighting down toward Eighth Avenue, the street looks like the inside of a giant arcade game, glowing red and blue and green. The buildings, with their inane products and cardboard food, seem to subside behind the wildly flashing signs. . . . The street is a fiesta, a commercial carnival."

Or is this teeming vision just another incarnation of Forty-second Street—yet one more chapter in the life of the Street of Dreams? The only permanent thing in New York is impermanence. The next chapter is still to be written. But it will come.

The auditorium of the New Amsterdam Theatre in a state of decay before the restoration began.

The New Amsterdam has been restored to much of its former glory.

WORKS CITED

Herein are listed the books that are readily available to our readers. Omitted are many unpublished materials, some of which appear in manuscript form and are difficult to access. We conducted interviews with the architect David Childs, of the firm of Skidmore, Owings & Merrill, and with many others involved in the rehabilitation of Forty-second Street, notably Cora Cahan of The New 42nd Street Inc. We also used reports generated by the architectural firms of Beyer Blinder Bell; Hardy Holzman Pfeiffer Associates; and Robert A. M. Stern. We drew on news clippings from the *New York Times* archives, the *New York Dramatic Mirror,* and other periodicals; and we unearthed material from the files and special collections of the New York Public Library for the Performing Arts. The data posted by the League of American Theatres and Producers were valuable for checking and double-checking our factual material on New York theatres. We also made much use of a database prepared by the Shubert Organization some years ago, which lists the shows that appeared at New York theatres during the early years of the twentieth century.

- Adler, Bill. *Fred Astaire: A Wonderful Life.* New York: Carroll & Graf, 1987.

- Aldrich, Richard. *Gertrude Lawrence as Mrs. A: An Intimate Biography of the Great Star.* New York: Greystone Press, 1954.

- Alpert, Hollis. *The Barrymores.* New York: Dial Press, 1964.

- Astaire, Fred. *Steps in Time.* New York: Da Capo Press, 1979.

- Baker, Roger. *Drag: A History of Female Impersonation in the Performing Arts.* London: Cassell, 1994.

- Baral, Robert. *Revue: A Nostalgic Reprise of the Great Broadway Period.* New York: Fleet Pub. Corp., 1962.

- Barrymore, Ethel. *Memories, an Autobiography.* New York: Harper, 1955.

- Benchley, Nathaniel. *Humphrey Bogart.* Boston: Little Brown, 1975.

- Bernheim, Alfred L. *The Business of the Theatre.* New York: Actors' Equity Association, 1932.

- *Best Plays* series. New York: 1899–2004. Various editors and publishers.

- Bianco, Anthony. *Ghosts of 42nd Street: A History of America's Most Infamous Block.* New York: HarperCollins, 2005.

- Bloom, Ken. *Broadway, Its History, People and Places: An Encyclopedia.* New York: Routledge, 2004.

- Bordman, Gerald. *American Theatre: A Chronicle of Comedy and Drama, 1969–2000.* New York: Oxford University Press, 2001.

- Cantor, Eddie. *My Life Is in Your Hands.* New York: Harper & Brothers, 1928.

- Carey, Gary. *Anita Loos: A Biography.* New York: Knopf, 1988.

- Carroll, John F. "Oscar Hammerstein I, 1895–1915: His Creation and Development of the New York Times Square Theatre District." Ph.D. dissertation, City University of New York (CUNY), 1998.

- Carter, Randolph. *Ziegfeld: The Time of His Life.* London: Bernard Press, 1988.

- Carter, Randolph, and Robert Cole. *Joseph Urban.* New York: Abbeville Press, 1992.

- Chach, Maryann, et al. *The Shuberts Present: 100 Years of Great American Theater.* New York: Harry N. Abrams, Inc., & the Shubert Organization, 2001.

- Churchill, Allen. *The Great White Way.* New York: E. P. Dutton, 1962.

- Fields, Armond, and L. Marc Fields. *From the Bowery to Broadway: Lew Fields and the Roots of American Popular Theater*. New York: Oxford University Press, 1993.

- Fordin, Hugh. *Getting to Know Him: A Biography of Oscar Hammerstein II*. New York: Da Capo Press, 1995.

- Foster, Charles. *Donald Brian: The King of Broadway*. St. Johns, NL: Breakwater Books, 2005.

- Fowler, Gene. *Good Night, Sweet Prince*. New York: The Viking Press, 1944.

- Gaige, Crosby. *Footlights and Highlights*. New York: E. P. Dutton, 1948.

- Goldstein, Malcolm. *George S. Kaufman: His Life, His Theater*. New York: Oxford University Press, 1979.

- Goodman, Ezra. *Bogey: The Good-Bad Guy*. New York: L. Stuart, 1965.

- Green, Stanley. *Broadway Musicals, Show by Show*. Milwaukee, Wisconsin: H. Leonard Books, 1985.

- Greene, Alexis. "The Petite Brunette and the Preferred Blonde." *SHOWmusic* 10, No 4. Winter 1994/95: 21–23, 62.

- Harding, A. *The Revolt of the Actors*. New York: W. Morrow & Company, 1929.

- Harris, Jed. *A Dance on the High Wire*. New York: Crown Publishers, 1979.

- Hecht, Ben. *Charlie: The Improbable Life and Times of Charles MacArthur*. New York: Harper, 1957.

- Henderson, Mary C. *The City and the Theatre*. New York: Watson-Guptill Publications, 2004.

- ———. *The New Amsterdam: Biography of a Broadway Theatre*. New York: Hyperion, 1985.

- Hischak, Thomas S. *Boy Loses Girl: Broadway's Librettists*. Lanham, MD: Scarecrow Press, 2002.

- Hopkins, Arthur. *To a Lonely Boy*. Garden City, NY: Doubleday, Doran, 1937.

- Irving, Washington. "Wolfert Webber, or Golden Dreams." In: *The Bold Dragoon and Other Ghostly Tales*, ed. Anne Carroll Moore. New York: A. A. Knopf, 1930.

- Jablonski, Edward. *Gershwin*. New York: Doubleday, 1987.

- ———, and Lawrence D. Stewart. *The Gershwin Years*. Garden City, NY: Doubleday, 1958.

- Jackson, Kenneth T., ed. *The Encyclopedia of New York City*. New Haven: Yale University Press, 1995.

- Jenkins, Stephen. *The Greatest Street in the World: The Story of Broadway*. New York: G.P. Putnam's Sons, 1911.

- Katcher, Leo. *The Big Bankroll: The Life and Times of Arnold Rothstein*. New York: Da Capo Press, 1994.

- Kemp, Kathryn. *God's Capitalist: Asa Candler of Coca-Cola*. Macon, GA: Mercer, 2002.

- Knapp, Margaret. "A Historical Study of the Legitimate Playhouses on West Forty-second Street Between Seventh and Eighth Avenues in New York City." Ph.D. dissertation, City University of New York (CUNY), 1982.

- Knight, Arthur. *The Liveliest Art: A Panoramic History of the Movies*. New York: MacMillan, 1957.

- Kobler, John. *Damned in Paradise: The Life of John Barrymore*. New York: Atheneum, 1977.

- Laffey, Bruce. *Beatrice Lillie: The Funniest Woman in the World*. New York: Wynwood Press, 1989.

- Landis, Bill, and Michelle Clifford. *Sleazoid Express*. New York: Simon & Schuster, 2002.

- Landmarks Preservation Commission. *New Amsterdam Theatre.* New York, October 23, 1979. Designation List 129 LLP-1027.

- Lesley, Cole. *Noel Coward and His Friends.* New York: William Morrow & Co., 1979.

- Loos, Anita. *Cast of Thousands.* New York: Grosset & Dunlap, 1977.

- McCabe, John. *George M. Cohan: The Man Who Owned Broadway.* Garden City, NY: Doubleday, 1973.

- McGill, Raymond, ed. *Notable Names in the American Theatre.* Clifton, NJ: J. T. White, 1976.

- Meredith, Scott. *George S. Kaufman and His Friends.* Garden City, NY: Doubleday, 1974.

- Minsky, Morton, and Milt Machlin. *Minsky's Burlesque.* New York: Arbor House, 1986.

- Moore, F. Michael. *Drag! Male and Female Impersonators on Stage, Screen, and Television.* Jefferson, NC: McFarland, 1994.

- Morehouse, Ward. *George M. Cohan, Prince of the American Theater.* Philadelphia: J. P. Lippincott Company, 1943.

- Morrison, Andrew Craig. *The Theatres of Forty-second Street.* Master's thesis, School of Architecture, Columbia University, 1968.

- Morrison, William. *Broadway Theatres: History and Architecture.* Mineola, NY: Dover Publications, Inc., 1999.

- New York Times editors. *New York Times Directory of the Theatre.* New York: Arno Press, 1973.

- Norden, Martin F. *John Barrymore: A Bio-Bibliography.* Westport, CT: Greenwood Press, 1995.

- Poggi, Jack. *Theatre in America: The Impact of Economic Forces, 1870–1967.* Ithaca, NY: Cornell University Press, 1968.

- Rice, Elmer. *Minority Report: An Autobiography.* New York: Simon and Schuster, 1963.

- Robbins, Jhan. *Front Page Marriage: Helen Hayes and Charles MacArthur.* New York: Putnam, 1982.

- Rogers W. G., and Mildred Weston. *Carnival Crossroads: The Story of Times Square.* Garden City, NY: Doubleday, 1960.

- Sagalyn, Lynne B. *Times Square Roulette: Remaking the City Icon.* Cambridge, MA: The MIT Press, 2001.

- Sheean, Vincent. *Oscar Hammerstein I: The Life and Exploits of an Impresario.* New York: Simon and Schuster, 1956.

- Stoddard, Richard. *Theatre and Cinema Architecture: A Guide to Information Sources.* Detroit: Gale Research Co., 1978.

- Stokes, I. N. Phelps. *The Iconography of Manhattan Island, 1498–1909.* New York: Robert H. Dodd, 1916.

- Taylor, William R., ed. *Inventing Times Square: Culture and Commerce at the Crossroads of the World.* New York: Russell Sage Foundation, 1991.

- Traub, James. *The Devil's Playground: A Century of Pleasure and Profit in Times Square.* New York: Random House, 2004.

- Tuttle, H. Croswell. *Abstracts of Farm Titles in the City of New York.* New York: The City of New York, 1934.

- Valentine, Maggie. *The Show Starts on the Sidewalk: An Architectural History of the Movie Theatre.* New Haven: Yale University Press, 1994.

- Young, William C. *Famous American Playhouses, 1900– 1971.* Chicago: American Library Association, 1973.

- Zeidman, Irving. *The American Burlesque Show.* New York: Hawthorn Books, 1967.

- Ziegfeld, Richard and Paulette. *The Ziegfeld Touch: The Life and Times of Florenz Ziegfeld, Jr.* New York: Harry N. Abrams, 1993.

PHOTOGRAPHY CREDITS

- Photograph Courtesy William Appleton: page 91

- AP Images / Wide World Photos / Emile Wamsteker: page 155

- Photograph Courtesy © Alan Batt / Battman Studios: page 20

- Photograph © Michael Berger / TimesSquareGallery.com: page 123

- Copyright © Beyer Blinder Belle Architects & Planners LLP. All rights reserved. Courtesy of Beyer Blinder Belle Architects & Planners LLP Kofman Engineering LTD. Project Manager & Architect: pages 223; 224

- Brown Brothers: pages 92; 158

- Photograph Courtesy © Frederick Charles, FCharlesPhotography: page 227

- © John Springer Collection/CORBIS: page 201

- Photograph Courtesy © Whitney Cox: pages 122; 220; 228; 229

- Culver Pictures, Inc.: pages 14 (left); 16; 66 (top left); 74; 93; 162

- Photograph Courtesy Drew Eliot: page 108

- Courtesy of Mary Henderson: pages 14 (right); 50; 83; 143; 219

- Photograph Courtesy © Zbig Jedrus: pages 190; 191

- Photograph © Elliott Kaufman/Elliott Kaufman Photography, New York: page 75

- Photograph Courtesy © Joan Marcus: page 188

- Courtesy The New 42nd Street Organization: page 32

- Museum of the City of New York: page 17

- Museum of the City of New York, The Byron Collection: pages 36; 38; 40–41; 42; 53; 54 (top); 62; 64–65; 66 (top right and bottom left); 67; 69; 81; 84–85; 115; 160

- Museum of the City of New York, The Theatre Collection: pages 2; 6; 39 (left and right); 44; 45; 46; 48; 52; 54 (bottom); 55 (left and right); 56; 57; 59; 68; 71; 72 (left and right); 76; 78; 80; 82; 86; 89; 96; 97; 98 (top and bottom); 99; 100; 102; 104; 105; 110; 111; 113; 116 (left and right); 118; 119; 126; 127; 128; 129; 131; 132; 133; 134; 136–137; 146; 147; 148; 149; 150; 161; 163; 164–165; 169; 171; 175; 179; 183; 194; 197; 200; 203; 204; 212; 214

- The New York Historical Society: pages 10; 15; 22–23

- The New York Public Library for the Performing Arts / Billy Rose Theatre Division: pages 47; 73; 114; 130; 135; 144 (left and right); 152; 167; 174; 177; 181; 184; 187; 206–207; 210; 217

- The New York Public Library for the Performing Arts / Billy Rose Theatre Division / photo by Marc Bryan-Brown: pages 19; 34; 60; 94; 124; 140; 156; 172; 192; 208

- The New York Public Library. Astor, Lenox and Tilden Foundations, Manuscripts and Archives Division: pages 12–13

- Ruby Washington / The New York Times / Redux: page 225

- Photofest: pages 58; 218

- Courtesy of The Shubert Archive, a project of the Shubert Foundation: pages 176; 196

- Photograph Courtesy © Beau States: page 226

- Courtesy Theatre Historical Society of America: page 211

- Robert A.M. Stern Architects: pages 30–31

INDEX

Abbot and Costello, 73
Abbott, George, 185
Abe and Mawruss, 87, 151
Abie's Irish Rose, 70–71, 72, 198
According to the Evidence, 162
The Acquittal, 166
Actors' Equity Association, 176
Actors' Equity Association (AEA), 166–168
The Adding Machine, 163
Adele, 136
Adler, Jacob P., 42, 43
Akins, Zoë, 171
Albee, Edward F., 59, 168
Alcazar de Paris, 217
Allen, Fred, 186, 187
American Airlines Theatre, 33, 188, 189, 190–191, 225
American Theatre, 18, 25, 35–47
    A. H. Woods and, 44
    burlesque at, 46
    Castle Square Opera Company to, 41, 43
    design and description, 37
    Elliott Zborowski and, 37, 41, 43
    fire and destruction, 46
    first electrically-lit theatre, 18
    Henry Savage and, 43
    impressive interior of, 37
    Marcus Loewe and, 45–47
    movies at, 217
    opening of, 37
    photographs of, 36, 38
    photographs of performances/ personalities, 39–42, 44, 45, 46, 47
    productions, 37–46
    renamed Loew's American Theatre, 46
    renovations, 44–45
    roof garden theatre, 37, 38, 39–43, 45
    site today, 46
    sold to Elliott Zborowski, 41, 43
    T. Henry French and, 37–43
    ticket prices, 37–38
    William Morris and, 44–45
Ames, Winthrop, 26
Anco, 28, 139
Anders, Glenn, 182
Anderson, Maxwell, 26
Anderson, Richard F., 110
André Charlot's Revue of 1924, 180, 199–201

Andrews, Ann, 185
Anglin, Margaret, 138
Antony and Cleopatra, 161
Apollo Theatre, 25, 209–219
    burlesque at, 27, 73, 216
    design and description, 195, 211–212
    destruction of, 218
    Ford Center for the Performing Arts on site of, 32, 90
    movies at, 216
    opening of, 212
    photographs of, 194, 210, 211, 217
    photographs of performances/ personalities, 213–214, 218, 219
    productions, 212–217
    rehabilitation project, 29, 216–218
Arlen, Michael, 151
Arms and the Man, 87
Astaire, Fred and Adele, 88–89, 103, 120
Astor Hotel, 25
Astor, John Jacob, 13–14
Atkinson, Brooks, 121, 202, 216
Back Pay, 151
Bailey, James, 18
Bailey, Oliver D., 71
The Band Wagon, 103
Bankhead, Tallulah, 205, 222
Barnard, George Gray, 96
Barrett House, 25
Barrymore, Ethel, 170, 177, 183, 185, 215
Barrymore, John, 70, 149, 150, 164, 168–170, 177, 185
Barrymore, Lionel, 63, 70, 152–153, 177, 212
Bates, Blanche, 69
Battling Buttler, 178
Belasco, David, 18, 25, 27, 39, 65–70
Bel Geddes, Norman, 120
Bennett, Richard, 87–88
Bent, 217
Berlin, Irving, 26, 53, 58, 88
Bernard, Barney, 151
Bernhardt, Sarah, 83
Bertelsman Tower, 224–225
Bertha, the Sewing Machine Girl, 44
Bial, Rudolf, 20
Bickerton, Joseph P., Jr., 135–136
The Birth of a Nation, 26, 112
Blackbirds of 1928, 118, 119, 120–121, 153
Blackbirds of 1933–34, 216
Blake, Eubie, 120
Blinn, Holbrook, 147

Bloom, Sol, 159, 165
The Blue Mouse, 87
Bogart, Humphrey, 139
Boleslavsky, Richard, 121
Bolger, Ray, 215, 219
Bolton, Guy, 116, 117–120
Booth, Shirley, 139
Boston Red Sox, 137, 138
Brady, William A., 86
Brandt Organization (family), 28, 29, 59, 74–75, 90, 121, 154, 186–189, 205, 216–217
Brian, Donald, 176
Brice, Fanny, 53, 56, 57, 137
Brinkley, Grace, 216
Broadhurst Theatre, 119, 151
Broadway, as "Main Street," 16
Broadway Theatre, 18, 37
The Broadway Whirl, 198
Brook, Peter, 103
Brounet, Arthur, 160, 175, 189
Brown, John Mason, 186
Brown, Lew, 215
Brownstones, 17–18
Bryant Theatre, 195
Buchanan, Jack, 180, 199
Buddies, 176, 177
Burlesque, 27–28, 46, 52, 72, 73–74, 121, 153, 154, 216
Burr, Aaron, 16
Business Before Pleasure, 151
Cahan, Cora, 32, 106
Cahill, Marie, 131, 132
Campbell, Mrs. Patrick, 85
Candler, Asa, 25, 169
Candler Building, 25
Candler Theatre, 25, 157–171
    as the Cohan and Harris, 165–168
    Cohen, Harris and, 161–162, 163, 164–168
    decline of, 171
    design and description, 159–160
    Elmer L. Reizenstein and, 162–164, 169
    John Barrymore, *Hamlet* and, 168–170
    movies at, 28, 171
    opening of, 161
    photographs of, 158, 160
    photographs of performances/ personalities, 161, 162, 163, 164–165, 167, 169
    productions, 161–171
    rehabilitation project around, 32
    Sam Harris and, 161–162, 163, 164–168, 170–171

    as Samuel H. Harris Theatre, 168–171
    Shubert brothers and, 170–171
Cantor, Eddie, 73, 178–182
Carr, Alexander, 151
Carrillo, Leo, 117
Carroll, Earl, 103, 139
Carroll, Leo, 182
Carter, Mrs. Leslie, 65–69, 177–178, 179
Castle Square Opera Company, 41, 43
Centennial celebration, 27
Chaplin, Charlie, 45, 46, 53
Charlot, André, 199
Charlot's Revue of 1926, 180, 182. *See also André Charlot's Revue of 1924*
Cheating Cheaters, 150–151
Childs, David, 224–225, 226
The Chocolate Soldier, 87
Churches, 17
CinemaScope, 28
The Circle, 176–177
Cirque Éloize, 75
The City, 87
The Clansman, 112, 116, 137
Clark, Bobby, 73, 88
Clement, Percival Wood, 18
Cline, Maggie, 39
Clinton Apartments, 17, 18
Coca-Cola, 25, 159
The Cocoanuts, 88
Cohan, George M., 25, 99, 112, 116, 136, 161–162, 163, 164–168, 171, 222
Cohan, Jerry J. and Helen F., 113
Cohen, Max, 28, 103, 139, 186
Colbert, Claudette, 153
Colton, John, 151
Columbus Theatre, 20
Connelly, Marc, 117, 137, 138, 178, 198
Constant Nymph, 180–182
Corbin, John, 170
Corio, Ann, 73, 74
Cornell, Katharine, 151
Cort, John, 139
Coward, Noel, 135, 185, 202, 204, 205
Cowl, Jane, 69, 70, 148, 175, 198
Craven, Frank, 116
Crewes, Laura Hope, 137
Crosman, Henrietta, 63, 69
Crothers, Rachel, 87
Dafoe, Willem, 189
Dagmar, 178
Dale, Alan, 80, 143, 166, 175–176, 185, 195–197, 202

Daly, Arnold, 85, 87
The Darling of the Gods, 69
Davis, Owen, 153
Dawn, Hazel, 151, 152
De Angelis, Jefferson, 85
De Koven, Reginald, 21, 79, 80, 86, 87, 88
Demi-Virgin, 151, 152
DeRosa, Eugene, 195, 211
DeSylva, B. G. "Buddy," 215, 216
Dietz, Howard, 103, 186
Dillingham, Charles, 26, 102, 121
Divine Sarah, 83
Dixon, Reverend Thomas, Jr., 112, 137
Dressler, Marie, 53, 54
Drew, John, Jr., 177–178, 179
Drugs, on 42nd Street, 28, 223
Duke, The, 33, 226
Dulcy, 137, 138
Durante, Jimmy, 73
East of Suez, 151–152
Edna, the Pretty Typewriter, 44
Edwardes, Felix, 120
Eisner, Michael, 106, 225
Electric lights, 18
Elite Private Address and Carriage Directory, 17, 18
Ellis, Evelyn, 72
Eltinge, Julian, 25, 143–146
Eltinge Theatre, 25, 141–155
    A. H. Woods and, 142, 143
    burlesque at, 27, 73, 121, 153, 154
    design and description, 143–147
    downfall of, 153–154
    Lambert Theatre Corporation and, 153
    landmark status to, 154
    moved to site of Lew Fields Theatre, 139, 154–155
    movies at, 153, 154
    photographs of, 147, 148
    photographs of performances/ personalities, 142, 144, 146, 149, 150, 152, 155
    productions, 147–153
    rehabilitation project, 32
    Shubert brothers and, 153
    success after success, 147–154
Emerson, John, 202
Empire Theatre, 18, 37, 96, 222
Erlanger, Abraham Lincoln
    background and reputation, 110, 121
    death of, 121
    end of Klaw partnership, 102, 117

fortune dismantled, 103, 121
    Liberty Theatre and, 110–111, 112–121
    New Amsterdam Theatre and, 96, 98, 99–100, 101, 102, 103
    partnership with Klaw, 21–25, 87, 96, 102, 110, 117. *See also* Theatrical Syndicate
    photograph of, 98
Erté, 215
Esmond, Jill, 205
Evans, Charles, 101
E Walk, 33
Fair and Warmer, 137, 150
Fairfax, Marion, 135
Fantana, 85
The Fascinating Widow, 145, 146
Fawcett, George, 44
Fedora, 44
Ferber, Edna, 183–185, 189
Fields, Armond, 127, 132
Fields, Dorothy, 120
Fields, Lew, 99–100, 127–129, 131– 132, 222
Fields, W. C., 73, 103, 212–215
Fifth of July, 217
Fifty Million Frenchmen, 88–90, 91, 92
Filmmaking, 26
Find the Fox, 139
Finkelstein, Mark, 28, 103
The Firefly, 87
Fiske, Harrison Grey, 87
Fiske, Minnie Maddern, 85, 86, 87
Fitch, Clyde, 87
Flint, Eva Kay, 121
Flying High, 215–216
Follies, 101–102, 104, 117, 178, 215
Fonda, Henry, 205, 217
Fontanne, Lynn, 117, 137, 138
The Fool, 197, 198
Ford Center for the Performing Arts, 32, 90, 205, 218, 225–226
Ford Foundation, 29
Forsaking All Others, 205
42nd Street Development Project, 29, 32, 106, 223
Frazee, Harry Herbert, 137–138
French, Samuel, 18, 37
French, T. Henry, 18, 37–43
Friml, Rudolf, 87, 88
Frohman, Charles, 18, 21, 24, 37, 96, 121, 134, 185, 222
The Front Page, 202, 203
Gable, Clark, 153
Gaige, Crosby, 147, 148, 162, 174, 175, 177, 186, 195, 198, 201, 211
Gale Quadruplets, 214, 215
Gallagher, Ed, 105

Galsworthy, John, 164, 168
"Gang, the," 25
Gentlemen Prefer Blondes, 201–202
George, Grace, 134
George White's Scandals, 117, 215
Gershwin, George, 26, 71, 72, 117, 120, 198, 202–204, 215, 219
Gershwin, Ira, 26, 71, 72, 120, 202–204
Geva, Tamara, 186
The Ghost Train, 153
The Girl of the Golden West, 69
The Girls of Holland, 86
Giuliani, Rudolph, 226
The Glass Menagerie, 117
Glass, Montague, 87, 151
Going Up, 116
Gold, 138
On Golden Pond, 29, 216–217
A Good Bad Woman, 137
Good Gracious Annabelle, 70, 71
Goodman, Jules Eckert, 151
For Goodness Sake, 88–89
Goodwin, Nat C., 99, 100
Gordon, Leon, 152
Gordon, Ruth, 154
Gray's Drug Store, 26
The Greeks Had a Word for It, 171
The Green Bird, 75
The Green Hat, 151
Greenwall, Henry, 43
Grey, Clifford, 88
Grid of streets and avenues (1811), 12, 16
Griffith, D. W., 26, 112, 201
The Guys in the Truck, 217
Hackett, James K., 132–134
Haight, Charles Coolidge, 37
The Hairy Ape, 189
Haley, Jack, 216
Half-price tickets, 26
Hall, Adelaide, 120, 121
Hamlet, 169, 170
Hammerstein, Arthur, 51, 54, 59, 71–72, 87, 176, 212
Hammerstein, Oscar I
    biographical sketch, 19–21
    death of, 72
    Hammerstein's Victoria and, 51–53, 56, 59
    laying foundation of theatre district, 18, 20–21, 25
    Lew Fields Theatre and, 25, 127–130, 133
    Manhattan Opera House and, 20, 133
    Olympia complex, 21, 51, 101, 189, 222
    Theatre Republic and, 21, 63–65

Hammerstein, Oscar II, 176, 185, 212
Hammerstein's Victoria, 21, 25, 26, 28, 49–59
    building and opening, 51–52
    ceding control of, 26–27, 59
    design and description, 51
    finding right formula, 53
    murder buoying popularity of, 56–59
    opening of, 51–52
    Oscar Hammerstein I and, 21, 51–53, 56, 59
    panoramic view showing (circa 1900), 22–23
    photographs of, 50
    photographs of performances/ personalities, 52, 53, 54–55, 57, 59
    productions, 51–59
    rechristened Victoria Theatre of Varieties, 53
    Rialto movie palace on site of, 59
    rooftop garden/theatre, 52–53, 59, 63–65
    site today, 59
    unconventional interior, 51
    Willie Hammerstein and, 21, 53, 54, 55, 56–59
Hammerstein, Willie, 21, 53, 54, 55, 56–59
Hammond, Percy, 171, 177, 178, 180, 202
Hampden, Walter, 85, 87
Happyland, 86
Harbach (Hauerbach), Otto, 87, 116, 117, 145, 176, 180
Harding, Ann, 153
Hardy, Hugh, 75, 106
Harlem Opera House, 20
Harlem Railroad Company, 17
Harris, Henry B., 133, 134–135
Harris (Henry B.) Theatre, 134–139. *See also* Lew Fields Theatre
Harris, Jed, 184–185, 202
Harris, Sam H., 25, 113, 116, 121, 136, 161–162, 163, 164–168
Harris (Sam H.) Theatre. *See* Samuel H. Harris Theatre
Harris, The. *See* Candler Theatre
Hart, Lorenz, 26
Hart, Moss, 188, 189
A Hat, A Coat, A Glove, 186
Have a Heart, 116
Haworth, Joseph, 53
Hayes, Helen, 117
Hayman, Al, 21
Hearst, William Randolph, 102

Hecht, Ben, 202
Heflin, Evan (Van), 121
Held, Anna, 101
Helen of Troy, New York, 178, 198
Hell's Bells, 139
Henderson, Ray, 215, 219
Herald Square Theatre, 18, 132
Herbert, Victor, 26, 99, 102, 131–132
Hermitage farm, 13
Herts, Henry B., 96, 97, 110, 134
Heyward, Dorothy and DuBose, 71, 73
Hilliam, B. C., 176
Hilton Theatre, 90, 218, 225, 226, 227
Hirsch, Louis A., 116
History of Forty-second street
    Broadway and, 16
    burlesque and, 27–28
    centennial celebration, 27
    churches and, 17
    decline of great thoroughfare, 28
    earliest city records, 12
    grid plan of Manhattan and, 12, 16
    John Jacob Astor and, 13–14
    John Leake Norton and, 13, 17
    map demarcating streets (1811), 12–13
    new Forty-second Street, 28–33, 223–229
    nineteenth-century development, 16–24
    onset of public transportation, 17
    origins of theatre district, 18–25
    Oscar Hammerstein I and, 18, 19–21
    post-World War II, 28
    residential and commercial expansion, 16–18
    Revolutionary War, 15–16
    stock market crash, 27
    television and, 28
    Wolfert Webber and, 14–15, 16
    between World Wars, 26–28
Hitchcock, Raymond, 164, 165–166
Hitchy-Koo, 164–166
Hit-the-Trail Holliday, 136
Hobart, George, 54, 176
Holland House, 21
Holman, Libby, 186, 187
Hopkins, Arthur, 26, 70, 162–163, 169–170
Hopwood, Avery, 150
Hotel Cadillac, 25
Hotels, 25
The Hot Mikado, 119

Houdini, Harry, 53, 55
The House Beautiful, 216
The House of Glass, 164
Howard, Leslie, 151
Howe, General Sir William, 16
How He Lied to Her Husband, 87
Hubert's Museum, 28, 222, 223
Hurok, Sol, 90
Hurst, Fannie, 151
Huston, Walter, 103
Icebound, 170
Illington, Margaret, 136
Information, Please!, 175–176
It Happened in Nordland, 131–132
Jardin de Paris, 101
The Jazz Singer, 26
J. B. McElfatrick and Son, 51
Jessel, George, 178
Jimmie, 212
Johnson, Hall, 90
Jolson, Al, 26
Jones, Robert Edmund, 103, 169, 170, 212
Justice, 164, 168
Kalich, Bertha, 44
Kalmar, Bert, 178
Kaufman, George S., 26, 88, 117, 137, 138, 178, 183–184, 185, 188, 189, 198, 202–204
Keaton, Buster, 53
Keith, B. F., 59
Kelly, Anthony Paul, 166
Kennedy, Madge, 137, 150, 212–215
Kern, Jerome, 26, 102, 116, 117, 185
Kid Boots, 178, 180, 181
King David, 106–107
King, Dennis, 88
Kirkwood, James, 198
Klaw, Marc Alonzo
    background and reputation, 110
    death of, 117
    end of Erlanger partnership, 102, 117
    Liberty Theatre and, 110–111, 112–121
    New Amsterdam Theatre and, 96, 98, 99–100, 101, 102
    partnership with Erlanger, 21–25, 87, 96, 102, 110, 117. *See also* Theatrical Syndicate
    photograph of, 98
Klaw Theatre, 117
Kleine, George, 159, 161, 165
Knickerbocker Hotel, 25
Knickerbocker Theatre, 114
Koch, Edward I., 29, 106, 223
Koehler, Victor Hugo, 79, 80, 90
Koster and Bial's New Music Hall, 20

Koster, John, 20
Kruger, Otto, 183
Lackaye, Wilton, 86
To the Ladies, 117
Ladies' Night, 151
Ladie's Union Aid Society, 17
Lady, Be Good!, 117–120
Laff That Off, 139
La Guardia, Fiorello H., 27, 74, 154, 216
Lahr, Bert, 73, 215–216, 219
Lamb, Thomas White, 45, 143–147, 159, 211
Lane, Nathan, 188, 189
Langner, Lawrence, 153
The Last Mile, 171
Lauder, Harry, 44, 45
LaVelle, Paul B., 147
Within the Law, 147–148, 174
Lawrence, Gertrude, 180, 182, 199, 200, 202, 204–205
Leblang, Joe, 26
Lee, Sammy, 120
Lehar, Franz, 100, 176
LeMaire, Charles, 215
LeMaire, Rufus, 178
Leslie, Lew, 118, 120
Levey, Ethel, 113
Lew Fields Theatre, 21, 25, 28, 125–139
    design and description, 130
    end of, 139
    as Harris Theatre, 134–139
    Henry B. Harris and, 133, 134–135
    H. H. Frazee and, 137–138
    It Happened in Nordland, 131–132
    James K. Hackett productions, 132–134
    jinx of, 133, 138–139
    John Cort and, 139
    movies at, 137, 139
    Oscar Hammerstein I and, 25, 127–130, 133
    photographs of, 126, 130
    photographs of performances/personalities, 127, 128, 129, 132, 133, 134, 135, 136–137
    productions, 131–139
    Selwyn brothers and, 135–137, 150
    Shubert brothers productions, 132
    as Wallack's, 28, 139
    Weber and Fields and, 127–129
Liberty Theatre, 25, 28, 109–123
    design and description, 110–111

downfall of, 121–122
fireproof escape routes, 111
Klaw, Erlanger and, 110–111, 112–121
movies at, 112
oddly-shaped plot of land for, 110
photographs of, 110, 111, 122, 123
photographs of performances/personalities, 113, 114–116, 118, 119
productions, 112–121
The Lie, 136
Liebler, Theodore A., 52, 85
Lillie, Beatrice, 180, 182, 185, 199–201
Lillie, Lawrence, 199
Lindsay, John V., 223
The Lion King, 107
Little Johnny Jones, 112, 162
Loewe, Marcus, 26, 45–47
Lonsdale, Frederick, 152
Loos, Anita, 201–202
Love Dreams, 198
Love, Honor, and Betray, 153
Lunt, Alfred, 137
Lyric, 21, 28, 77–93
    competing with Syndicate, 83, 85, 86, 88
    conservative interior of, 79–80
    decline and condemnation of, 90
    early performances at, 80–88
    façades of, 78, 79
    Ford Center for the Performing Arts on site of, 32, 90
    movies at, 90
    opening of, 80–83
    photographs of, 78, 81–82
    photographs of performances/personalities, 80, 83–85, 86, 89, 91–93
    Reginald De Koven and, 21, 79, 80, 86, 87, 88
    rehabilitation project, 29
    Shubert brothers and, 79, 80–88, 99
    worthy productions at, 88–90
MacArthur, Charles, 202
MacDonald, Jeannette, 87, 117
MacDonough, Glen, 131
Madame Sherry, 138
Madame Tussaud's, 28, 32, 122, 171, 222, 225
Madam Sherry, 100
Madison, Martha, 121
Maggie Pepper, 134–135
The Magic Ring, 117

Magnolia, 117
Mamoulian, Rouben, 153
Mandel, Frank, 176
Manhattan Mary, 215
Manhattan Opera House, 20, 133
Manners, J. Hartley, 117
Mansfield, Richard, 80–83, 99
Mantle, Burns, 121, 134, 137, 148,
   163, 178, 185, 197, 201, 202
The Man Who Came to Dinner, 188,
   189
Map, of Jonathan Randel (1811),
   12–13
Marcin, Max, 150, 164
Marlowe, Julia, 85
Marshall, Everett, 215
Marx Brothers, 88
Mason, John, 150
Maugham, W. Somerset, 151–152,
   176–177
Mayo, Margaret, 112, 115
McClendon, Rose, 72
McCullough, Paul, 88
McHugh, Jimmy, 120
McMurray, Fred, 186
Megrue, Roi Cooper, 87
Menken, Alan, 107
The Merchant of Venice, 42, 43
Merman, Ethel, 215, 216
The Merry Widow, 100, 176
Metropolitan Opera Guild, 117
Metropolitan Opera House, 18, 96
A Midsummer Night's Dream, 99,
   100, 103
Mielziner, Jo, 216
Miller, Marilyn, 102
Mills, Florence, 120
Milstein family, 46
Minsky, Billy, 27, 72, 73
Minsky brothers, 72, 73–74
The Mirage, 195–198
Miss Prinnt, 54
A Month in the Country, 153
Moore, Carlyle, 87–88
Moore, Tim, 120
Morrison, Craig, 122, 159
Morris, William, 26, 44–45
Morris, William, Jr., 45
Morton, Michael, 148
Mother Goose, 99
From Mourn to Midnight, 138
Movies, 26–27, 28
   at Apollo Theatre, 216, 217
   Bill "Bojangles" Robinson in,
      119
   at Candler Theatre, 28, 171
   at Eltinge Theatre, 153, 154
   at Harris/Wallack's, 137, 139
   at Liberty Theatre, 112

   at Lyric, 90
   Marcus Loewe and, 45–47
   multiplex emporium, 32
   at New Amsterdam Theatre,
      103
   over time, on 42nd Street,
      26–27, 28, 222–223, 226
   at Selwyn, 186–189
   Syndicate and, 112
   at Theatre Republic, 70
   at Times Square Theatre,
      206–207
   wide-screen CinemaScope, 28
Mr. Moneypenny, 121
Mundin, Herbert, 180, 199
Murder at the Vanities, 103
Murder on the Second Floor, 153
Murfin, Jane, 175
Murray, John L., 18
Murray's Roman Gardens, 18, 25,
   28, 222
Nazimova, Alla, 153, 178
Nesbit, Evelyn, 56–59
New 42nd Street Inc., 32–33, 75, 90,
   106, 122, 205, 218, 224–225
New Amsterdam Theatre, 95–107
   city landmark designation,
      29, 103
   cost of, 99
   design and description, 96–99
   Disney acquisition/renovation,
      32, 106–107, 225, 226,
      228–229
   end of era, 28, 103
   Klaw, Erlanger and, 96, 98,
      99–100, 101, 102, 103
   movies at, 103
   opening of, 21, 25, 99
   photographs of, 96, 97, 98, 99
   photographs of performances/
      personalities, 98, 100, 102,
      104–105
   productions, 99–103
   rooftop theatre, 25, 101–102
   timely building of, 96
   Ziegfeld productions, 100–102
New Forty-second Street, 28–33,
   223–229
New Stagecraft, 70
New Victory, 32, 74–75, 222, 226
The New York Idea, 86, 87
New York Theatre, 101
Niblo, Fred, 136
Nichols, Anne, 70–72, 198
Nicolls, Sir Richard, 13
The Night Boat, 117
Nightclubs, 25–26
The Ninth Guest, 153
Nixon, Samuel, 21

No, No, Nanette, 137
Norton, John Leake, 13, 17
Norton, Martha, 13
Novelli, Anthony, 161
Novelli, Ermete, 85
The O'Brien Girl, 117
Old Heidelberg, 80–83
Olivier, Laurence, 153, 202, 205
Olympia, 21, 51, 101, 189, 222
O'Neill, Eugene, 25, 26, 138, 189
O'Neill, James, 85
Opera, 18, 20, 43, 59, 69–70
Oppenheimer, Jacob and Joseph,
   88
Under Orders, 151
Othello, 103
Our Mrs. McChesney, 183, 185
Ourselves, 87
Paradise Roof Garden, 52–53, 63–65
A Parlor March, 101
Payne, Ben Iden, 164, 168
Pelléas and Mélisande, 198
Pennington, Ann, 117
Percival apartment house, 18
Perkins, Osgood, 202
Peter Ibbetson, 70
Pigeons and People, 171
The Piker, 152–153
The Pink Lady, 100
The Pit, 84–85, 86–87, 198
Plymouth Theatre, 26
Pollock, Channing, 85, 150, 197, 198,
   201, 216
Polly of the Circus, 112, 115
Poor Girls, 38–39
Porgy, and *Porgy and Bess*, 71, 72,
   73
Pornography, 28, 29, 33, 139
Porter, Cole, 185
Potash and Perlmutter, 151
Potash and Perlmutter in Society.
   See Abe and Mawruss
Power, Tyrone, Sr., 117
Price, of tickets. See Ticket prices
The Prisoner of Zenda, 134
Private Lives, 202–205
The Prodigal Daughter, 37–38
Producers, prominent, 25, 26, 27.
   See also specific names
Producing Managers' Association,
   166–168
Prostitutes, on 42nd Street, 28, 223
Putnam, General Israel, 15–16
Ragged Army, 186
Rains, Claude, 182
Randel, Jonathan, Jr.
   grid of avenues and streets by, 12,
      16
   map of (1811), 12

study of Manhattan, 12
Rector's, 25
The Red Feather, 86
The Redskin, 117
Reed, Florence, 148–150, 151, 197
Reeve, Christopher, 217, 218
Rehan, Ada, 83
A Reign of Error, 51–52
Reinhardt, Heinrich, 116
Reizenstein (Rice), Elmer L., 162–164,
   169
Réjane, Gabrielle, 83
Republic. *See* Theatre Republic
The Respectful Prostitute, 186
Resurrection (Tolstoy), 52–53
Revolutionary War, 15–16
Rialto, 25, 26–27, 28, 29, 33, 59, 222
Rice, Elmer. *See* Reizenstein (Rice),
   Elmer L.
Rice, Tim, 107
Robin Hood, 21, 86
Robinson, Bill "Bojangles," 119, 120,
   121, 216, 222
Robson, Eleanor, 117
Rodgers, Richard, 26
Rogers Brothers, about, 114
The Rogers Brothers in Ireland, 112
The Rogers Brothers in Paris, 112,
   113, 115
Rogers, Will, 53
Romance and Arabella, 137
Romberg, Sigmund, 83
Rose of the Rancho, 69
Rothafel, S. L. "Roxy," 26–27, 59
Rothstein, Arnold, 174–175
A Round of Pleasure, 115
The Royal Family, 183–185
The Royal Vagabond, 166, 167
Ruby, Harry, 178
Rudnick, Max, 27, 121, 153, 154
Ruggles, Charles, 178
Run, Little Chillun!, 90, 92–93
Russell, Lillian, 101, 117, 131, 222
Ryskind, Morrie, 204
Sag Harbor, 63
Sally, 102
Salomy Jane, 117
Samuel H. Harris Theatre, 168–171
Sanger, Frank, 18
Savage, Henry, 43, 100
Scandals series, 117, 215, 219
Schaff, George, 170
Schwab, Laurence, 216
Schwartz, Arthur, 103, 186
Segal, Vivienne, 88
Selwyn, Edgar and Archibald
   "Arch," 222
      amassing theatres, 25. *See
      also* Apollo Theatre; Selwyn

Theatre; Times Square
Theatre
background and image, 174
dissolution of Selwyn and
Company, 201
Harris Theatre and, 135–137,
150
Within the Law by, 147–148,
174
Spring Cleaning by, 152
Selwyn Theatre, 25, 28, 173–191
as American Airlines Theatre,
33, 188, 189, 190–191, 225
decline of, 186–189
design and description,
174–175
Eddie Cantor and, 178–182
movies at, 186–189
photographs of, 175, 176,
190–191
photographs of performances/
personalities, 174, 177, 179,
181, 182, 183, 184, 187–188
productions, 175–182, 183–
186, 189
renovations, 33, 189
The Royal Family, 183–185
Sunday night performances,
186
The Shanghai Gesture, 151
Shaw, Billie, 154
Shaw, Fiona, 122, 123
Shaw, George Bernard, 85, 87, 134
Shaw, Oscar, 215–216
Shean, Al, 105
Sherman, Martin, 217
Shipwrecked, 139
Shooting Star, 186
Show Boat, 102, 185
Shubert brothers (Sam, Lee, and
Jacob J. "Jake"), 21, 24–25, 79,
80–88, 99, 117, 129, 132, 153,
170–171
Shuffle Along, 120
Silvers, Phil, 73
Silvers, Sid, 216
Sissle, Noble, 120
Skinner, Cornelia Otis, 186
Skinner, Otis, 83, 85
Smathers, E. E., 88
Smith, Alfred E., 121
Smith, Harry B., 101, 116
Smith, Kate, 215–216
Smith, Queenie, 120, 178
Smith, Robert B., 116
Sothern, E. H., 85
Sothern, Sara, 197, 198
Spring Cleaning, 152
The Spring Maid, 116

Stahl, Rose, 134, 135
Stanley's, 25
Stevens, Risë, 87
Stock market crash, 27
Stothart, Herbert, 176, 212
Strauss, Oscar, 87
Streetcars, 17
Strike Up the Band, 202–204
The Student Prince, 83
Stuyvesant, Peter, 14
Stuyvesant Theatre, 70
Subway Express, 121
Sweet Kitty Bellairs, 69
Syndicate. See Theatrical Syndicate
A Tailor-Made Man, 166
Take a Chance, 216
Taliaferro, Mabel, 112, 115
Tallant, Hugh, 96, 97, 110, 134
Taylor, Laurette, 85, 117
Taymor, Julie, 75, 107
Television, 28
Thaw, Harry Kendall, 56–59
The Theatre, 21
Theatre district. *See also*
Theatre district
decline of Forty-second Street
and, 28
new Forty-second Street and,
28–33
origins of, 18–25
Oscar Hammerstein I and, 18,
19–21
panoramic view (circa 1900),
22–23
rise of, 25–26
between World Wars, 26–28
Theatre Republic, 21, 61–75
Abie's Irish Rose at, 70–71,
72, 198
A. H. Woods and, 70
Anne Nichols and, 70–72
as the Belasco, 69–70
Billy Minsky and, 27
building and opening, 63
burlesque at, 27, 73–74
David Belasco and, 25, 65–70
handsome façade of, 62, 63
Minsky brothers and, 72, 73–74
movies at, 70
Mrs. Leslie Carter and, 65–69
photographs, 62, 64–65,
66–67, 75
productions, 63, 69–74, 75
reincarnation as the Victory
and New Victory, 32, 74–75
renovations, 65–69
rooftop garden/theatre, 52–53,
59, 63–65
ticket prices, 73

Theatre system
"combination system," 24
Klaw and Erlanger Syndicate.
See Theatrical Syndicate
"stock" system from England,
21–24
Theatrical Syndicate, 21–25, 83, 85,
86, 87, 88, 102, 110, 112, 117, 139
This Year of Grace, 185
Thompson, Ernest, 216–217
Thompson, Fred, 120
Three Faces East, 166
The Three Musketeers, 88
Three's a Crowd, 185–186
Throckmorton, Cleon, 153
Ticket prices, 26, 37–38, 43, 51, 73
Tickets, sterling-engraved, 175
Tickle Me, 176
Tierney, Harry, 198
Times Square, 25, 222
"Times Square Action Plan," 29
Times Square Center Associates,
29
Times Square Theatre, 28, 151,
193–207
decline of, 205
design and description, 195
hits from Selwyn to, 178
movies at, 205, 206–207
new development on site of,
33
photographs of, 194, 196,
206–207
photographs of performances/
personalities, 197, 200, 201,
203, 204
productions, 195–198, 199–205
property for, 195
tough beginning, 195–198
Tip-Toes, 120
Touring shows, 26
Tracy, Spencer, 171
Treasure, tales of, 14
Trentini, Emma, 87
On Trial, 162, 163, 164, 169
The Trial of Mary Dugan, 153
Tucker, Sophie, 44
Tumble In, 176
Twin Beds, 136
The Two Orphans, 99
Tyler, George C., 102, 138
The Unknown Purple, 87–88
Up in Mabel's Room, 151, 152
Urban, Joseph, 88, 101, 216
Vallee, Rudy, 215
Van Brugh, Johannes, 13
Victoria. See Hammerstein's
Victoria
Victory, 74–75

The Voyage of Suzette, 38
Wake Up and Dream, 185
Walker, James J., 121
Walker, June, 202
Wallack's, 28, 139. *See also* Lew
Fields Theatre
Walsh, Blanche, 52, 53
Walt Disney Company, 32, 106–107,
224–225
Ward, Aida, 120
The Warrens of Virginia, 69
Washington, General George,
15–16
"The Waste Land," 122, 123
Wayburn, Ned, 99
Webb, Clifton, 186, 187
Webber, Wolfert, 14–15, 16
Weber, Joe, 99–100, 127–129
Weiman, Rita, 166
West, Mae, 53, 55, 146, 205
Westover, Albert E., 63, 130
West, Roland, 87–88
We, the People, 163–164
Wexley, John, 171
Wharton, Edith, 18, 202
Wheeler, Jedediah, 122, 123
White, George, 117, 214, 215,
216, 219
White, Stanford, 56–59, 131
Whiting, Jack, 216
Whiting, Richard, 117
Whitney, Fred C., 87
Whoop-Dee-Doo, 99–100
Wildfire, 117
Williams, Bert, 53
Wilner, Max, 27, 216
Wilson, Frank, 72
Winchell, Walter, 180, 185
The Witching Hour, 134
Wodehouse, P. G., 88, 116
The Woman of Bronze, 138
A Woman's Way, 134
Woods, A. H., 25, 44, 70, 142, 143,
148–154, 222
Woods, Al, 26
The Wooing of Eve, 117
Woollcott, Alexander, 151–152, 180,
185, 199–201, 202, 212
Wright, Haidee, 183, 185
Wynn, Ed, 73
The Yellow Ticket, 148–150
Youmans, Vincent, 216
Zborowski, Elliott, 18, 37, 41, 43
Ziegfeld, Florenz, Jr., 25, 26, 39, 86,
88, 100–102, 103, 104, 117, 121,
178–180, 212, 215
Ziegfeld Follies, 28
Zimmerman, J. Frederick, 21

223 W. 42d
George W. Thedford
Coal